THE
SKETCHBOOK
WAR

RICHARD KNOTT

THE
SKETCHBOOK
WAR

SAVING THE NATION'S ARTISTS
IN WORLD WAR II

The
History
Press

'Oh, but you should be an artist. I had one with my squadron during the last war, for weeks – until we went up the line.'

Evelyn Waugh: *Brideshead Revisited*

First published 2013

The History Press
The Mill, Brimscombe Port
Stroud, Gloucestershire, GL5 2QG
www.thehistorypress.co.uk

© Richard Knott, 2013

The right of Richard Knott to be identified as the Author
of this work has been asserted in accordance with the
Copyright, Designs and Patents Act 1988.

British Library Cataloguing in Publication Data.
A catalogue record for this book is available from the British Library.

ISBN 978 0 7524 8923 0

Typesetting and origination by The History Press
Printed in Great Britain

Contents

Acknowledgements

There are many people whom I should thank for their help in writing this book. I am particularly grateful to Christianna Clemence, Edward Ardizzone's daughter, and his grandson, Tim Ardizzone, for so willingly loaning me correspondence and photographs, as well as being so generous with their time. Mrs Anne Ullmann, the daughter of Eric Ravilious, has also been very supportive and helpful. Vincent Freedman, Barnett Freedman's son, has been most generous, allowing me to make use of the extensive Barnett Freedman archive at Manchester Metropolitan University. Jean-Pierre Gross and his sister Mary West have been very helpful and allowed me to include photographs of their father. Mary West also kindly sent me the letter which Edward Bawden wrote to her with his fond memories of Anthony Gross, written in 1987. My thanks are also due to the Estate of Edward Bawden for permission to quote from the artist's letters.

The Special Collections Archivist at Manchester Metropolitan University, Jeremy Parrett, has been extremely helpful in guiding me through the Freedman archive and providing me with a number of photographs. Dr Laura MacCulloch (Curator of British Art, National Museums, Liverpool) has also been a valuable guide. I am also grateful to Sara Bevan at the Imperial War Museum and Colin Simpson, Principal Museums Officer, at the Williamson Gallery, Birkenhead. In addition, I would like to thank the following: Fran Baker, Bruce Beatty, Ronald Blythe, Julie Brown (Towner Gallery, Eastbourne), Ged Clarke, Stephen

Courtney (Curator of Photographs, National Museum of the Royal Navy), Betty Elzea, Colin Gale (Archives and Museum, Bethlem Royal Hospital), Hannah Hawksworth (The Royal Watercolour Society), Simon Lawrence (at the Fleece Press), Polly Loxton, Michael MacLeod and Peyton Skipwith.

The following institutions have also been useful in the writing of this book: The British Library, both in London and Boston Spa, Yorkshire, The British Library Sound Archive, The Royal Watercolour Society, The Higgins Art Gallery and Museum, Bedford, the National Museum of the Royal Navy, The Henry Moore Foundation, The Ministry of Defence Art Collection, The Imperial War Museum, The National Archives, Regen-Williamson Art Gallery, Birkenhead, The Walker Gallery, Liverpool, and The Towner Gallery, Eastbourne. I should also like to thank my commissioning editor at The History Press, Jo de Vries, for her enthusiasm for this project.

My wife Vanessa has, as always, been an invaluable and generous confidante in the writing of this book. I am most grateful to her.

Every effort has been made to contact copyright holders. It has not been possible, however, to trace the copyright holders of all the photographs contained in the book and I would be pleased to hear from any copyright holder via the publisher.

Finally, I would like to apologise for any errors I have made in telling this story of my nine war artists. I hope that the great regard I have for them all outweighs any inadvertent mishaps or inaccuracies.

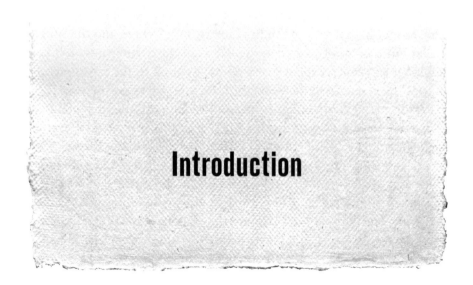

Introduction

I first learned about the vast treasury of war artists' work by the luckiest of chances. I was trying to track down the whereabouts of a painting by R. Vivian Pitchforth which he had completed in the middle of the war. It was of seven white Sunderland flying boats in Plymouth in 1942: it was striking and evocative – and yet I knew nothing about Vivian Pitchforth. Then, to my surprise, I found that the original was in the possession of Bendigo Art Gallery in Victoria, Australia. Not in Plymouth. I wanted to know why.

That was the start of it all – I became fascinated by the kind of life war artists led, and particularly what it was like for those of them who were nearest to combat. That led me to a whole series of related questions. Who were these artists? Who chose them? How dangerous was such a life? How close to combat did they get? What did the ordinary soldier and airmen think of them? What was it like to sketch in the midst of shellfire and mayhem? Did they carry guns, or simply cling on to pencil and sketchbook? Why did three artists lose their lives? What were they like as men – were they set apart somehow, or indistinguishable from those fighting beside them? Later, as I discovered more about the nation's war artists, I realised that there was a story to be told about Sir Kenneth Clark of the War Artists' Advisory Committee and his flawed plan to keep artists alive during the war, and the extent to which it failed.

In writing *The Sketchbook War* I have consulted relevant files at the Imperial War Museum, National Archives, Manchester Metropolitan

University, Sheffield Local Studies Library and Archive, and the Walker Gallery in Liverpool, as well as the letters of the participants and their published accounts. I spent many hours listening to the taped recordings of interviews conducted with those who survived the war. Held by the Imperial War Museum, they are a wonderful resource and have allowed me to gain a privileged insight into the characters of each of them. Listening to them reminisce in relative old age about the war years proved inspiring – somehow hearing the mischief in Edward Ardizzone's voice as he uncovers the past, for example, brought me much closer to an understanding of the man himself. It was strange to hear 'my' artists coughing, breaking off for a cigarette, laughing at some prank long ago, drinking tea (tea cups clinking in the background), admitting to fading memory, or struggling with becoming hard of hearing. Such human foibles rendered them even more real than might have been the case with measured prose in a plain journal.

Occasionally, in telling the story, I have allowed myself a certain amount of writers' licence, but even those forays into the imaginative hinterland are securely rooted in fact. A valuable additional source of material has been the paintings themselves. At certain points in telling the story, I have turned to the artists' paintings and sketches. For example, early in the book there is a description of Henry Moore swimming off the south coast on the day war broke out. That painting – *3rd September 1939* – I saw at an exhibition at Leeds City Gallery; I was very moved by it – the stark coming together of a blue late summer's day and the looming blood-filled threat of war – and knew that I wanted Moore's perspective on that September day to be the first sight of the war the reader gets. Each time a war artist sketched the war as he or she saw it, it added to the pictorial record of those six tragic years. I was grateful too for the way that the sum total of a war artist's work, with its sequence of dates and locations, provides a different kind of diary or journal. I liked the way I could 'read' such an account, and follow an artist through their war experience by looking closely at what they had painted, canvas by canvas. I have listed those particular paintings which figure in the text at Appendix C.

1

The Secret List

It is a summer Sunday in September 1939, a few weeks after Chamberlain had announced that the country was at war with Germany. The scene – not a typical one for this book – is a large country house in the Berkshire Downs. There has been a lunch party hosted by the local MP, Sir Ralph Glyn. John Betjeman and his wife have breezed over from Uffington. Lord and Lady Esher and Sir Kenneth Clark and his wife, Jane, are there. The weather has been kind enough for them to take a post-luncheon stroll around the grounds. Perhaps there is something about the late summer sun glowing on the red brick of Ardington House, or the wisps of white cloud in a blue sky; the bleached yellow of post-harvest corn-fields, and the fading greens of the garden. At all events, the conversation turns to art. And the war, of course …

Inevitably, they see the new war in the light of the old conflict two decades before; bowed heads are shaken over 'the destruction of the flower of a European generation' and the loss in particular of artistic talent. Lord Esher, it is, who suggests 'a secret list of the most promising artists and writers of military age and to ask the government to steer them, with equal secrecy, into safe war jobs.' There is much nodding and Betjeman agrees to begin the task of putting a list of names together. When the lunch party breaks up and the guests' cars sweep away up the gravelled drive, the plan has been hatched. Lulled by a good lunch and the beauty of an English garden, they were intent on saving the nations' artists, if uncertain as to whose names might appear on the list and how it might be put together.

There were disagreements as to whether the 'secret lists' should include writers, musicians, even scientists and economists, amongst others. But the greatest conviction and momentum was behind the scheme for artists and designers. The 'plan to save the nation's artists' emerged through the autumn of 1939 and, remarkably, by the end of the war, British war artists had produced some 6,000 works of art: paintings in oil, watercolours, sculpture, drawings and sketches.

The Sketchbook War focuses on nine war artists: Edward Ardizzone, Edward Bawden, Barnett Freedman, Anthony Gross, Thomas Hennell, Eric Ravilious, Albert Richards, Richard Seddon and John Worsley. The principal reason for this choice – a not so secret list – is that each of them was much closer to the front than the majority – they all went abroad; many of them approached the front line; they heard guns firing in earnest; two were torpedoed; two were taken prisoner; and three died, two of them in 1945, the last year of the war.

This is a book about artists, rather than art itself. It tells how the artists' way of life and temperament came up against the grinding and relentless nature of warfare. If in the months before 1939 you saw yourself as an artist, focused on a career with no room for the prospect of war, how did you manage with the transformation to artist in military uniform? The artists in this story show courage, tenacity, inventiveness, and persistence. They are transported overseas; battle with fresh demands on technique, weather, illness, discomfort and hardship; value freedom and their own abilities; keep the world of the non-artist at bay; and, finally, survive, or lose their lives in the most tragic of circumstances. For all of them it was clear that the war artist shared with the war photographer the uncomfortable truth articulated by Robert Capa: "'If your pictures aren't good enough," he was fond of saying, "that's because you're not close enough"'.

2

3 September 1939

Henry Moore lay on his back, floating, looking up at the blue of the sky, imagining the shadows cast by the legions of German bombers, when, as the phrase went, 'the balloon went up.' The water was warmer than he had thought and, on another occasion, he might have felt buoyed by a sense of peace. Lifting his head, he could see the cliffs, stern and white, beetling above the pebbled beach where his pile of clothes lay crumpled: this was Shakespeare Cliffs near Dover. He had a dim memory of lines from *King Lear*: the blind Gloucester brought to the teetering edge where, could he but see, the view was of the beach far below, then the English Channel, and, in the distance, France, a smudge on the horizon on a clear day like this. Irina, Henry's Russian-born wife, was swimming close by. He noted her white skin and bony back; her yellow bathing cap rising and falling in the white-topped blue of the water. In that moment, Henry could see into a blood-red future: Chamberlain's and Hitler's war on the point of beginning, with who knew what end. On cue, the distant wail of an air raid siren – the first of the war – drifted across the water.

Later artist now – not swimmer – Moore would capture the moment, turning the late summer idyll into a grim foretaste of things to come. The cliffs would acquire a red tinge; the sea would turn thick and red as blood; and he would draw eight stiff-backed women bobbing like corks in the water, wearing gasmasks and expressions of desperate anguish as they looked, with trepidation, to the east.

This sketch, a mix of pencil, wax crayon, chalk, water colour and pen and ink – just 12 inches by 15¾ inches – marked two moments: the first war art of the 1939–1945 conflict; and the end of a world where artists could expect to make a tolerable living from their work; where paintings sold, dealers flourished and galleries stayed open. From that hot September day in 1939, the war would ensure that nothing would stay the same. Moore, in common with most artists, foresaw increasing difficulties with work – he worried about his ability to focus on anything meaningful in such a febrile atmosphere. Having been in the trenches in the 1914–1918 war, he hoped that this time he would be able to do something more constructive than enduring the mayhem and bloodshed at the front.

Early in October 1939, Moore wrote to the Director of the National Gallery in London, Sir Kenneth Clark: 'I hate intensely all that Fascism and Nazism stand for and if it should win it might be the end in Europe of all the painting, sculpture, music, architecture, literature which we all believe in …'[1] Underlying the worthy sentiments was a question which Moore contemplated in common with other artists: what should artists do in wartime? Just then, however, Clark was preoccupied with seeing 'that the National Gallery pictures were in safety'[2] and was looking for a suitably protected site in the United Kingdom to store them. Soon there was an exodus of great canvases to Wales, to be entombed in 'a vast, abandoned slate quarry … not far from the hellish town of Blaenau Festiniog.' Clark had overseen a rehearsal for such an event the previous year: 'The Gallery was shut, the rooms were empty, the remaining pictures were standing all around and the man came in and said that Munich had taken place.'[3] Back then, with the crisis over, the plans could be put away with a huge sigh of relief. This time, though, it was for real. Indeed, 'the National Gallery was able to complete the move of nearly all of its collection of 2,000 paintings by the evening of the 2nd September.'[4] War started the next day, with sirens and a first blackout.

Within months Sir Kenneth Clark found himself at the Ministry of Information, cast in the unlikely role of the head of the film division. He believed it was because 'in those days films were spoken of as "pictures", and I was believed to be an authority on pictures.'[5] He did not take the post too seriously. Clark was young – thirty-six in 1939, the same age as some of the artists he would later commission – tall and thin, with a patrician glint in his eye and an oily sheen to his hair. As well as the survival and wellbeing of the gallery's paintings, he was also increasingly concerned about what happened to artists in wartime. The issue was raised again by Lord Esher, who had been party to the discussion on the issue at the luncheon date at Ardington House on the downs in September. Clark replied: 'The work I am doing on behalf of artists seems to have been exaggerated. I am nothing more than a member of two committees which the Ministry of Labour has appointed to draw up lists of artists for the Central Register.'[6] The present focus, Clark wrote, was camouflage and propaganda; nothing more. He proposed 'a fresh committee constructed on rather broader lines'. Its focus should be to 'make a record of the war'.

With the benefit of hindsight, when the war was over, Clark claimed that his principal aim had been to 'keep artists at work on any pretext, and, as far as possible, to prevent them being killed.'[7] He believed that his 'only worthwhile activity' during the war period was the War Artists' Advisory Committee (WAAC) which he was instrumental in setting up and subsequently chaired. As a result thirty-seven war artists were eventually given full time salaried contracts, while literally hundreds of others were given commissions of varying lengths. Most artists found themselves on the Home Front, drawing ruins, ships in dock, families sheltering in the London Underground while the bombs fell above them, portraits of officers and men, women armament workers, barrage balloons – the war as the citizens suffered it. Others, though, were despatched abroad. Nothing was sure in that bleak time, least of all the prospects for those artists who were in uniform and had left the UK to observe the war at close quarters. The enemy did not distinguish between men with rifles in their hands, or just sketchbooks and pencils.

The initial proposal to the Ministry of Information by Clark was made on 29 August and finally approved on 7 November, and the WAAC met for the first time on the afternoon of 23 November 1939, in the old board room of the National Gallery. High ceilings above them; good intentions around the table. It was the first of many meetings – all of which were deemed 'secret' – and the sifting of suitable artists' names began the following week. The committee met 197 times in all, a remarkable average of nearly three times a month for the duration of the war. Mindful of its responsibilities, it was uncertain about where its work would lead. How could they know what lay ahead?

There were some key principles, however, some of which were articulated by Esher in a letter to Oliver Stanley, Secretary of State for War, on 20 February 1940: 'The artists should be unaware of what was being done to save them … there should be no demand to release these men from military service, but only that they should be used for work of comparative safety.' The final principle was that selection should be left to 'competent and distinguished judges'. For its part the committee was insistent 'that the artist should always have seen what he painted'. The basic purpose was clear too: to make 'an artistic record of the war in all its aspects'. But how it would work and evolve in practice was less clear-cut. Equally uncertain were the selection criteria, although some judgements were fixed early on: abstract artists were deemed inappropriate – Ben Nicholson's name, for example, was marked 'No recommendation' on the artist's index card. The first 'sifting of names' looked at 504 artists and 800 were considered in the first sixteen weeks.

3

The Sifting of Names

Outside, London fog swirled on a late November afternoon. Inside, in the National Gallery's board room, Sir Kenneth Clark presided over a meeting of the WAAC. As the light faded, the ritual of the blackout arrangements was completed, shutting out the remains of the day. Clark sat stiff-backed and expectant as he looked round at the familiar faces. Seated strategically nearby was the committee's secretary, E.M. O'R. Dickey, whom he had known before the war. Thoroughly good chap, art lover, been a bit of a painter, worked with the Board of Education, 'so he really knew a great deal of how to work with these funny people.'[1] Around the table were the 'competent and distinguished judges' – artists with enough establishment pedigree to pass muster: Muirhead Bone, Walter Russell, and Percy Jowett, the principal of the Royal College of Art. Nearby was the Home Office representative, T.B. Braund.

Completing the group were the representatives of the armed services whose presence was designed to keep the committee grounded and focused. There was Colin Coote, an old friend of Clark's from peacetime, whose credentials as an art lover were sound enough. With an army background, he was the War Office's point man, his CV boasting a First World War DSO and a spell as a member of parliament. Clark had been to school with the Admiralty's R.M.Y. Gleadowe and he was unconvinced by him, while the RAF's William Hildred gave the distinct impression of having his mind on greater things.

Hildred's previous work had involved civil aviation and a period at the Treasury. He had firm views on the art he liked – and didn't like. In January 1940 he was to give cautious, sniffy approval for two artists to be attached to the Royal Air Force. 'I think therefore,' he wrote, 'we ought to ask the Treasury for sanction forthwith to the appointment... to be paid for from Air Votes at a salary of £650 per annum inclusive.'[2] He was, however, unconvinced by both nominees, Paul Nash and Edward Bawden, thinking them both 'a bit leftist'. Moreover, he didn't much like Bawden's work. The Permanent Under Secretary agreed. Nevertheless Hildred recognised that he was a guardian of the RAF's status and appearances must be maintained: 'The Minister would not be agreeable to the Admiralty and War Office having accredited war artists and the Air Ministry not being in the same position.'[3]

★★★

Henry Moore went swimming that September Sunday when war broke out. Albert Richards, a student at the Wallasey School of Art, heard Chamberlain's speech declaring war while he was drinking Horlicks in a Lyons Corner House overlooking Westminster Bridge. He 'went pale ... [was] shocked, expecting imminent bombing.'[4] Not yet twenty, he will have wondered what the declaration of war meant for his anticipated studentship at the Royal College of Art (RCA) in London – and what happened to artists in wartime. He was not alone. The respected painter, designer and wood engraver Eric Ravilious cycled from Castle Hedingham in Essex over to neighbours that day for a cup of tea. The war was the only topic of conversation. That same day he signed up for a part-time post (at 15s a week), monitoring German aircraft on behalf of the Royal Observer Corps.[5] He was on duty in the early hours of the following morning and worked all hours of the day and night thereafter, conscious that German bombers bound for London could well fly over Castle Hedingham.

While William Hildred was fretting over the prospect of Edward Bawden as one of the RAF's war artists, Bawden himself was reflecting on what a war artist scheme might look like. He was sure there would be such a thing, just as there had been in the Great War. Now thirty-six – the same age as Kenneth Clark – he had been too young to be caught up in the fighting on the Western Front. Now he contemplated what this new conflict might have in store for him. On 9 September, he wrote to his friend Eric Ravilious inquiring, 'What part do you intend to play in the general mess?'[6] He sent his friend some useful addresses for obtaining wartime camouflage and propaganda work. His own first thought had been to work in the field of camouflage. He wrote to Clark in the hope that something more fulfilling than that might be possible. 'Don't get tied up with camouflage!' was Clark's advice. Clark was not always consistent. At much the same time he wrote: 'Camouflage has got an advantage over propaganda ... it is sufficiently remote from a painter's normal activity not to have a bad effect on it.'[7]

★★★

The committee began its difficult task of identifying names. Some were all too readily rejected – James Boswell and Clive Branson's links with the Communist Party were enough to see them summarily ruled out. But as for the rest, who should end with a neat, approving tick alongside their name, and a formal letter of invitation?

'Let's make a start, gentlemen. Could we discuss Edward Bawden?'

'There is an ascetic quality about him. He is tall, slim and courteous, with a disabling shyness, despite the fact that his career is well established. They say that, as a student at the Royal College, he "couldn't bring himself to enter shops or ride on buses" – so he walked everywhere.[8] He is a man well equipped for self-reliance: vegetarian; doesn't drive, or even own a car; has never possessed a camera; spurns the telephone. He seems deeply content with his own company. He has the talent and the discipline for the role in my view ...'

Edward Bawden was born on 10 March 1903 at Braintree, Essex, the son of an ironmonger. A self-contained man, Bawden had been a solitary, self-sufficient boy, flitting here and there with butterfly net and art materials. As an adult, he was scathing about Braintree, indeed he thought it merited bombing, and apologetic about his own boyhood – the 'Sissy Years', he would have entitled that chapter of his (unwritten) autobiography. Braintree High School he hated and he made his dislike evident: he was 'badly behaved, rebellious and unpopular'.[9] Later, he went to the Friends' School at Saffron Walden and Cambridge Municipal Art School, before winning a £60 per annum scholarship to the RCA.

Bawden's contemporaries at the Royal College included Henry Moore and Vivian Pitchforth – two future war artists – as well as Eric Ravilious and Douglas Percy Bliss, who became Bawden's inseparable friends. From 1925, Bawden, Bliss and Ravilious lived together in London's West Kensington. Bliss remembered the 'gravy-coloured sitting rooms'.[10] Bawden thought Ravilious 'a bit of a layabout', but they were very close, despite their differences: Bawden found women scary; avoided drink and cigarettes; newspapers and films too. Life-drawing unsettled him; oil painting was virtually taboo – he hated the smell of turps, wrinkling his nose in distaste. He took the view that 'oil paint was prose, and watercolour poetry'. The two were close friends, but did not agree on everything: Bawden, for example, regarded reading as a means of learning about the world, while to Ravilious it was a leisure pursuit – for fun. Bawden was 'one of those melancholy people to whom laughter is medicine … He had never been to a football match, to Lords, to Wimbledon.'[11]

A painting by Ravilious of Bawden working in his studio, in 1927, shows a straight-backed Bawden at his easel, all shyness forgotten in the intensity of his concentration, paints and brushes methodically laid out, ginger cat washing itself amiably in the tranquility of the room, the artist's jacket discarded and workmanlike braces looped over a loose-fitting grey shirt. Bawden's face has a haughty, aristocratic look, and his hair is swept back from a high forehead. One wonders how he would cope with the discomfort and disruption of war.

In that year of 1927, Bawden and Ravilious would cycle out together from Bawden's Braintree house, seeking places of mutual interest to paint and freedom from intrusive observers for the anxious Bawden. 'They cycled for miles in stifling weather much to the discomfort of the poor Boy [Ravilious], who tired easily.'[12] See them, two artists, absorbed in landscape, straw-hatted, easels set up in the cool shadow of a copse of willow trees, slapping at flies and sweating in the heavy August heat. Through the late 1920s and 1930s, the two men's careers in art flourished and they earned a wide range of commissions – linocuts, wallpaper designs, calendars, diaries, menus, murals etc. Bawden's clients included Shell, London Underground, the Empire Marketing Board, Twinings, and Fortnum and Mason.

In 1932 Bawden got married and his father bought Brick House, Great Bardfield in Essex as a wedding present; subsequently, Eric Ravilious and his wife, Tirzah, shared the house with the newlyweds. The house was

imposing if austere, with a wide street frontage and a front door opening directly on to the street. Attic windows peeped out from the tiled
roof. The street was sleepily rural. Charlotte Bawden was her husband's
opposite in many ways, extroverted where he was much more restrained.
It was neither Mrs Bawden's extroversion, nor her husband's quiet self-
containment, that caused the Raviliouses to move out. The amicable
parting of the ways was the result of Tirzah Ravilious' persistently regular rustling-up of Queen of Puddings for dessert.

In 1936 the Bawdens' son Richard was born (the future war artist
Tom Hennell was his godfather). Bawden himself was underwhelmed
by parenthood, even in comfortable retrospect: 'I still don't like children. They're wet smelly things and make an awful lot of noise.'[13] But he
loved Great Bardfield, his garden and rural Essex. The war would make a
nomad of him. It was not at all what his peers expected: John Nash, for
example, commented in a letter to Ravilious: 'I am sure (Bawden) would
not deign to notice a state of war!'[14] On the contrary, his stint as a war
artist would stretch over six years and thousands of miles.

Brick House, Great
Bardfield: the house
shared for a time in the
1930s by the Bawden
and Ravilious families.

'That's probably enough to be going on. So what about Ravilious?'

'He's widely known as "Rav" or "The Boy". He's smooth, charming and witty, although some people talk of his "emotional reticence" and a "withdrawal" which gets in the way of "any binding intimacy".[15] He is tall and thin with light brown eyes. His "curling eyelashes" are "like a girl's".[16] He breezes through life, eyes twinkling, persistently whistling in a way that people find endearing ...'

Eric Ravilious was four months younger than Edward Bawden: he was born in Eastbourne, Sussex on 22 July 1903. Where Bawden had a middle-aged look about him, Ravilious looked boyish. He arrived at the Royal College at the same time as Bawden, and in much the same way, having won a similar scholarship. Eric liked pretty girls, beer and sport. Once Ravilious discovered that Bawden had a waspish sense of humour, they became close. They were competitive nonetheless, and demonstrably different. Bliss would, occasionally, find Bawden at the breakfast table absorbed in a book, 'his social temperature near freezing'.[17] Ravilious was more approachable. Both were influenced by Paul Nash, who taught them at the Royal College. Both went to Italy in the 1920s: oddly, the straitlaced Bawden was the more enthusiastic, stirred by the grandeur and sense of history. Ravilious complained about the heat, the cold and his bowels; he caroused with Henry Moore in Florence and took long walks by the Arno. Like Bawden, he was unmoved by the shadow of Italian fascism. Ravilious was 'curious about everything except politics,' one contemporary wrote.[18] Later, during the war, John Nash's wife, Christine, noted that Ravilious 'never reads a paper or listens to the news'.[19]

Bawden was best man at Ravilious' wedding. Just before the ceremony he wrote to fellow artist Barnett Freedman telling him that Eric was very keen that Freedman should attend: 'We – that's Him and Me – are both going in our ordinary clothes so there'll be no need for you to appear funereally clothed unless you wish.'[20] Ravilious and Bawden shared a deep mutual respect: 'Eric admired Edward's dour creativeness, his sheer professionalism, and Edward believed in elegance and fastidious taste with which Eric was endowed.'[21]

'Who's next on the list? Ah, yes, Thomas Hennell. Now, what do we make of him?'

'Hennell is on good terms with both Bawden and Ravilious. They regard him as a genius. He is tall, gaunt and troubled. No one doubts his tenacity. For example, he bicycles around the country, his drawing board protected from the weather thrust down the back of a scruffy sweater, determined to sketch for posterity the fading fabric of English agriculture. He has been 'seen in winter sturdily propelling at a steady five knots a huge, ancient black bicycle … with lumpy packages and a suitcase tied on the grid.'[22]

Once, on the trail of subject matter in Langdale in the Lake District, Hennell resolutely marched his bike and its accoutrements up the long bind of Wrynose Pass, before turning south up a fell-walkers' path on Wetside Edge (aptly named – he would have got his boots and tyres thoroughly wet) to the high ridge leading to the Old Man of Coniston; then down through the quarries and woods of Tilberthwaite to Ruskin's house at Brantwood overlooking Lake Coniston. Even without a bike, this is a hefty trek.

He was born in 1903 in Ridley, Kent, where his father was the local vicar. A carefree childhood ended when he was sent to boarding school, latterly Bradfield College in Berkshire. Subsequently he trained at Regent Street Polytechnic in London before, in the late 1920s, embarking on a brief career as an art teacher, notably at Kingswood School, Bath. He did not take to it, recognising that he was 'a very indifferent schoolmaster'.[23] He lived in austere, cheerless rooms in Bath – 10 Bladud Buildings – and wrestled with the despair arising from an obsessive, unrequited passion for the education reformer Marion Richardson, who was eleven years older.

He first met Bawden and Ravilious in 1931. One breakfast time they found him, 'a total stranger – pumping water and splashing it all over himself at their kitchen sink …'[24] Raised eyebrows; a moment of disconcerted stillness in the shadowed kitchen; a ticking clock; then a nod from Bawden to his friend, followed by a disarming Ravilious smile and a frank question. To which Hennell, in his 'deep, booming parsonic' voice, explained that he was renting the other half of Brick House for the night. Bawden thought him 'very intense, solitary … profoundly serious.'

Instinctively sombre, Hennell's equilibrium was brutally disturbed when his proposal of marriage to Marion Richardson was turned down, sometime in 1931 or 1932. For part of 1932 he lived near the Tate Gallery. That same year, and for the next three years, he would suffer from mental illness. Diagnosed with schizophrenia, he 'expressed many paranoid views of a bizarre type … he was at times agitated and occasionally violent.'[25] He spent much of the years to 1935 in hospitals. Even after his discharge in October 1935, and the judgement of 'recovered', he suffered hallucinations. Photographs of him at the time are revealing: shirt collar size too big for his thin neck; haggard expression, deep-sunk, anguished eyes; chiselled lines dragging his face down; a permanent frown tightening his forehead. He did not look like a man who would be able to resist whatever darkness a war might bring.

In the summer of 1939 Thomas Hennell and Edward Bawden, together with Muriel Rose, Director of The Little Gallery in Chelsea, set out to savour continental Europe while they still could. In the last weeks of August, before the war began, they visited the French Alps. It was very hot: reluctantly Hennell was dissuaded from swimming in the Alpine lakes, no doubt tempted by cold water in a blistering summer. They 'managed to see the German pictures [from the Prado]'.[26] On 1 September, they made a fleeting visit to the Zurich International Exhibition. The fast-moving European crisis caused it to be closed in a hurry; the English artists 'were in the grounds having lunch ... it was then we heard of fighting having commenced on the Polish frontier.'[27] Undeterred, Hennell proposed moving on to Basel to see the town's collection of Holbeins, but Bawden was less keen, anxiously pointing out the numbers of people evidently on the move, heading for the safety and comfort of home. Bawden won

Edward Ardizzone.

the argument and they set off by train for England, a journey subject to frequent stops, confined to the discomfort of the crowded, steamy railway carriage. Later, Bawden remembered 'that Hennell preferred to observe English standards of dress when travelling abroad';[28] on this occasion he went so far as to unfasten his shirt collar as the train meandered through the haze of a dying summer.

'Mm, not convinced! He doesn't seem fit for what we have in mind. Who's next? Ardizzone?'

'Well, if Ravilious has the look of a professional cricketer – lean, comfortable with himself, a spiral of smoke drifting up from a cigarette in his tanned hand, fringe of hair tumbling over his forehead – then Hennell resembles a farmer on the verge of bankruptcy. Bawden? A stern and unforgiving priest! And Edward Ardizzone? Well, he has the appearance of a classics master in a middle-of-the-road public school. He's charming, spreads a calming influence, open, direct. "Warm and gregarious"[29] is a good description. He loves a pint and pubs; never stops sketching – wonderfully infectious laugh. You'd like him.'[30]

Edward Ardizzone was known at school as 'Ardizzone, fat and bony'. It was a name that would cause him trouble later in life too, once Britain was at war with Italy. He was born in exile – in Haiphong (now Vietnam), the eldest of five. His father, who was French, but Italian by blood, worked for the Eastern Extension Telegraph Company, while his mother was half Scots and half English. She was the one with the artistic blood. When he was five, Ardizzone sailed to England, and lived in East Bergholt, Suffolk – Constable country. His parents were frequently abroad, leaving Ted in the tender care of a large, volatile grandmother. Unimpressed with school, he doodled his way through it; struggling with wielding authority as a prefect, but always trying to do the right thing – 'I was a conformist'.[31] In 1918, he was determined to 'join the Army as soon as possible and fight for King and Country'. Flustered, he made 'a boob of the interview' when he tried for a commission in the Artists' Rifles; he was rejected on health grounds – 'a misdiagnosed aortic murmur'[32] – when he tried to enlist in Bristol in October 1918. For him, this war was over in a moment.

He had no thought of being a professional artist; instead, he did a six-month course at a school of commerce, acquiring the ability to take shorthand at 120 words per minute. He was employed by the Warminster Motor Company in Wiltshire, and then went to London, working as a clerk variously for the China and Japan Trading Company, Liverpool Marine and General Insurance, and Eastern Telegraph. He earned £10 per month. He attended life-drawing evening classes, joined the Territorial Army (it meant an extra week's holiday from work) and played rugby for the Exiles. It was his father's gift of £500 (he had been given a work bonus) which prompted the shift to a career as a professional artist. By the time the war broke out, he was well regarded, successful and thirty-eight years old. He looked older, with a spreading waistline, a bad back, and a balding pate. His war correspondent's licence noted that he was 5 feet 10½ inches, with 'brown hair, grey eyes' and a 'heavy' build.

'Sounds ideal. Let's move on. Can you just run through the next few on the list? We can look at the detail later – at the next meeting perhaps.'

'We have some very young men to consider. John Worsley, for one. He's just twenty, studied fine art at Goldsmiths College in London before working briefly as a freelance illustrator until he chose to go to sea. He's a midshipman in the Merchant Navy. Then there's Albert Richards, who's even younger than Worsley and another Liverpudlian. Born in December 1919 into a working-class family, his scholarship to the Royal College was awarded this year. Anthony Gross is closer in age to Bawden, and the only one of those we've mentioned who went to the Slade School in London. He is instantly recognisable – beret, oil paint in his nails; a European cut to his clothes, a southern French suntan. I imagine with his French connections and ability to speak the language he would be keen to get involved. And we should also look at Barnett Freedman – you'll recall he designed the George V Silver Jubilee stamp? He teaches at the Royal College. Sound chap in my view.'

'Excellent. Well, I think we've done a good afternoon's work. Remind me, when's the next meeting?'

4

War Drawings? Theatre of War?

The weather that September was perfect: 'singularly beautiful,' one writer described it. 'It hung like a golden apple on a bough, soon to be detached. The sun, through windless days, shone on the cherubic aluminium roundness of the tethered barrage balloons.'[1] People's hearts were less sanguine, however, with so much uncertainty in the air. Eric Ravilious, for one, hated upheaval and was very unsettled – 'exceedingly restless,' he wrote in a letter to his wife Tirzah on 2 September, 'but not unhappy at all.'[2] He contemplated enlisting in the Artists' Rifles before being advised against it.

Similarly uncertain was the Yorkshire artist Richard Seddon. He found the prospect of war deeply perplexing: 'my plans, like those of many people, fell about my ears.'[3] It was a 'disastrous interruption'.[4] After three years at the Royal College, he had just been awarded a scholarship at the Tate Gallery. It was not to be: a telegram to his home in Sheffield came from the RCA, telling him not to return to London. He tried to enlist at once, without success, turned away because neither the army or the navy had enough equipment to cope with the sudden flood of recruits. As the autumn drew in, the hills around Sheffield became increasingly cloud-capped; valleys filled with mist. A hard winter lay ahead.

If it wasn't to be the army or navy, then Seddon saw himself painting camouflage, or else being a war artist, like Paul Nash in the Great War. Nash had been one of his teachers at the Royal College and Seddon wrote to him 'to find out what was afoot in the art world'.[5] The reply

Richard Seddon: 'I've been put in for a War Office Order, sir, to make war drawings in the theatre of war.'

was sobering. There was, Nash wrote, 'no demand for [artists'] work and no impulse to do any'. He also wrote to Edward Bawden, another of his tutors; the reply when it came was on the thinnest of paper in Bawden's 'spidery and inhumanly neat calligraphy'. Bawden was warm and responsive, but had little in the way of concrete information or guidance; he lamented the new-found difficulty of 'meeting one's friends ... even of knowing what they were doing or where they can be found',[6] and suggested that 'a particular restaurant should be selected as a common room, so that one could go there for a meal, and perhaps meet someone like yourself.'[7] Bawden recognised that artists needed each other to face what lay ahead. Seddon, meanwhile, fretted, unable to paint. He tried the army again and was told to wait.

In December, Seddon received another letter from Bawden, this time with more information: war artists were being appointed; they were largely to be drawn from those who served in the last war; and would number no more than fifty. 'Like you,' Bawden wrote, 'I would willingly go to the front to record war scenes.' He was resigned at that point to being a Home Office Camouflage Officer: he thought the prospect 'tepid'.

The uncertainty was frustrating, but you couldn't fault Seddon's persistence. He wangled his way into the army, through 'a friend of my sister's';

the adjutant who facilitated it 'risked a rocket from the War Office' for doing so. Nor did he give up on his ambitions to be a war artist. On one weekend leave, he met Percy Jowett, the Principal of the Royal College and a member of the WAAC, who explained how the committee was operating – under the Ministry of Information; with three other members apart from Jowett himself, including Kenneth Clark; and planning to use some younger artists who were serving in the forces in some capacity. They would, Jowett said, 'make records in the actual theatre of war'.[8] Seddon's eyes lit up and he confirmed that he would like to be considered for such an opportunity. That evening, dancing at the Trocadero in London, he couldn't put the possibility out of his mind. Joy, the WAAF he was whirling round the dance floor that evening, had similarly pulled strings. 'I wonder,' Seddon said, 'whether it took as much influence to get into the last war.'[9]

There was a distinctly bumbling amateurism about Seddon's engagement as a war artist.[10] Percy Jowett wrote suggesting that he should speak about the arrangements to his commanding officer. It led to a very woolly series of short discussions. 'I've been put in for a War Office Order, sir, to make war drawings in the theatre of war,' Seddon said, three times, eyes front, to rising levels of seniority. 'War Drawings, eh? Theatre of War, you say? Umm …' Finally, the colonel said, 'Oh well, that's all right. You can carry on.' So Seddon did, never receiving any further guidance of any kind. He understood that 'nothing but essential duties were to be allowed to interfere' with his painting. The months of waiting and volunteering, persistence and determination had paid off. He would soon be crossing the Channel to confront the German Army, with sketchbook, paper and paint-box.

★★★

Eric Ravilious leaned back, one hand on his tin hat, and looked up at the night sky above Essex. He could hear aircraft engines and occasionally see shadows passing across what he supposed was a bomber's moon. He sat there, uniformed observer and 'resting' artist, mug of coffee in his hand, Royal Observer Corps heavy boots on his feet, wrapped up against the weather in what he described as a 'life-boatman's outfit'.[11] He worked odd hours as part of a team of two. He was, he joked, 'saving the country', and all for 15s a week, though his 'only luxuries here are beer and cigarettes'.[12] Ale, fags – but no art. That seemed to have come to a conclusive stop.

He took, however, a whimsical pleasure in the arcane ritual of passwords and the careful logging of aircraft sightings. Not to mention the splendour of spectacular sunrises. There was little danger in this 'observing'; indeed, it seemed like boy scout camp. For example, he played darts and 'progressive ping pong' with the soldiers who guarded the hilltop post. The soldiers' boots, as they careered around the table, sounded like thunder. Food was more of a preoccupation than the enemy: he munched tasty sandwiches prepared by the 'aged granny from Wood Green'[13] who had been billeted on Bank House, Castle Hedingham, where the Ravilious family lived; mushrooms and blackberries were picked from the fields and hedgerows in quiet moments (at this stage of the war there were plenty of those); while the splendour of Castle Hedingham Observation Post's oyster party – oysters, brown ale, and

Bank House, Castle Hedingham, home of Eric and Tirzah Ravilious when war broke out.

bread and butter – seemed out of keeping with wartime. Occasionally barrage balloons drifted over, high above them; eventually they would be shot down or else the wind blew them over to Sweden. At times, when the weather was good, night duty could be uplifting, looking up at the stars from the post's hilly location, but it could be uncomfortable too: 'the rain [is] coming down so hard on the corrugated iron and the oilskins and a high wind' – all of which made listening for aircraft in the night very difficult.

It couldn't last – neither the torpor of that first autumn of what was soon dubbed the 'phoney war', nor Ravilious' rural obscurity. He found waiting for the war to begin in earnest 'nerve-wracking'; the unexpected lull was 'in an awful sort of way … a holiday'.[14] He certainly hoped for an escape from the hilltop eyrie to some kind of work that was more suited to his artist's skills, although, as autumn turned to winter, he was not optimistic about a rapid clarification of the role, number and location of war artists. There were some who regarded the phoney war as a blessing in disguise: the WAAC's Colin Coote later observed, 'I have always said that Hitler was a most useful honorary member of the committee, not because he vaunted himself as an artist, but because he allowed the 'phoney' war to last nine months. This gave us time to assign artists to the most suitable fields.'[15] For the artists, though, there were months of uncertainty.

Towards the end of October, Ravilious received a letter from the artist John Nash, who had virtually stopped working and whose brother Paul, he wrote, was in Oxford compiling a list of artists who should be protected from the most dangerous aspects of the war. John Betjeman was sniffy about the latter exercise, referring to Nash's 'rather futile conferences'.[16] By mid-November, Ravilious began to think there might be a real prospect of work. He wrote to Helen Binyon on 26 November that 'the war artist scheme is a good one, if they ever start it'.[17] At much the same time, the WAAC began its sifting of names, but Ravilious, in common with other artists, was in the dark about its progress and deliberations. Increasingly he recognised that life in the observation post was far removed from art. Moreover, observing was demanding: 'They don't let us relax at all,' he wrote to his father-in-law, Colonel F.S. Garwood in Sussex. 'The beds in the hut are merely properties never used.'[18] He took a brief respite from the observation post in December when he went to a wintry West Country to draw a series of landmarks, including the white horses in the chalk uplands at Westbury and Uffington. There was a price to pay for the trip: the cold and wet – and working outdoors – gave him rheumatism in both shoulders.

Then suddenly, at an unlikely time, things started to move. At mid-morning on Christmas Eve – a Sunday – Ravilious received a letter from the Admiralty. It was signed by R. Gleadowe, the WAAC's naval representative, and dated 23 December 1939. Ravilious tore open the buff envelope and ran his eyes down the letter for its principal content: 'you and John Nash have been selected to work for the Admiralty on a part-time basis … the sooner you get to work the better … It would be a great disappointment to the Admiralty, the Ministry of Information and, I may add, myself, if you should feel unable or unwilling to undertake work of this kind.'[19] Splendid news! It felt like a Christmas box from the Admiralty. He celebrated with rum, coffee, tea and port.

Before the year ended, he caught the train up to London for two interviews that typified the upheaval the war had perpetrated on people's lives: there he was, an established artist (and novice aircraft observer), summoned to meet two senior civil servants, both recently translated educationalists. The Admiralty's man, Gleadowe, had been Head of Drawing at Winchester as late as 1939, and was previously Slade Professor of Art at Oxford; while E.M. O'R. Dickey, at the Ministry of Information, had been the former Staff Inspector for Art with His Majesty's (School) Inspectorate.[20] The outcome of the interviews was a six-month contract and a fee of £325 for everything that Ravilious painted during the period. He was also entitled to a maintenance allowance of £1 a day, or 5s if on board ship; a uniform grant of £15; and he could apply for any necessary materials. He wasn't to know that Muirhead Bone's fee – Bone was the first war artist commissioned by the Admiralty and a member of the WAAC – was £1,000 a year.[21]

It was agreed that Ravilious and Nash would both be given the rank of captain in the Royal Marines. On 20 January 1940, Ravilious received a letter from John Nash suggesting that captainships were ten a penny. Nash was delighted that the decision about which uniform to wear meant they avoided the laughable 'WC' (for War Correspondent) on their hatbands. He did some gardening in his new uniform to break it in. Ravilious looked good in his: 'trim and boyish'.[22] A contemporary described him as wearing 'uniform with a certain degree of insouciance. His carefree collar and wayward tie would certainly have aroused the spleen of any senior officer of that most spick and span of martial outfits.'[23] With some relief, no doubt,

Dickey wrote to Gleadowe on 27 January that MI5 could find no objection to Ravilious and Nash. Waiting for the commission to begin seemed painfully slow and the weather was grim. Early in February, Ravilious cycled on icy roads to see Bawden in Great Bardfield, falling off regularly as he struggled to keep the bicycle upright on the glassy surface. At Bank House, the water pipes were frozen; so too the artist's ink bottle – his pen could not penetrate the surface. Later, the milk and soda water turned to ice.

★★★

Edward Bawden, meanwhile, had heeded Clark's advice to avoid camouflage and bided his time, although he was apprehensive about what the future might hold. A letter was sent on 27 December 1939 inviting him to be an official war artist, and on 2 January 1940 he and Paul Nash met Sir William Hildred from the Air Ministry at the Orleans Club in London for lunch to discuss the proposal. Soon after he was asked to submit some examples of his work to the Secretary of State for Air. By the middle of the month the negotiations had reached a point where 'an outfit grant of £15 to provide a suitable uniform for wear when working

Eric Ravilious, Barnett Freedman and John Nash, artists in uniform, April 1940.

with the Forces in France' was proposed. The War Department, according to Dickey, were also keen to recruit him, and he wrote to Bawden on 12 January noting that there was 'competition for your services'.[24]

For his part, Bawden wanted to get to France, declaring that he 'would like to get to the front and live in close touch with the RAF and make documentary pictures for a period of – say – six months.' He kitted himself out and waited through February. He received formal notification of the appointment on 2 March 1940: '£650 a year; appointment can be terminated at one month's notice on either side; uniform that of a special correspondent; all work belongs to the Crown; transport first class on boat-trains, channel boats; and in France, third class in England.'[25] Arrangements were hazy about hospital treatment ('free?'); death – 'in accordance with the regulations applicable to civilians', whatever that meant; and, indeed, there was a large question mark over the work to be undertaken. The question of an artist's status – military personnel or civilian – would prove to be of critical importance later in the war.

Bawden would not be alone in heading for France: Edward Ardizzone was similarly charged. In the days before the war began, Ardizzone had been digging trenches in very hot weather. He sent a postcard to his daughter Christianna on 29 August 1939 saying that his 'hands are getting quite hard and horny like the Elephants child's aunt the ostrich.' On the reverse of the card, Ardizzone had drawn a sketch of himself at work wielding a pickaxe.[26] He was posted for a time to the ominous sounding Lower Hope[27] in Kent with an anti-aircraft battery; then a further posting to Plumstead marshes, before falling victim to pneumonia (those Dickensian Thames fogs?) that winter. Returning to duty as a second lieutenant to a battery on Clapham Common, he 'felt like death'. A telegram informing him of his newly won war artist status changed everything. He celebrated by buying himself a pair of splendid cavalryman's boots which, to his chagrin, hurt his feet ('gave me hell' he recalled many years later – he sincerely hoped 'that some German is wearing them to this day!').

A formal letter suggesting a four month contract was sent to 'Bombardier Edward Ardizzone' at 162 Anti-Aircraft Battery, Woolwich on 21 December 1939. Getting MI5's approval took most of January and caused a minor hiccup late on: 'I now hear today that this approval applies only to work at home'[28] – not for France! Eventually the paperwork was sorted and on 27 March 1940 his 'Release from Service' was signed:

Digging trenches: Ardizzone's sketch on a postcard to his daughter: 'My hands are getting quite hard and horny.'

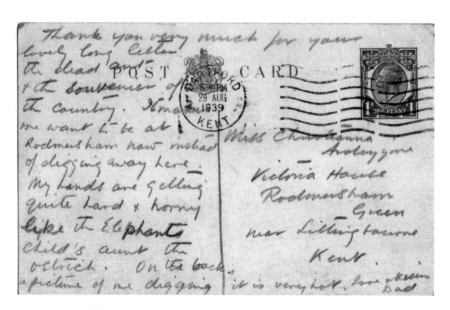

Reluctant trench digger and future war artist Edward Ardizzone sends a postcard to his daughter, Christianna, August 1939.

Second Lieutenant E.J.I. Ardizzone was 'to be released immediately for an indefinite period to take up the appointment of official war artist'.[29] Ardizzone began packing his sketchbook, paints and cavalryman's boots for service abroad. Shortly before embarking for France, he met up with Bawden in a pub in Shaftesbury Avenue. There they are, in soft tavern light, over-coated against the London winter, supping flat ale and making plans for springtime in France – two watercolourists against the Boche. Bawden warmed to his companion, listened to what he felt was good advice – the man knew how to behave, he felt, officer material even, all that Territorial Army background. On 31 March 1940, they travelled together to Calais, at first, and then on to Arras near the Belgian border, a city over which the fighting had raged during the Great War.

Things were beginning to happen at last: Percy Jowett, Principal at the RCA, wrote to Barnett Freedman on 16 April 1940 noting that the college was losing one or two students to the war each week.[30] Artists were making plans: for example, in February 1940, Anthony Gross, wrote to fellow artist Eric Kennington: 'What I want to do now is to get to France by some way or other and paint in and behind the lines there.'[31] When the war broke out, Gross had been in Paris, but he immediately headed for London. He remembered the wise words of his friend Dick Pearsall: 'Best job you can get if another war comes along is as a war artist.' Early in March 1940 he was given a short, one-month commission from the WAAC, but he was denied the chance to return to France, working instead at Caterham in Surrey and on the Yorkshire moors, based at Catterick. For his part, however, Barnett Freedman was on his way to France.

On 1 March 1940, Freedman received a letter from the War Office inquiring whether he was 'desirous of accepting appointment' to serve with the British Expeditionary Force in France.

His acceptance was dated 4 March. Ten days later he received a letter from WAAC's Colin Coote asking how his preparations were going and proposing a date for travel. In the event, 10 April was fixed as the embarkation date. On the 26th Coote wrote again, informing Freedman that the Director of Military Intelligence, BEF, 'has now ruled official artists will be free to move in the BEF zone without being conducted.'[32] Freedman embarked on a flurry of shopping: art materials (oils, turps, brushes, Indian ink, pencils, drawing pins etc) from Winsor & Newton (the cost was just over £14) and equipment from Harrods (a long list that included torch, balaclava, talc, Listerine,

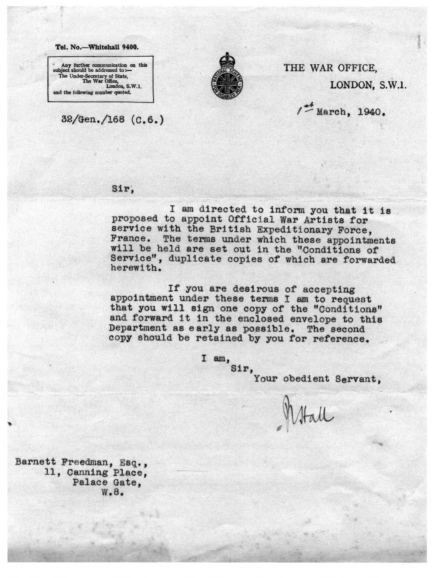

Tel. No.—Whitehall 9400.

Any further communication on this subject should be addressed to :—
The Under-Secretary of State,
The War Office,
London, S.W.1.
and the following number quoted.

32/Gen./168 (C.6.)

THE WAR OFFICE,
LONDON, S.W.1.

1st March, 1940.

Sir,

      I am directed to inform you that it is proposed to appoint Official War Artists for service with the British Expeditionary Force, France. The terms under which these appointments will be held are set out in the "Conditions of Service", duplicate copies of which are forwarded herewith.

      If you are desirous of accepting appointment under these terms I am to request that you will sign one copy of the "Conditions" and forward it in the enclosed envelope to this Department as early as possible. The second copy should be retained by you for reference.

I am,
Sir,
Your obedient Servant,

Barnett Freedman, Esq.,
11, Canning Place,
Palace Gate,
W.8.

The War Office letter of March 1940 asking if Barnett Freedman was 'desirous of accepting appointment.'

vests (2), pants (2), a 'soldier's comfort', shoes and shoe trees). Finally, he received a movement order: he was to travel on the 07.30 boat train from Folkestone to Calais on 10 April. With Ardizzone and Bawden already in France, the war artists' military campaign had begun.

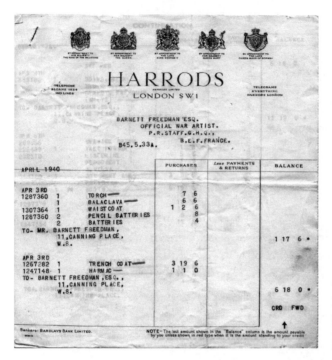

'Balaclava, talc, Listerine, vests (2)' – page 1 of Freedman's Harrods shopping list, 1940.

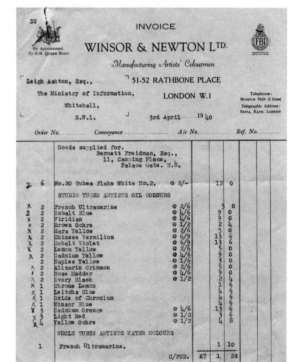

What the well-prepared war artist takes to the front: the first page from Freedman's order from Winsor & Newton.

5

A Cold and Phoney War

The slush on the dockside persistently seeped into his boots and an east wind cut through his new uniform. Yesterday's snow had already lost its soft whiteness; it had turned yellow, churned up by ratings' impatient boots. The short day had seen a fleeting thaw, a rare event in this bitter winter of 1940, but it would freeze again overnight. Eric Ravilious thrust his hands deep into his uniform pockets, wondering whether such hankering after warmth was somehow *infra dig* for officers. He smiled to himself, tilting his head back to look at the sky, a forlorn island of blue in a tumult of towering grey clouds. There was a hint of sun, but it was shrouded by a veil of mist. The roofs of the dockyard buildings were deep in untrammelled snow. A chimney breathed smoke into the clouds. Ravilious contemplated a cigarette, but chose instead to keep his hands in his pockets. Only the need to hold a sketchbook would tempt them out, and sure enough, thinking of it, he could not resist the temptation of harsh light and washed-out colours. He began to sketch, the cold temporarily forgotten.

He stood looking up at the knife-edged prow of a great ship, observing the spider's web of ropes draped down from its height to the bollards on the quay, gun-grey metal in the yellow slush. A sailor in a peaked cap looked down from the deck high above, his figure surrounded by the diminishing pocket of blue in the wintry sky. Thin figures were walking reluctantly up the gangplank in a landscape almost devoid of colour. Ravilious remembered with a pang the trees and meadows of rural Essex, but there was something about the stark military grey and the dull maritime blues which stirred him. So this is Chatham Dockyard, Ravilious thought – I'm in the navy, of all things! The water looked icy with thin February light reflected off an oily sheen. I can catch the way the light plays on the ship's side and on the flat estuary water, he thought. It felt good to be working again ... He couldn't take his eyes off the ship's shapely bow, imagining it driving the waves apart. The ship loomed above him and he shivered with something more than the cold.

The process through which the Admiralty had put him had been slow, dragging on either side of Christmas 1939 and involving exchanges of letters between London and Castle Hedingham, and of cautious minutes within the Admiralty. The officials were intent on keeping costs down: Dickey, in writing to Gleadowe on 22 December, noted that 'we shall not wish to spend any great sum of money.'[1] A month later he told Gleadowe that Ravilious should not receive a 'salary in the sense that Sir Muirhead Bone is receiving a salary'. Moreover, the Admiralty would get 'the whole of the output ... during the period of employment'. This was clung on to as a principle by the officials: 'Ravilious' output is ours to do with what we like, is it not?'[2] For his part, Ravilious was excited about the commission: 'I felt that I wanted to make an exploration in some new country there and then after the quiet life in the Observer Corps.'[3]

On 26 January 1940, a letter confirming the appointment was sent – MI5 having finally cleared him – with further reminders of the proper protocol: 'It will be necessary to submit all your preliminary sketches, as well as finished works, for censorship.' On 10 February 1940, Ravilious became officially attached to the Admiralty and, two days later, he arrived at a bitterly cold Royal Naval Barracks at Chatham. He immediately sent home for his 'red and white striped dressing gown – its weight won't matter I think as from the look of it there is no fetching and carrying for Captains.'[4] He liked the officers' Mess on HMS *Pembroke* – 'a wonderful place, huge and tasteless' – and the officers themselves ('very pink and jocular and "damn it sir"').[5] He tried hard to make himself presentable to the naval brass hats, essaying conscientious salutes and trying to make his uniform suitably ship-shape, although he was discomforted by his being dressed in khaki amidst the ubiquitous navy blue. As the spring of 1940 approached, the weather did not improve, snow falling with grim regularity from a series of resolutely wintry skies. Ravilious painted until his hands were so numbed by the cold that he couldn't continue. He worried about his wife and family back home in Castle Hedingham, imagining them being gassed by the Germans – 'a spray might easily reach Essex' – and he encouraged Tirzah to have 'soap and water … rubber boots and gloves' to combat any drifting clouds of gas.[6]

He was not only preoccupied with German gas; a more serious threat were the German mines that occasionally were left exposed by the tide on banks of damp sand … Up betimes; mug of hot tea and a hurried cigarette, then an ungainly scramble aboard, hindered by the voluminous folds of a long naval coat and the need to clutch sketchbook and pencils. It was a bright dawn, for once; the snow had gone and instead there was a cloudless sky, with a low sun bisected by the horizon. They headed for the sands at Whitstable on an outgoing tide. There was a sense of apprehension on board amongst the men in black waterproofs and gum boots. Once on the sands they trudged, head down, across the slushy ice. The mine was half out of the water, black and rusting, in a place

Ravilious 'trying to make his uniform suitably ship-shape'.

more suited to oysters than explosives. Time to 'render the mine safe' – RMS, as Ravilious learned the jargon had it. 'Rendering is so nice and understates the job perfectly.'[7] For his part, he concentrated hard on preserving the moment – *this* would make a painting! – and left it to the naval bomb disposal man, Lieutenant Commander G.A. Hodges, to fulfil his side of the bargain, making the mine safe. Ravilious held the image in his mind – a big sky, rising sun, barrels, tall oars aloft and coiled ropes slung over shoulders; men wading purposively through pools of sea water, or standing, hands in pockets, waiting for the time to return to somewhere warmer, and a belated breakfast, when they would look out from a noisy mess through windows misted with condensation at a cold, unwelcoming sea, and a world rendered slightly safer.

At the end of February 1940, Ravilious moved further east, to Sheerness on the Isle of Sheppey, staying at the Royal Fountain Hotel. He wrote to his wife, Tirzah, from there on the 27th: 'Will you thank Tom Hennell for the books and say I'll write to him.'[8] He liked Sheerness, its 'lovely Regency buildings' and heart-warming still-lifes of 'buoys, anchors, chains and wreckage'.[9] He thought it resembled Venice. Chatham's estuarine river was replaced by open sea, a bleak white-capped English Channel. Somewhere to the east, great armies were massing. It was more apparent in Sheerness that there was a war on. It remained cold: on an expedition to the Nore lightship the wind cut like a knife. Snow tumbled from grey cloud on a nithering east wind. He wondered when the war would mean more than cold-numbed fingers, breezy excursions on the Channel, and manoeuvring his way through naval protocol.

★★★

It was still cold at the end of March when Ardizzone and Bawden landed in France. For his part, Ardizzone struggled initially with what 'official war artist' status meant. Heavens, he thought, I'm a civilian now! Or am I? Gone were the days when, as a second lieutenant, he knew whom to salute and who, in turn, should salute him. Now, it was all very muddling really: he was obliged to wear 'WC' – for War Correspondent – on his shoulders, for example. WC! Embarrassing, frankly. Moreover, what were war artists supposed to *do* in a war zone? In theory, it seemed, they were free to roam about unconducted, sketching unhindered, but in practice, with no transport of their own, they were at the mercy of those with jeeps.

It was a cause of irritation: Barnett Freedman wrote asking for his own driver and transport. In a terse response, Colin Coote refused the request.[10]

Once in the field, different problems arose: there was no escaping the fact that a solitary man intently sketching military installations was all too liable to end up arrested as a suspected spy. In the early days, Ardizzone was chauffeured to see trenches, graveyards and the pill-boxes lining the Belgian frontier. Stone, mud and concrete – all so dead, somehow. Edward Bawden had the same unsatisfactory experience. The two war artists wondered what they had let themselves in for. Moreover, the landscape fitted their mood: it was devoid of trees, flat and melancholy with history. 'Beastly country,' Ardizzone thought, 'wet, cold and just fields growing beet.'

A fourth official war artist soon followed Bawden, Freedman and Ardizzone across the Channel. The portrait painter Reginald Eves was commissioned 'to paint all the Corps Commanders' pictures', including Lord Gort, the British Expeditionary Force's Commander-in-Chief (C-in-C), a task which struck Lieutenant-General Alan Brooke as sufficiently impressive to merit an entry in his diary. 'As he charges £1,500 for a picture in private life he ought to be good. Unfortunately he does not present one with the picture when it is finished as it belongs to the state.'[11]

In the first days of April, Ardizzone and Bawden took rooms for a while in the Hotel Commerce in Arras, fussed over by a shared batman. They enjoyed the local wine and hospitality, before being billeted separately.[12] Arras was dour, small and grey. It was also GHQ for the British Army in France. Ardizzone's attic room in the small house of silk-stocking worker Monsieur Donat was gloomy, ill-lit and low ceilinged. Worse, for a man with a bad back, the bed was damp. Ardizzone's heart sank, until he sensed that it was a room he could work in. He set up his drawing materials under the round attic window, took off his boots and enjoyed the play of the evening light on his drawing paper. Not so bad, eh? He could live like this well enough.

His natural sense of *joie de vivre* was soon challenged, however. He fell victim to an acute attack of lumbago. It was so distressing that Bawden was required to minister to his fellow artist, prescribing tots of brandy. He even held the chamber pot for his immobile friend, laughing as he watched Ardizzone's troubled contortions. Lumbago seemed to be an apt symbol for the paralysis and gloom that afflicted Arras as the population waited for the war to arrive at its door. Freedman succumbed briefly to illness too, while Edward Bawden was not immune – at one point his landlady provided him with a hot water bottle to warm his painful stomach. As if in expectation of what was to come, Arras' citizens all wore funereal black. What little colour there was came courtesy of the army, and that did not extend much beyond dull khaki and a few blazons of colour from forage caps and tartan trews. The cafés were unprepossessing and the nightlife non-existent. Ardizzone fell into a comforting routine, drawing under the window in his room during the days and wassailing in the evenings at the war photographers' mess. Despite the relative ease of such a life, he hankered after something more meaningful, contemplating living cheek by jowl with the troops, rather than being holed up in his cosy Arras attic.

From the outset Edward Bawden had wanted to be close to the action: 'Mr Bawden … would like to get to the front and live in close touch with the RAF.'[13] In the event he began his time in France with the 2nd Northampton Regiment, rather than the air force. The Northamptons, he found, were 'nice, simple fellows … who tear about wagging their tails, fetching sticks and retrieving balls.' Bawden left Arras on 10 April 1940, 'dressed like a journalist and looking like an officer', and headed for the Belgian frontier. 'One night I would be sleeping in a richly fur-nished chateau and drinking champagne and eating the best of food and the following night on straw in a barn with no food or drink.'[14]

Like Ardizzone, Bawden found himself initially at the mercy of a Conducting Officer (CO) whose role was to shepherd the artists around sites that were thought to be suitable subjects. He was escorted around a series of white-stoned cemeteries and forlorn, abandoned trenches from the previous war; it seemed that the CO was trying to establish a suitably melancholy mood. There was an endless supply of concrete pill-boxes to draw. The dullness of it all – not a German in sight – was alleviated by occasional variations to the routine. Once, Bawden was placed under arrest as he was painstakingly drawing a gun. On another occasion he was able to sit in on a court martial and sketch. The accused had urinated into a fire grate when he was in his cups: sitting in the court-room, Bawden enjoyed his own anonymity, and the challenge of drawing figures. He worked away with his Indian ink and sketch pad, absorbed in the task of catching the mood – the accused standing in front of five officers sitting behind a U-shaped arrangement of desks.

Licence to Sketch: Barnett Freedman's War Correspondent's Licence, Number 106.

A sergeant sat to Bawden's right, facing the officers, hands clasped in his lap. Such parochial drama was of much greater interest than the war whose phoniness seemed destined to become a permanent state.

Bawden and Ardizzone would not meet again in France, but as the former left for the frontier, Barnett Freedman turned up, larger than life and crackling with energy. Ardizzone described him as a 'card', noting that he was 'short, stout (with) a bald head, a fresh complexion and (a) … gingery quality'.[15] Freedman was thirty-eight, just 5 feet 6 inches tall, and a raconteur, with a loud voice, considerable charm and boundless cheek. A fellow artist remembered him as 'a small, squat man, with a very large head, very white pock-marked skin, with hair like loose tobacco … his whole presence was really very big, and to me, immensely attractive.'[16]

On Freedman's arrival in France a very senior general had proposed that he, rather than Eves, might wish to paint the all-powerful Lord Gort's portrait. Freedman declined forthwith, causing a startled reaction. He was adamant at first: 'No. I am not interested in uniforms.' Then he marginally relented: 'Oh well, perhaps I might, if he's got a good head.'[17] In the event it was Eves who painted the C-in-C's head:

rugged, stern-eyed, strong-jawed. Freedman travelled some 30 miles north of Arras, to Thélus to record the building of an aircraft runway.

Eventually Ardizzone left Arras, accepting an invitation to a battery manned by a Highland regiment, on the Belgian border in the village of Merris. It stood on a low hill. Looking south, there was an interminable plain devoid of trees, brightened by occasional farmhouses, glimpses of red brick in the grey and green. North into Belgium, there were some feeble hills. The army dominated the village and its sense of hierarchy was reflected in the allocation of billets: officers had a kitchen and a sitting room; the sergeants took over a small estaminet, while the men slept in straw in the village barns. The move transformed the way Ardizzone could work. Instead of being driven from one mournful site to the next by a watchful sidekick, he could wander around freely, talking to troops, sketching architectural features that he knew he might otherwise forget, and relying on his visual memory for the way people looked and moved. All that and champagne at 4s a bottle! He liked soldiers, taking the view that 'fighting troops were marvellous'; for their part, they warmed to him: 'My dear Ted, come along with us!'

★★★

On 9 April, just as Edward Bawden was contemplating leaving Arras and Barnett Freedman was doing his last minute packing, Eric Ravilious arrived in Grimsby, after a brief stopover at home. The town did not impress him: he thought it devoid of trees and malodorous. Where Arras was grey, Grimsby was 'a meaty red colour'. He would though have been cheered by a letter from the WAAC's secretary, E.M. O'R. Dickey, who 'thought [his] first six drawings delightful'.[18] Grimsby's Royal Hotel he found unpleasant: pretentious and clumsily refurbished. Trains rumbled past his bedroom throughout the night. Moreover, drawing was tricky, since the wind was relentless and the location exposed, whipped by icy gales roaring in from the North Sea. In a letter to his father-in-law he wrote that he chose the mulligatawny soup whenever he could to keep the cold at bay. One bright moment in the gloom was when he lunched with the officer in charge of the dockyard – he was the first socialist Ravilious had met in the senior service.

He left Grimsby fairly soon, heading home – a relief after the bleak flatness of the Lincolnshire coast. His next posting would be to Norway

Edward Bawden, official war artist, in uniform.

aboard the destroyer HMS *Highlander*. On 12 May, three days before the ship sailed, he had made a will: 'I give and bequeath all that I have to my wife' – apart from one painting which he left to Edward Bawden. He seemed to foresee trouble: 'I want the property, paintings, books, junk, furniture and the rest of it to pass to my wife and children *as soon as* I die.'[19]

The war might have seemed never to have started in earnest – quiet skies, desultory manoeuvres – but disrupted lives were becoming the norm. The young Merseyside artist Albert Richards had studied at the Wallasey School of Art, before winning a scholarship to the Royal College of Art in London. He took up his place in January 1940 but was called up on 3 April, joining the Royal Engineers as a sapper and being posted to Suffolk. The previous month Tom Hennell had written to the WAAC offering his services: he was rejected. Anthony Gross had left his home in France and had been commissioned to do some drawings in Shoeburyness. Henry Moore and Graham Sutherland were wondering how they might usefully contribute to the war effort. It was all very unsettling.

★★★

Richard Seddon was also in France. He was fresh from college, boyish, sporting a wispy moustache and trying hard to look soldierly. He had arrived in France with his unit, not officially commissioned by the WAAC, but with an artist's brief nonetheless. He would have approved of Ravilious' comment to John Nash: 'Why artists should be so privileged as to expect other people to fight for them I don't know.'[20]

The weather in France had at least taken a turn for the better: 17 April was warmer, while the 21st was a 'glorious spring day … carpets of cowslips, anemones and wild violets, the cuckoo singing and fresh tracks of roe deer.'[21] Seddon's lorry, at the tail of a convoy, 'like the guard in a railway train', slowly nosed its way towards Germany, across the old battlefields of the First World War. Led by Lieutenant Jimmy Cullen, Seddon's unit was based in the village of Mancy, 40km from Metz, where France met Germany – in Alsace Lorraine, disputed territory for many years. Seddon was never quite sure if he was *in* the Maginot Line, or simply looking at it.

They killed time, not Germans, as spring turned to early summer, April to May. To the east, Germany seemed empty, often in haze; not a soul in sight. Cullen practised firing his revolver at a tin can perched on a wall; the men sunbathed, occasionally raising sleepy heads to gaze out at the Maginot Line. Seddon painted and sketched, using materials he had bought in the French towns through which his convoy had trundled. He kept his sketchpad in the 'capacious' knee-pocket of his battledress. He had taken 'a supply of watercolour paper and [his] battered old paint-box and made endless sketches … as J.M.W. Turner used to do …'[22] It was as if time had stopped.

Seddon set up his studio in a 3½ ton lorry, duly christened the Demon Barber, the letters daubed in white paint on the front bumper. It housed a large case of paper and a drawing desk. Seddon's art intrigued the rest of the unit: a soldier and his 'etchings'. These, and his ability to speak the lingo, were seen as part of a damnably clever strategy for captivating French girls. His fellow soldiers frequently came calling, wide grins on their faces as they leant on the lorry's tailboard and watched the artist at work. It was unnerving that war was so peaceful. It was blisteringly hot and no one moved far or fast if they could help it, only the hens and Lieutenant Cullen. Subject matter for the would-be war artist was strictly limited: ploughed fields, misty Germany ('There didn't seem to be anybody there'); little else. Seddon reflected on the benefits of being a war artist with a small unit, tucked away in the backwaters of the conflict, far better, he thought, than 'a big outfit of several hundred' – much less 'regimental bull'. Cullen was an idiosyncratic leader of men, choosing to shift his men from their unsatisfactory accommodation to a brothel in the town ('under conditions of public school respectability, and the highest comfort'). Only the madam remained, the girls having fled south away from the war.

What war? The weeks passed in a blur of heat and sleep. Seddon worked on a painting of the unit's machine-gun nests, since there was no other war to draw. He included a flight of German reconnaissance aircraft, idly droning in the distance, close enough to sketch but too far away to shoot. A lone Heinkel, nicknamed Heinrich, droned over-head with the regularity of a local bus. In truth, the machine-gun posts provided more in the way of secluded reading outposts than military sites, littered as they were with magazines and newspapers. Seddon knew in his heart what he thought the war artist should achieve: 'not to report facts, nor mould opinion … [but] to seize, when it came, that immediacy of vision that … is always right and always true.'[23] He wanted to avoid painting the war 'with passion … I must be detached and serene'. He also wanted to paint action, fighting – the 'battle when it began' – rather than the ordinariness of a soldier's life. He 'didn't see soldiers peeling potatoes as war art'. It seemed to him that the war artist's dilemma was to 'find a worthy subject'. He worked hard on a landscape of a First World War battle site – they had driven through white-crossed cemeteries on rolling green slopes on their way to this new war's outpost – 'a tricky moonlight scene, as our convoy snaked down the hairpin bends to the Marne, over the bridge that stood pearly in the cold light'. As the spring of 1940 edged towards summer, the lorry-studio began to fill with paintings.

It was eerily peaceful, just waiting for the war to burst into life. Night duties could be tense; there were noisy evenings in French cafés and sometimes they went to Metz to drink; sentries patrolled in the darkness; men read and smoked on the makeshift latrine on the hillside above the orchard; gunfire at Luftwaffe reconnaissance sweeps was banned, though the fiery Lieutenant Cullen once seized Seddon's rifle and took a pot-shot at a solitary enemy aircraft. He missed. 'I came to shoot Germans, not to sit around,' he said. The chance would soon come.

★★★

So phoney was the war that, back in England, Anthony Gross decided that there was no point in staying away from his family in Villeneuve-sur-Lot: he wrote to Dickey at the WAAC, saying that he 'was just leaving for France, so should anything turn up all of a sudden could you please get in touch with me ... I will be back like a shot.'[24]

6

Old Battle Ground

Ardizzone enjoyed the sleep of the innocent on the night of 9 May. He was oblivious to the thunder of artillery that had rolled along the frontier from the very first dawn light. It was a glorious late spring morning, but the oblivious war artist's ample chest rose and fell with the satisfaction of a man who had dined well the night before. He liked a leisurely start to the day, not the urgent sound of a batman with a bombshell to drop. It was to be a rude awakening.

'Captain Ardizzone, sir! The Germans have gone and invaded, sir! It's all kicked off at last! Wake up, sir!'

Ardizzone pushed the blankets back, swung his legs clear of the bed, struggled with his socks, and decided in the interests of warfare to forego his morning coffee, though the smell of it was wafting up the stairs. The sun streamed in through the attic window, a band of light passing across the jar of brushes on the table under the window and on to the bare floorboards of the attic room. The trusty batman – news imparted – was now polishing Ted's cherished cavalry boots, with his own right boot firmly placed on the artist's chair and his head bent, concentrating on the production of a military sheen to the leather to the exclusion of all else. He had opened the window and Ted could hear the gathering hubbub in the streets as the news spread. Moments later he was down in the tumultuous streets of Arras, assailed by the noise of military vehicles, shaken by the signs of intense activity and confusion. 'Where's that blessed batman when I need him? Right, we need to pack up.

And I mean now. We're moving up to Advanced HQ at Lille. Most important, this — these pictures need to be sent back to London as soon as you can. Make up a parcel of them before we go. Is that clear? Come on, look sharp, old chap!' So in their respective ways, both Captain Ardizzone, war artist, and the German Army were hell bent on reaching Lille as soon as possible — the latter with France in its sights; the artist with a war to draw.

The German advance into the Low Countries on 10 May dispelled the phoney war once and for all. Ardizzone spent that chaotic morning sheltering from a blazing sun under a convenient chestnut tree, conserving his energy. Not much point in rushing around like a headless chicken. He chatted briefly to Reginald Eves, who had taken time away from his queue of would-be portraitures – they had after all other things on their minds now — while around them the ant-heap of the British Army indulged in an unmilitary frenzy. Eves sat on a cane chair, holding court, while Ardizzone sat at his feet in the welcome shade. Once Eves had left, Ardizzone felt as if he was the solitary centre of a whirlpool swirling on all sides around him. Told that he could not be driven the 30 or so miles north to Lille before that afternoon, he had a solitary lunch in a gloomy and deserted photographers' mess, musing on what dangers lay ahead.

At the Carlton Hotel in Lille, journalists who had been racking their brains for some sort of story for months past, were leaning over typewriters hitting the keys with regained enthusiasm. The briefing by General Macfarlane was an unseemly scrum of photographers and journalists, either side of a long table, with everyone leaning expectantly towards the uniformed figure at the end. 'This, gentlemen, is the basic situation — the Germans have already crossed the Albert Canal and are carrying all before them. If you wish you may travel north, but I advise the utmost caution.'

Hitherto, the British and French had been held back from entering Belgium – the shock of the sudden German advance rapidly put paid to that and triggered a rush for the frontier, sometimes with the most gung-ho of approaches: cavalry officers from the Royal Lancers, for example, 'celebrated their call to arms by knocking back a bottle of champagne for lunch.'[1] They might not have been so euphoric, despite the long wait for action to begin, if it had been realised 'that Hitler and his generals were doing everything in their power to persuade the British and French to advance quickly into Belgium.'[2] The war had become a contest between the ill-prepared and unsuspecting on the one hand, and the relentless and disciplined on the other.

General Macfarlane, the Director of Military Intelligence, was even more anxious the following day, 11 May. He told Brooke that 'the Belgian situation was bad and that the Germans had broken through at Maastricht.'³ Early that morning, unaware of the gloomy intelligence to which Brooke and others were privy, the eager Ardizzone and a few companions set out for the frontier. It had the feel of a jaunt, rather than a military operation. They arrived at the Belgian frontier at 06.00 a.m. Convoys of lorries and tanks thundered north along straight roads lined with trees. The impression the lorries gave was reassuring, with each vehicle a regulation distance from its predecessor, and speeds uniformly resolute. Excited Belgians waved and cheered.

Breakfast was in a café on the town square in Tournai. Ardizzone sketched while the others smoked and talked, sitting outside in the early morning sun. His pencil skated over the page: tall, gabled buildings looking down serenely on cobblestones; lines of artillery, Bofors guns shrouded in tarpaulin; a covered lorry with troops craning their necks to see out, arms resting on the tailgate; a cheerful-looking soldier leaning nonchalantly, shoulder propped against the wooden frame, one dusty boot across the other, with the cavalier air of a man who could sort your plumbing or clean the windows. As the coffee cooled, the air raid sirens began to whine and the sound of heavy guns and exploding bombs seemed to get closer. Time perhaps for us to move on, chaps, do you think? Ardizzone put on his tin hat and glanced upwards, wondering when the German planes might swoop down from this clear blue sky.

They headed northeast towards Brussels 45 miles away, driving along a broad highway, through countryside that reminded Ted continually of Kent: wooded valleys, low rounded hills, green orchards, the thin steeples of country churches. The road scarcely bothered to bend. In other times it would have been softly tranquil, a rural paradise, but not now – long lines of military transport rumbled on, diesel fumes thick in the air. A stick of well-placed German bombs had flattened houses by a railway line and the tracks themselves were twisted violently into crude iron sculpture. Ardizzone kept his tin hat firmly on his head and drew a hurried sketch of his colleagues standing amongst the contorted railway metal, taking photographs. The road was littered with broken bricks, shattered tiles and dust.

In Brussels they were feted, since they were among the first men in uniform to reach the city centre. After pulling into the station square, their jeep was surrounded by a cheering mob, hailing the arrival of the heroic and intrepid 'Anglais'; it wasn't a time to reflect on what was to come in the forthcoming weeks, the sour taste of defeat. The diminutive Conducting Officer was swamped in a luxurious embrace from a buxom, blonde Belgian with hungry lips. Tentative requests for coffee in the hotel were denied – open some bottles of champagne, yes, and brandy, for our English brothers-in-arms! The car outside was draped with lilac blossom. The conquering heroes – yet to conquer anything and years away from doing so – enjoyed the moment while it lasted, and then headed back to Lille, noting the machine-gun posts dotted regularly along the roadside, with guns angled to ensure a clinical line of fire at the anticipated German aircraft, expected to swoop low over the dense traffic. The communal dinner in Lille that night, held under ornate gold-framed mirrors in a chintzy hotel restaurant, was a convivial affair of toasts, heavy French wines and animated conversation. The camaraderie, however, did not disguise a dissatisfaction with what that day had brought – it had been like something out of a film, not much like war at all.

The next day, 12 May, compensated for that and presented a poignant target for the war artist. Ardizzone began to sketch the growing stream of refugees, mostly old men and women, mothers and children, steadily heading away from the fighting. His soldiers always had an irrepressible quality when he sketched them. Ardizzone presented them as buoyed up by the adventure and each other's company, and the need to look suitably martial. Ted's refugees, on the other hand, looked crumpled, heads bowed, exhausted and despondent. Hope and dignity had already gone. The sides of the road were busy with young men on bicycles, single-mindedly pedalling south. Later, there were more forlorn and desperate people, dressed in their Sunday best and pushing hand carts loaded with whatever they were not prepared to leave for the triumphant Germans to pick through. The perverse pride in appearance did not extend to footwear: often worn-out boots or carpet slippers. The retreating Belgian troops looked harassed and feeble, in tattered variations of uniform, carrying equipment that was dusty and oil-streaked.

A grim-faced Ardizzone, hands resting on each knee, stared through the jeep's fly-spattered windscreen, taking in the extent of bombed buildings and crumpled brickwork, broken glass, the tangles of fallen girders.

A line of guards marched against the tide of refugees, their military precision in stark contrast to the slow shuffle of the dispossessed. Periodically, the Luftwaffe, unopposed, roared in from cloudless skies, dropped bombs and strafed the roads before flying off at great speed. Away to the east, their returning aircraft bounced across grassy airfields before the pilots clambered free and, high on victory, bellowed to each other above the noise of idling engines, drinking coffee while mechanics climbed on oil-streaked fuselages, preparing for the next operation.

Ardizzone's driver took them into Louvain. Unbeknown to him, Generals Brooke and Montgomery had motored through the town that day too: Brooke recorded in his diary that the 'town had been heavily bombed and was burning near the station'.[4] The British top brass were keen to see the front; they saw refugees mingling with 'the normal Sunday church-going parties,' and worrying signs of Belgian lack of resistance. The enemy were close and advancing inexorably. The silence and emptiness gave the clearest possible signal that Ted and his colleagues were moving into real danger. The driver stopped the jeep in what had, the previous day, been a peaceful, fashionable part of town; it was burning now, with mounds of rubble everywhere. So this was what war looked like. It saddened him that, although people had fled, their pet dogs had been left behind to greet the enemy.

The sketch that Ted made of Louvain that day had an ominous look to it: a solitary figure in a grim street, over which two empty flag poles stood out. The windows were shuttered as if for a hot afternoon's siesta; there were deep shadows, no trees, and a sense of something waiting to happen; an imminent arrival expected.

The return to Lille was unsettling, though the danger seemed at some remove. On the dusty roads of Belgium, people remained panic-stricken, wide-eyed and desperate, sheltering from the onslaught as best they could. In the far distance, German transport could be seen, slowly picking its way through the valley floor. The noise it made was faint, carried away sometimes by the light summer breeze. Once Ted saw, and sketched, a group of nuns, heads bowed as if intent on prayer, huddling together in a ditch, grey habits patched with dust. They looked, he thought, 'like the women at the base of the Cross in Tintoretto's "Crucifixion"'.[5] That night the constant noise of anti-aircraft fire made sleeping difficult.

A few days later, Ardizzone witnessed the fall of Louvain and its occupation by the Germans. Courtesy of a Belgian soldier and 'a fat smiling

Belgian lieutenant acting as a traffic policeman'[6] he acquired a bottle of white wine. 'Should we have a little snifter?' Why ever not? The cork slid out with a satisfying noise and the sun gave the white wine a golden glow. It tasted, however, appropriately sickening. Around them, 'the air was full of a thick red dust which combined with the hot afternoon sunshine to make a reddish gold haze.'[7] As well as the war artist and his companions, grimacing over what was an unpleasant bottle of wine, there were soldiers drinking bottles of beer, putting on an impressive air of nonchalance. The Germans, however, were 'just over the other side of the bridge', and there was a clear necessity to destroy it before the first German patrols began to cross the river.

In the middle of the bridge was an improvised barricade of wire, while at the western end was a mattress and two easy chairs, with a few exhausted soldiers taking advantage of the minimal comfort they provided. As well as being starved of sleep, the men were impatient to receive the order to blow the bridge – and contemplating doing it anyway, knowing that enemy patrols were lurking close by on the other side. Nonetheless, they 'were having a nap before they blew it up.' Eventually a dispatch rider roared up and soon after the bridge exploded in a towering cloud of grey smoke. Shattered masonry was thrown high in the air: Ardizzone was awed by the sight, and then acutely aware that the tumbling bricks were being scattered far and wide, raining down around him as he sped away from where the bridge had been. A sniper's bullet whistled close by and instinctively Ardizzone ducked behind a wall, a position from which he could see that the bridge had been severed.

There was now an eerie silence, and an even more ominous absence of people. Machine-gun posts were emptied; lorries had fled, and the impression was that the town had been summarily conceded to the enemy. The British had gone. As Ardizzone drove away from Louvain, he saw long lines of refugees moving more slowly than the soldiers, but perhaps with a greater sense of resolution. A consoling omelette and beer in a bar outside Brussels did not dispel the defeatist mood – there were no garlands of flowers now, just sullen looks and huddled groups of the resentful.

Parched from the brick dust of Louvain, they stopped briefly for more beer as they motored south on the Tournai road, sweeping gladly through level crossings, knowing that a delay waiting at crossing gates was ill-advised, an open invitation to any marauding enemy aircraft.

Once a large bomber swept in, but veered away at the last moment. In the distance they could see a town burning and later they came to a convent fiercely ablaze. The nuns had gone – perhaps cowering in a ditch somewhere – and the building would soon be just charred rubble, but Ardizzone wandered through the garden, moved by its sense of peace, with its wide lawn, spreading mulberry tree, and impassive stone saints. It lifted him temporarily, but the prevailing mood as they journeyed on to Tournai was gloomy. Tiredness added to the conviction that there was worse to come.

Soon after Ardizzone found himself in Lille, a town whose charms passed him by. It brought out the metropolitan and disdainful in him: 'It struck me as a large ugly town – not unlike Birmingham.'[8] He didn't like the brash bars – 'flashy (and) got up in the American manner.' Moreover, his room at the Carlton Hotel was improbably grand, but not somewhere he could work up the sketches he had completed on his journeys through Belgium. He set out to find a studio where he could work in peace. Air raid sirens were a persistent nuisance, but few bombs fell. He was content: the studio was unfurnished, but a little ingenuity brought him a chair and a small table. He took off his fine cavalryman's footwear, rubbed his toes where the boots had wrought their damage. He put them neatly alongside the chipped skirting board. He put his brushes in a glass jar, lit a pipe, spread paper on a large drawing board and looked out over the red roofs of Lille. Such light! Once his concentration was challenged by the sight of 'two pretty girls in their camisoles … leaning out of an attic window sunning themselves and combing their blond hair.' Lovely, just lovely! Burning Belgium seemed a long way away in this peaceful enclave. He worked happily until his stomach began to rumble and he recognised his need for sustenance and company. He washed his brushes, knocked his pipe out on the window sill, scattering flecks of tobacco and spittle on the tiles, put on those damn boots and repaired to the Metropole bar. The cries of 'Ted old boy, what's your poison?' and 'Have a little tincture on me, old chap!' warmed the cockles of his heart.

The idyll of red roofs and pretty girls didn't last long. There were orders to leave for Arras within the hour: Ted was back where he had started weeks before, but the mood had changed. Somehow the ghosts of the previous world war loomed larger: this was, after all, old battle ground. Rooms were hard to find and there was fear in the air. He had a

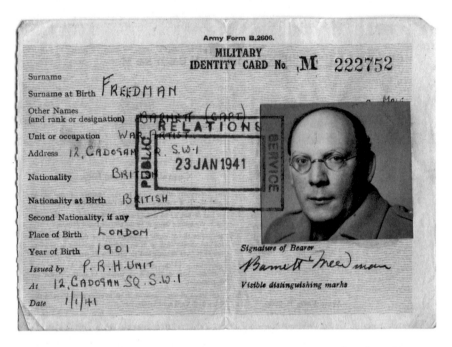

'His whole presence was really very big' - Barnett Freedman stares out from his military ID card, 1941.

strong sense that away to the north some disaster was under way, or even over. There was a false alarm when the sirens wailed one night at 10.00 p.m. – it sent everyone scurrying to the cellars, chambermaids chattering like sparrows amidst the champagne and sparkling wines, while the more taciturn men congregated in the rows of bottled clarets and burgundies. The next day, the retreat continued, to Amiens this time, some 60 miles south. His billet was in the Grand Hotel, whose apparent grandeur did not compensate for the absence of sheets on the beds or water in the taps.

Ardizzone unpacked and left his room; he was soon standing outside the city's cathedral. He pulled out his sketchbook and rapidly drew the great edifice, its walls everywhere protected by neatly stacked sandbags. They looked like the defences of some city in the Peninsular War, tight-packed angled constructions that dwarfed the two uniformed figures entering the cathedral's main door. As he drew, he could hear both the chanting of vespers and an air raid in progress, guns in counterpoint to the pure voices. He would remember for the rest of his life the 'plainsong in Amiens Cathedral and the sound of the guns echoing through it.' Later, back at the Grand, the hotel foyer was choked with assorted bags and luggage, a hazard for scurrying chambermaids and an image that caught the mood of impermanence and flight. Undeterred, Ted unpacked his drawing materials and contemplated with pleasure the thought of working the following day. Then he went to bed, curled up with a good book and a sense that not everything was wrong with the world – there were things to draw; human voices which could stir the heart while bombs were dropping just a few miles away; a comfortable bed; sleep …

Then that cheerful chappie Barnett Freedman burst in! Cue an exchange of artists' adventures. Then, more sombrely, an officer hammering at the door: 'Get up at once. We are leaving in half an hour!' Half an hour was over-optimistic – there was some desultory waiting in the foyer, but there was no escaping the fact that this was the most serious retreat yet. When they left Amiens it was with 'only the luggage we could carry, in my case, a haversack'. The rest of the luggage in the foyer would be in German hands within hours. Ardizzone and his haversack were bound for Boulogne on the Channel coast. In less than two short weeks, he had travelled a long way, at first with buoyant hopes towards the invading German Army, then rapidly back through towns and landscape where the soldiers of the Great War had dug their trenches and slowly edged back and forth over four long years. It was all a pretty poor show, he thought, not at all the kind of adventure that had seemed just the thing for the would-be war artist. He wondered how – if – he could avoid the disaster to come.

7

Of Scapa Flow and Rearguard Defences

While Ardizzone was heading towards the French coast, looking nervously at the sky for enemy aircraft, Eric Ravilious was aboard the destroyer HMS *Highlander* leaving Scottish waters for the cold beauty of Norway. *Highlander* was to be part of an expeditionary force, headed by the aircraft carriers *Glorious* and *Ark Royal*, and charged with the recapture of the Norwegian port of Narvik. Ravilious sailed for Norway from Scapa Flow in the early afternoon of 24 May 1940. He stood on deck, exhilarated by the way the sun turned the sea into a gun-metal sheen; by the line of ships steaming in obedient single file for the open sea; the tumult of hills to the south; the delicate lines of the ship's wake; the near empty deck, just a solitary figure in water-proofs dwarfed by *Highlander's* camouflaged smokestacks. The wind whipped the pages of Eric's sketchbook and spray dampened both his cigarette and his drawing paper. He felt something like optimism, in this bleak period of the war, cocooned by the ship, buoyed by the sense of voyaging and the unmistakeable power of the Royal Navy, its ships spread across the water as far as the eye could see.

The ship impressed him, with its cleanliness and order. He enthused about it in a letter to Tirzah on 17 May 1940: fresh paint, flowers on the tables and the portholes covered with chintz curtains. The stark, remote beauty of Norway was uplifting to him: he loved 'working on deck long past midnight in bright sunshine' and the crew of the destroyer were impressed with the artist's ability to retain his concentration while guns fired and enemy aircraft criss-crossed the skies. It was, he wrote, 'the first time since the war (that) I've felt any peace of mind or desire to work'.[1] He was intrigued by an existence where he didn't see land, women or darkness for weeks on end. He saw arctic terns; wore a lifebelt in bed; wondered at the deep pure blue of the ocean and went ashore to sketch, shaken by the contrast between the simple beauty of the landscape – green turf, sky heavy with snow, hills patched with white and brown, ruffled deep blue and wintry sea – and the harsh remainders of fighting, the black silhouettes of half-sunken ships nose down in the bay.

Through late May and early June Ravilious sketched contentedly, wrote letters home and enjoyed the life at sea, while HMS *Highlander* carried out its duties helping to protect the aircraft carrier *Glorious*. By 8 June, however, while *Highlander* had stayed on station with *Ark Royal*, *Glorious* was sailing for Scapa Flow. She was soon to be surprised, then destroyed, by the German battleships *Scharnhorst* and *Gneisenau*, in just two hours of intense gunfire. Safe, for the moment, on *Highlander*, Ravilious recognised how lucky his ship had been. *Glorious*, by contrast, was doomed and, when she sank, took 1,500 men with her to the bottom of the ocean.

★★★

At much the same time as Ravilious was on board *Highlander*, reflecting on what might have been, Ardizzone and Bawden were increasingly aware of the sudden transformation from apparent stalemate to chaotic retreat. Ardizzone was caught up in the urgent rush west, towards the port of Boulogne. Bawden had become acutely aware that hitherto friendly units were trying to offload their official war artist as quickly as they could. Instead of contemplating what to draw, he focused his mind on the here and now, where he could sleep once night fell and how to get from one place of safety to the next. In Armentières he watched bombs fall and fires start, smoke dirtying the sky and swirling through the streets, the soft red of the buildings contrasting with orange flame.

When Ardizzone reached Boulogne, he found it was full of dispirited soldiers and refugees. The Dutch soldiers, in their grey uniforms, looked like Nazis – a grim reminder of what was closing in from the east. The town was thick with suspicion and anxiety. It was 'in chaos with some of the French naval garrison dead drunk, and others destroying the coastal batteries.'² BEF Adjutant-General Sir Douglas Brownrigg had been ordered 'to evacuate all "useless mouths" from Boulogne'.³ Ted killed time and waited. He had his first taste of night-time air raids and was shocked by the ferocious din and intense bursts of colour in the sky. Once late at night, scurrying back to the hotel, with his tin hat bouncing on his head as he ran, he saw 'a German plane flying very low like a great black bat in the moonlight'. It was tipping mines into the harbour. At the Hotel Meurice, the raids didn't stop till dawn, and sleep was all but impossible.

The weather was glorious, more suitable for a seaside holiday than the unfolding of a military disaster. Ardizzone occasionally went up to the ramparts above the town and sat on the grass, sketching, glad of a self-imposed task that seemed to mark an adherence to duty. It also took his mind off what perils might emerge from the clear blue sky. At one point, he joined a group which took a cab out to Wimereux, 3 miles to the north. It was a dispiriting visit: the town's pre-war sparkle had gone, to be replaced by a sense of desolation. 'The tall hotels and villas along the beach had their shutters up and looked like a many-coloured cliff against the dark blue sky.' Ardizzone paddled disconsolately, khaki trousers turned up to keep them dry.

That night's air raid was more than usually terrifying. Barnett Freedman was understandably apoplectic, sounding off at Ardizzone in a flurry of explosive curses: 'That's a bloody fine room you have chosen me under the roof, isn't it? I'm not bloody well staying in it. I thought the whole bloody thing would slide into the street.' The ceiling of the room at the Hotel Meurice had collapsed. They fled the building, glad of each other's reassuring presence, and headed for the beach front, past burning cars, bomb craters, twisted lamp posts and bodies, broken and scattered. Any attraction that Boulogne, or indeed the whole sad military enterprise, had had was long since gone. Later they learned that the Germans were rushing, like floodwater, through a gap between Amiens and Arras. The end seemed to be close, but the detail of what that entailed was obscured in mystery. All too aware of the growing power of the Luftwaffe over the town, Ardizzone and a few others commandeered a mansion in the countryside outside. He felt acutely aware of his sudden lack of value. Indeed, his whole unit was now redundant – 'we were completely out of action … no use whatever, we were a nuisance to everyone and we knew it.' Falling

Apparently oblivious to everything but his canvas - Barnett Freedman at work in France 1940.

back on a thin strip of Channel coast to face the inevitable, the BEF's need for war artists and photographers had long since gone. What they needed were boats.

There were twelve men holed up in the house above Boulogne. It was big, built of white stone and nestled in a protective ring of trees. It had been evacuated in a hurry – there were hats and coats still on the hall-stand – and there were constant reminders of a civilised world: books, a piano, a nursery with a cot and children's toys. Once night fell, they watched the fires over Boulogne while Freedman played Handel and Bach on the piano, accompanied by the sound of distant guns. Later, a bomb fell very nearby, reminding them that, despite the unreal calm of the house, the war had become disconcertingly close.

As it turned out, the following day was to be Ardizzone's last in France. That morning a red-faced, elderly colonel collared him outside Boulogne's Crystal Bristol: 'You're officers. Don't let the townspeople know. Get all the soldiers together you can. I have come from Abbeville. The Germans are just behind me.' Soon they were told that embarkation for England would be in 90 minutes. The announcement came as panic began to spread through the town. German planes roared over, 'like dark moths coming over the harbour.' Ardizzone left France on an old grey-painted Channel steamer, looking back at long lines of RAF personnel snaking along the quay. Barnett Freedman was missing, having decided to retrieve his one oil painting of the BEF in 1940: the runway at Thélus. Ardizzone thought him inordinately brave. Nonetheless, he enjoyed 'a little party' on board, drinking whisky and eating sandwiches below decks. It put him in fine fettle for greeting the white cliffs as they steamed towards Dover.

As for Barnett Freedman, he got back home on an ammunition boat. Before leaving the burning city, he ate a defiant final meal on French soil. It consisted of three bottles of champagne and a tin of bully beef, which he enjoyed alone, sitting on the quayside railway tracks. As for Ardizzone, clutching glass and sandwich on board, he could not help worrying about the whereabouts of Edward Bawden, of whom he had heard nothing.

★★★

On his way to Dunkirk, Bawden had rolled up his paintings in a cylindrical tin which he clutched under his arm, while above him the skies were filled with German aircraft. The clouds of smoke were choking and the noise was deafening. Darkness brought little respite, with gunfire filling the night. Approaching the port, he ditched all his equipment except his art materials (what would the Germans have done with them?) Marching into the town, they ran the gauntlet of ragged French soldiers jeering them. It discomforted him, as did the looters sweeping like locusts through abandoned houses. It was as if there was an army of burglars on the march. He reached the quayside in the company of a Canadian major, and they watched with dismay the frantic self-preservation of a group of British generals on the Dunkirk quayside, swagger sticks pointing at likely boats bound for England. He turned to the major, with a wry smile. 'Rats always go first!' he said. German bombers flew over in waves, dropping bombs, and the fires relentlessly spread. There was an acrid, oily cloud of smoke that hung low over the sea. It seemed wise to abandon the stone quay, though he memorised the images of air raid shelters; men scurrying for shelter, descending into the depths with anxious glances upwards; tall ruined buildings with no roofs, just gaunt girders licked by flame; wounded soldiers on blood-stained stretchers; men taking ignominious shelter under the tables of a bombed out café. He sheltered under privet bushes in a small park, close to three Scottish soldiers smoking fags with an air of desperation, while the fires around them drew closer.

Towards nightfall, he finally got on a boat heading for England. Below decks, the men lay exhausted, uniforms torn and bloodied, only half aware of the escape across open sea in the darkness. In the morning, Bawden was back in England, initially in some anonymous port (he later decided it was Harwich), before going to Aldershot for debriefing. He slept for an inordinately long time and then began to paint what he had seen in the preceding few days, capturing the confusion of the defeat that soon became recast as a kind of victory. Back at Brick House on 31 May he wrote to Dickey that he regretted leaving France 'at the moment when things were becoming hot'. He had been pleased that he had got 'the right technique for recording my impressions'.[4] He received £16 in compensation for his gear lost in the confusion of Dunkirk, but the War Office baulked at paying for his sketching bag, stool and board, his brush case and two brushes.

Back in the methodical atmosphere of his studio, he reflected on what the nature of war artistry was: 'The man who is drawing in the field must accept what he sees, self-conscious arrangement is hardly possible, the scene is always changing and masses of men are moving about and not posing to be drawn. In fact it was a rough life: I simply had to draw reasonably well, whether in a cookhouse or in a repair depot for tanks or a court martial. I think it was the most valuable experience I have ever had to be pitched straight into what was happening in France.'[5]

While Barnett Freedman returned to England safely, he was not happy about the experience. Later, he wrote a report on the sequence of events. It was critical of the arrangements for war artists. Right from the outset, things had been unsatisfactory – no one had met him on his arrival at Calais on 10 April; indeed 'no one had any knowledge of my coming'.[6]

He had been taken ill at his hotel in Arras; had resented being taken to the Belgian frontier ('I had seen it often before in civilian life'). When he met up with Ardizzone he was disillusioned to be told that 'unless I could get a personal invitation from the OC of some Regiment or Company I would be likely to remain in Arras forever.' Transport was a nightmare. He wanted a car, driver, a special war artists' licence and 'temporary field rank'. Moreover, he posed the question that all war artists must have considered, and which would come to matter so much later in the war: 'The dangers of doing this work,' Freedman wrote, 'are not inconsiderable. I would welcome some definite assurance that my wife would receive some sort of reasonable compensation if I were killed.'

★★★

The first letter which reached Richard Seddon in his French rural outpost was from his former tutor, Edward Bawden. Sent from GHQ, Bawden's unhappiness was apparent: 'I find my fellow officers here almost insupportable in their narrowness and lack of any conversation or ideas.'[7] He admitted to keeping away from them 'in this small estaminet in the far corner of the square' – it was a refuge, since his fellow officers rarely went there. He suggested that Seddon might drive over 'sometime soon'. Moments after reading this, Seddon heard a motor bicycle approaching. It was 'Crasher', Lieutenant Cullen's dispatch rider, his face encrusted in road dust; the drama of his message not remotely apparent. 'Listen, Sarge – and don't any of you say I'm a liar because this is from HQ. The Dutch have ceased fire. Jerry has gone across Holland and Belgium. Then the bloody Belgians have packed up! They're in France!'[8] Abbeville had fallen; Arras too. And Sedan. It dawned on the unit soon enough: 'That's where the bastards are! Between us and the sea!' Seddon, Demon Barber, paintings – all were totally cut off, and a very long way from home.

It was the sudden end of an unreal period when time had seemed to stand still. Cullen's unit thought they had been sitting pretty, in the perfect cushy number, but now? Sergeant Jack Howard took a grim pleasure in the state of play: 'Sitting *bloody* pretty. We're so damned pretty we've only got about a hundred thousand Huns to fight through if we move at all. And if we don't move …'[9] So the following morning, they began a long trek west across northern France, in a very different frame of mind from when they had trundled in the opposite direction a month before. They travelled by night, resting up during the hours of daylight, reaching Neufchâtel, about 50 miles from the Brittany coast, on the fourth day. It was a Sunday morning in the middle of May and the town was ominously quiet, with very few people on the streets. They were holed up there for the next three weeks, while to the north, troops fell back towards Dunkirk, with the Germans in relentless pursuit. Seddon's unit was unaware of the pace of the advance, its direction and the way it left them stranded.

It was a time of collapsed plans, botched hopes and creaking logistics. Seddon had an acute sense of the bumbling, makeshift conduct of the campaign thus far. While the rain fell, he sketched one of many imitation anti-tank guns designed to confuse and delay the German advance. Made of wood and canvas, and parked at a road junction near a tobacconist's shop, it had 'a long wooden pole prodding blindly forward in place of a gun barrel … It was,' he thought, 'a worthy graphic symbol of our entire Division.' He called it '*Rearguard Defences*'.

Neufchâtel grew emptier as the Germans approached. There was already a steady flow of refugees from Abbeville, 30 miles away and in enemy hands. Like Ardizzone, Seddon was deeply disturbed by the condition of the refugees: they were white-faced, terrified and wide-eyed, stumbling away from the horrors they had seen. They begged for bread and talked of the wholesale destruction of Abbeville. Lieutenant Cullen and his men felt like castaways, deprived of information and with no sense of what lay ahead. Seddon lost himself in his painting, holed up in the lorry-studio, absorbed with his work, 'while the generals disagreed'. Once, he and Cullen drove 17 miles to capture a parachutist in the grounds of a château. He turned out to be an RAF pilot 'making small talk and holding a dainty cup of tea in a slightly trembling hand.'

At dawn on 7 June — the day before the town was destroyed by the Germans — the unit moved out of Neufchâtel. The mood was bitter: 'OK! let's get going. We've humped this stuff right across France and all the way back again. I hope they start using some of it soon!' They weren't to know that the Dunkirk operation, whereby hundreds of thousands of troops were ferried back home across the Channel, was over. 'Nobody told us a thing.' The isolation in which the unit had found itself in the middle of May was increasing. They had no map and no idea where they were going. Cullen was bitter: 'It's a bloody wonder to me, they managed to give us rifles!' He and his men kept looking up to the skies, looking for German dive-bombers, occasionally checking out the proximity of ditches which might provide a sudden, desperate refuge. There was something deeply ominous about the landscape – deserted villages and broken telegraph poles – and there was a strong feeling that finding a safe route home was becoming impossible, while their convoy of lorries was blundering into a trap as a dust-streaked, triumphant enemy closed in.

Near the coast, they found themselves at the back of a long convoy grinding its way uphill; the unit's job was to look after damaged lorries that had fallen by the wayside. The road was arrow-straight, with tall trees providing regular pools of shade. For the moment there was no sign of trouble, just the smell of diesel fumes and the whining of laden trucks in low gear. Then it all happened in a moment: one of the unit's lorries broke down; the bonnet was raised; nervy glances were directed at the sky; French Army lorries ('shabby and decrepit') suddenly appeared and *poilus* could be seen running pell-mell for cover in the trees. Gunfire soon followed, including the dull thump of mortars. So this was what action felt like, after all that idle waiting. French soldiers with fixed bayonets lurked in the valley below the road, while explosions ahead suggested that the convoy was under heavy tank or aircraft attack.

Seddon's unit hurriedly reversed their lorries to the dubious shelter of the houses further down the road, while Seddon himself moved through the woods to get a clearer view of what lay ahead, making his way through long grass and nettles, with the safety catch eased off his rifle and his heart thumping. Eventually he was able to look down on what was left of the convoy. There was dust, smoke and the crackle of fire as vehicles burned. Also the wary preliminaries of surrender: German soldiers standing tall – even at that distance there was no mistaking the respective positions: German triumph against British humiliation. There was nothing for it, but to slip back to the houses where he had left the remains of the unit. War artist he may have been, but someone had to take a lead: he encouraged the rest to make for Fécamp. 'Which way would that be?' A confused shrug. 'Half a dozen of us with rifles can do nothing up that hill, but we can try to get through to Fécamp and bring back some anti-tank guns.'[10]

The lorry-studio – the Demon Barber – was abandoned, and with it a treasured supply of tank wheels, a case of excellent Bourgogne, ten pairs of army boots, 3,000 cigarettes, half a large cheese and ten watercolours, all of the war. Notwithstanding his precious artwork, it was the leaving of the wine and cheese which pained him most. He was confident that if he made it home, he could reproduce the paintings from the drawings in the sketchbook he had in the map pocket of his battledress. They roared off in the lorry, five of them in the cab and more in the back. At one point they came across an 'elegant French officer' presiding over a long line of anti-tank guns. He was profoundly unhelpful when asked to send the guns forward to relieve the convoy: 'No petrol!' he explained with a Gallic shrug, and shrugged again when the proximity of petrol pumps was pointed out to him. Another shrug: 'Wrong sort.' Seddon was furious: 'Are the French all cowards, then?' There was so much unspoken between the sweat-stained, dusty war artist, lost and a long way from home, and the resplendent Frenchman 'and his spotless guns and his men idling in the square'. Seddon had yet to discover that most of the BEF had slipped back across the Channel and the French felt abandoned. What love and trust there had been among the Allies was temporarily lost.

★★★

Eventually, after a minor collision with another British lorry, they arrived at the coast – a surprise for the map-less Seddon, who thought it was at least 40 miles away. 'Half the time we didn't know where we were.' They drove along the promenade, past a coastguard station and holiday villas, shuttered for a summer season that would not now take place. At the far end of the promenade, the road started to climb. As the lorry tackled the incline, fierce machine-gun fire erupted from a clump of trees on the hill's leading edge. They dived for cover into the ditch, returned fire and then applied field dressings to the wounded. Further down the hill, they were sufficiently hidden by the shoulder of the slope to hold a council of war in the middle of the road. The hill was clearly not to be attempted: the Germans were well dug in and in considerable numbers. The only alternative was the beach, threatened by incoming tides and difficult walking, with its shifting shingle. But no Germans so far as Seddon could see.

High chalk cliffs towered above the strange and desperate party: five men from Seddon's own unit; half a dozen men from the 51st Highland Division;[11] a couple of French soldiers from the French Tenth Army; two

French coast guards and a mournful dog. A fishing boat, close in-shore, chugged past, its crew apparently oblivious to the drama on the beach. Rather than persisting with the forlorn trudge along the shingle – too visible and vulnerable – they elected to stay put, on a stretch of beach where twisted columns of chalk stood tall and cast long shadows as the sun fell away towards the horizon, and England. The white cliffs turned pink with the declining sun. Seddon took out his battered sketchbook and set to work, more preoccupied with capturing the play of light on the rocks and the stark pre-eminence of the cliffs than worrying about a German patrol emerging high above them, into the fading sunlight. That he could do nothing about.

Once, two German aircraft swept along the coastline and Seddon's introductory lectures on camouflage came in useful. 'Get in off that white chalk, you!' he shouted. 'Lie along the edge of that big patch of seaweed. They'll never pick you out there. And keep your face down, they can see your face at a thousand feet!'[12] It was the fishing boat that had excited the attention of the German pilots, however, and their aircraft swooped towards it before unleashing two arcs of gunfire which blew the boat apart. It was over in a moment, and the aircraft turned away, regained height and disappeared, heading inland. Fifteen minutes later, the men on the beach saw a destroyer far out in the haze to the west, and, after a prolonged and increasingly desperate bout of sema-phore signalling – *SOS British soldiers!* – they were seen and taken on board. Seddon had to wade through the surf, then swim as his army greatcoat was lifted and spread by the waves. He worried about keeping his rifle and his sketchbook dry.

A little later, Seddon stood on the destroyer's bridge, bedraggled and dripping seawater, tin hat and dignity gone, facing the immacu-late Lieutenant Commander Michael Meyrick. It was only then that the artist learned the present state of the war: the debacle at Dunkirk and the collapse of France. He contemplated the disaster while he sketched, undeterred by the fact that the sketchbook's pages were still damp from their soaking. He drew ('for dear life') from a sheltered point on board where he felt relatively safe: he was out of sight, and could look back to the shore from where gunfire was peppering the ship. On the cliffs, Rommel's tanks and artillery kept up an unremitting barrage. A 'hole as big as a soup plate' appeared in the metal bulkhead above Seddon's head. HMS *Boadicea* returned fire and all seemed well enough until the arrival of nine Junkers aircraft which hit the ship with two sticks of bombs. The destroyer shook, heeled over; the lights went out and, finally, the engines stopped. 'For an encore, the ship blew up.' The order came to abandon ship and Seddon was ordered to put on a life jacket. 'I was in the water half an hour ago,' he said. 'It seems a pity to have to go back in again'.

Instead of abandoning ship, the captain and crew chose to jettison everything of any significant weight – 'shells, long copper gun charges, depth-charge carriers, signalling equipment … boxes and bales, gratings and so on …'[13] The ship wallowed without power, rudder or electricity; there were floods in the engine room, and she drifted with the tide, uncomfortably close to shore, so much so that the captain was worried about voices carrying across the water to the Germans on the cliffs. Rescue when it came was from a sister ship, HMS *Ambuscade*, which was able to tow *Boadicea* across the Channel. It was a painful, limping and blood-stained return to England: at one point Seddon tried to sketch one of the dead sailors from the burned-out engine-room. 'I felt that here was a challenge to my pencil, the material for a work of art that would be a silent cry of the human spirit.'[14] It was beyond him: he could not bring himself to draw the burned corpse.

The sight of the mainland – low green English hills – lifted the spirits ('that's bloody Dorset!'). They arrived back in Portsmouth at 10.00 p.m. Seddon and the rest were dirty and in uniforms that were ripped and stained with blood and oil. The welcome home was anything but warm: a plain-clothes policeman interrogated Seddon on the quayside, with withering intensity, much exercised by the fact that the artist was in a much-damaged naval uniform and didn't know the number of his rifle. 'Where did you get it?' he asked. 'I grabbed it fast to return fire when we were attacked. Someone else grabbed mine.' Seddon 'patiently explained that we had been a little pressed for time'.[15] Later, two customs officers came on board the broken ship, skirting gingerly around the holes in the deck and stepping over the chaos of ropes, wires and cables. They were most concerned with the quarantine arrangements for the two dogs aboard. So ended Richard Seddon's time in France. He had the sand and mud of France on his boot soles, little else, while the Germans, masters now of most of Europe, had taken possession of some thirty or forty of Seddon's pictures, left behind in the confusion of the retreat. He half seriously imagined them, years later, in some German war museum, to be wondered at by the citizens of Hamburg or Berlin.

★★★

The defeat in France was a kind of victory: Bawden, Freedman, Ardizzone and Seddon were escapees from the breathtakingly rapid German advance to the French coast; so too were some 338,000 Allied troops who were rescued from Dunkirk alone.[16] For those war artists who were determined to be close to the front, the reduction of Britain to the status of island fortress presented difficulties. Anthony Gross, for example, had returned to France just a week before the Germans began their frenetic attack. A few weeks later, on 26 May, he wrote to Dickey in London: 'I have found myself stuck down here by the latest happenings. However, by degrees I have unravelled the tangled threads of visas and permits and *sauf conduits* and hope unless there are some new restrictions to leave France by the end of the week.'[17] It was July before he and his family sailed from Bordeaux, bound for Glasgow, in one of the last ships to leave.

Barnett Freedman had spent his time with the BEF 'leaping from crag to crag over the roads of northern France'.[18] He had been billeted for a time in Airaines in Picardy, some 18 miles south of Amiens. He had a studio in the house of a Maurice Ricaut (who was sufficiently warm towards the English war artist to be sending him greetings at Christmas 1949). Once back in England, Freedman embarked on a campaign of trying to return across the Channel. It did not go down well with Colin Coote. On 11 June 1940, Kenneth Clark wrote to Freedman, evidently upset by a letter he had received from him: he read it to Coote 'in moving tones … to which he replied, "Not a dog's chance," and was deaf to all my expostulations'.[19]

A week later, Coote wrote to Freedman giving little in the way of encouragement over Freedman's lost luggage and equipment sustained in the flight from France. It was the beginning of a tetchy correspondence. The dispute over compensation rumbled on for a year. Coote could be waspish: he wrote to Freedman on 18 July 1940 informing him that he must travel third class on the railways. 'I am fully conscious that this is not the proper class for an artist of your eminence.' Freedman replied a few days later: 'I am not,' he wrote, 'an eminent artist as you are so good to suggest'. Instead of the return to France he wanted, Freedman was posted to 'Fixed Defences Thames and Medway', to a Colonel Bingham in Sheerness. Undeterred, he settled down to work.

★★★

War artists, 1940: 'What Should We Draw Now?'

You cannot underestimate the disruption the war brought to all our lives – take Richard Seddon, for example – remember he missed out on his post at the Tate. You couldn't get worse timing – a golden opportunity lost because of the war: halls of great paintings exchanged for a rough khaki uniform. It all felt so temporary – our initial contracts with the War Artists' Committee were invariably short term – Ted's, for example, was for just four months. It didn't exactly make you feel secure. And then there was that MI5 nonsense! My goodness, what a fuss – such suspicion of humble artists: the assiduous vetting and lingering doubts. Presumably they were ferreting out the communists amongst us, before it emerged that we would be fighting Hitler alongside the Reds. What on earth did the security services think people like us could do to threaten the state? What secrets did we have?

In the months before France fell we were close to the action, but not close enough, watched over by nervy regular officers with tobacco-stained moustaches and instructions to keep us out of trouble. It was as if someone higher up had decreed, 'We can't afford a dead artist on our hands – just let them draw silent guns, crumbling remains from the last war, and troops sharing a fag well behind the lines. That sort of thing'. We should have been commissioned officers, so it was clear to others where we stood, and, to be honest, the PR staff weren't always the most helpful. Barnett was so cross about it all: at one point he wrote 'I am sick of the job' – [he crossed out 'disgusted with'] – 'and if anyone could get me a commission in the army I would willingly bloody well go.' [20] Bullets flying, the army in retreat, German tanks hot on our heels – there was at least some possibility of our being blown to pieces. The reward Freedman got for his being brave enough to speak his mind was Colin Coote's outrage: 'I can see no alternative to dismissing so cantankerous a fellow'.[21] Bawden was another who believed that the War Office should have conferred commissioned rank on us. He had been frequently held up during the German advance and once was not allowed to leave a building without being subjected to a barrage of questions.

How free were we? The committee certainly took the view that we could pursue whatever we wished. I know that the army man,

Coote, believed that each of us had total freedom. We were not 'stinted of money or opportunity'. Well, maybe that was the case later in the war, but in 1940 we were lost without transport and a willing driver.

And then there was the perennial problem of what to draw. We wanted to record the war as we saw it, but how the heck were we supposed to do it? We soon realised that the most intense moments of danger were the least possible to sketch. Once shells started flying you kept your head down, and the sketchbook was temporarily discarded. Who can blame us? What would you have done? So we painted what we could, what we saw in the slipstream of the fighting, once that listless spring of 1940 turned to the summer of defeat. Ted, for exam-ple, drew soldiers on parade; flat landscapes and farmyards; officers in quirky military caps; green shoots on shrubs and trees; fat-arsed sergeants around beery mess tables; a pipe-smoking soldier squatting down while a line of washing in the fenced garden behind him flaps in the breeze. He had such an acute eye for that neat juxtaposition of the domestic and the military. As early as August 1939 he had drawn the mobilised troops of his anti-aircraft unit leaving a drill hall in Putney – ordinary blokes looking browned-off. If you look at his work now, you would think the early part of the war was a series of lengthy lunch breaks in shady woods, men leaning on jeeps and drinking warm beer; troops in picnic mode lying in a field looking up at distant flak, church spires and burgeoning trees beyond the end of a meadow. It all changed later – he caught the desolation in Louvain well enough: the lost dog deserted by its owner, long since turned tail; the machine-gun posts and sandbags; the bombed ruins and the broken bridge.

It was uncomfortable a lot of the time and we longed for home comforts, though perhaps that feeling varied depending upon your age. Seddon was to all intents and purposes a student still, with a young man's view of what constituted comfort; but Ardizzone, Bawden and Freedman were all in their late thirties, and Reginald Eves was in his sixties – and just a year from his death. Ted was a martyr to his lumbago and a damp bed in early spring was not conducive to his wellbeing! There was a temptation for all of us to drink too much and eat unwisely or irregularly. Billets might be hotels, but this was not a time for exceptional customer service! Rooms were often cold and cheerless, and the nights increasingly became illuminated by gunfire and air raids. Seddon, for example, spent time sleeping in a roof space above a pig sty, listening to the night-time scurrying of rats.

We fitted into the army's way of doing things very differently: some of us found the protocols and 'bull' deeply off-putting, and it made us turn in on ourselves. Bawden, for one, despaired at army officers' lack of conversation or ideas. Ted, of course, was fine, relying on that easy charm, the smile and bonhomie. Seddon thought himself lucky he was a long way from the beating heart of the army, tucked away at the edge of things. That came back to haunt him of course, when he found himself on the edge of Germany and forced to drive through the darkness in the hope of escape.

We were desperately lucky, it should be said, to get back to England in one piece – you would have thought that one of us at least would have been caught up by the Germans – but we all survived for a time at least. After the evacuations from Dunkirk and Boulogne, we were left wondering what was coming next. What would we artists draw now? Sketches of German invaders driving tanks across the weald of Kent, perhaps; burning buildings and blackened rubble; forlorn figures trying to sleep in underground shelters; the last-ditch efforts of a nation on its own and besieged. Each of us was alone too, sketchbook at the ready, wondering what the next commission might be and where we would be sent.

8

Exhibition, 1940

On 7 June 1940, when Richard Seddon's unit was moving out of Neufchâtel unaware of the events at Dunkirk, the secretary of the WAAC, E.M. O'R. Dickey, dictated a letter to Captain Ravilious. He wanted 'to let you know that we hope to be able to arrange an exhibition, opening at the beginning of July, of the work so far done by artists who have been employed on the committee's recommendation.'[1] Ravilious was asked to submit any work he wished to be included by 20 June. He duly identified a large number of paintings: of the campaign in Norway, of aircraft carriers in cold seas, of Scapa Flow, of defusing mines. One painting was of HMS *Glorious* steaming, in strange light, for the Arctic – and sunk the day after Dickey's letter.[2]

So, Dickey, talk me through the arrangements one last time – venue? The Spanish Rooms in the National Gallery ('immediately on the right of the entrance').[3] *When will it be hung?* Friday, 28 June. *When is the Press Viewing?* The following Monday, 1 July. There's to be a Private Viewing on the 2nd, and the general public will be admitted from the 3rd. *Who should be invited?* 'anything in the nature of a formal opening would be unsuitable …' but 'representatives of Government Departments, the artists themselves and others who have been connected with the arrangements for war artists' – let's have them there! No formal invitations – (there's a war on after all, and paper is short!) *What happens if the invasion has begun?* Invite the Germans! No, this is a British civil servant, remember, exhibiting an urbane *sangfroid* – the thought of German panzers thundering towards London was clearly not to be countenanced, certainly not discussed.

And which artists and which paintings? Well, many of the names suggest themselves: Muirhead Bone, of course, 'busily employed since 1 January in recording naval subjects of outstanding interest'; the four War Office men: Freedman, Ardizzone, Bawden and Reginald Eves. Mr Bawden's 'whereabouts were for some days a matter of speculation, [but he] returned by Dunkirk, and was fortunate enough to bring his drawings safely back.' *Who else?* Two Air Ministry men, Keith Henderson and Paul Nash. Some naval bods, including Captains Ravilious and Nash, John that is. We've included 'Mr Anthony Gross, who is an exceptionally rapid worker. [He] has made a series of numerous sketches of army training at home.' Much more to come from him, you can't help feeling. There are more of course … Hubert Freeth with a posthumous portrait of Commander Jolly RN; Midshipman Worsley drawing 'life on board an auxiliary cruiser in the North Sea'. *Other subject matter?* Well, aircraft and tank manufacture, the making of battledress, shipbuilding (by Stanley Spencer actually), making munitions, ARP control rooms … Finally, there are two women represented! Miss Evelyn Dunbar and a couple of lithographs from Miss Ethel Gabain. It promises to be very exciting.

★★★

The most memorable war art from the 1914–1918 war focused on the horrors of the western front: the territory over which the fighting had taken place reduced to a treeless hell, a morass of mud and pulped bodies; or blinded troops feeling their way back to Blighty. Subject matter for the 1939–1945 war artists encompassed anything from the manufacture of weapons, for example, to sailors clinging to the upturned hull of a lifeboat in heavy seas in the darkness of an Atlantic night. A key difference between 1940 and 1914 was that the Home Front in the former was also the front line. After Dunkirk, and for many months, there was little in the way of offensive action to record, certainly in Europe. Instead the war artists recorded bomb damage, strewn and mangled corpses, a population under fire. Some artists stepped carefully around Londoners forced to sleep on the underground platforms to avoid the bombs; others drew aircraft on their runways, or ships in dock; they worked on portraits of busy, high-ranking officers, or women munitions workers, hair in turbans, leaning over lathes.

Some war artists had already seen enough action in France to realise that capturing the reality of the battlefield was fraught with difficulty. Ardizzone, for one, commented on the problems of sketching shellfire or manoeuvres when the distances over which modern warfare was fought were so vast. For his part, Richard Seddon was dismissive of much war art: 'If you look through war artists' work it's folding parachutes, loading guns, peeling potatoes – any passer-by could have drawn it.'[4] Faced with the creaking shambles of the retreat in 1940, Seddon learned an important lesson. He had aspired to paint something entirely different, the true nature of action in battle, but then for the first time he realised that it was possible to draw only the preliminaries of fighting and the aftermath; 'the action itself is un-paintable, in any sense that conveys the noise, the stink and the tension.'[5] Reflecting after his close encounter with German gunfire aboard ship and the subsequent explosion, when returning to England, he commented: 'How the hell do you paint that?' Despite the difficulty, he felt that war art should be just that: art that illustrated war.

A second difficulty related to censorship: Eric Ravilious at one time was refused permission to paint an admiral's bicycle, and it was inevitable that the closer an artist got to sensitive information, the more likely the censors were to refuse any attempt to let the drawing see the light of day. For all that, while artists might have subjects suggested to them, in the main they felt free to draw what they liked. Some appeared to be a law unto themselves in terms of where they went and their ability to keep ahead of an interfering officialdom.

The extent to which artists were able to get close to the action was an issue: like Freedman, Ardizzone was critical of the way that obstacles appeared to be put in the way of getting right to the front in the battles of 1940. In fact, the speed of the German advance gave him a chance to get much closer to the action than the War Office had intended. Much later, in Italy, he would come up against the problem again: he had found himself staying with a guards brigade up in the Apennines and had crossed swords with a brigadier who 'wasn't a very nice man'. Ted was subjected to a bellowed 'What's an artist doing here?' from the irate old buffer.

And then there was the question which drifted in the back of each artist's mind, like smoke on a battlefield. Was the overall purpose of it all just plain propaganda, the boosting of morale – that example of courage; those brave men and women; this devastation from which we shall rise again?

★★★

AN OFFICIAL
EXHIBITION
OF PICTURES
BY WAR
ARTISTS
Open to the Public
on Wednesday, July 3rd at the
National Gallery, Trafalgar Square
and will remain open until further
notice. Hours 10 to 6 on weekdays.
ADMISSION IS FREE

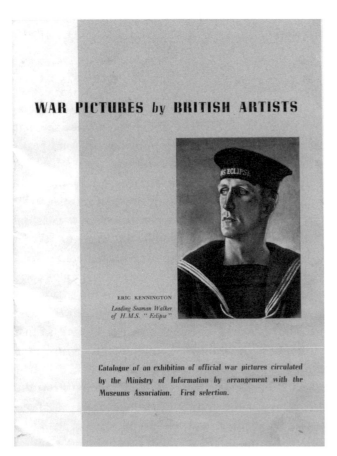

'There's to be a
Private Viewing
on the 2nd, and
the general public
will be admitted
from the 3rd ...'
The Catalogue
for the War Artists'
Exhibition at the
National Gallery.

Not everyone regarded war art as necessary or welcome: on 28 June, for example, a letter was sent from HM Stationery Office which read: 'I venture to express regret that (your Ministry) proposes to take hard-pressed Civil Servants from essential war work in order that they may devote an afternoon … to looking at pictures painted by war artists … [It] makes one wonder whether the French debacle was not largely due to the French High Command and the other officers spending their time looking at pictures in the Louvre … instead of spending their time with the business of getting on with the war.' The letter ended with a complaint about the 'gross waste of paper' the invitation represented, through 'sealing securely the flap of the envelope, and then covering the back of the envelope, including the flap, with a white label, containing the address, which is securely gummed all over.'[6] That was one stony-hearted Londoner who would have ignored the chance to see exactly what Ravilious, Bawden, Ardizzone and the rest had produced. For many others, the exhibition was a bright light in a dark world.

★★★

Eric Ravilious stood on the steps of the National Gallery; then half-turned to look back over Trafalgar Square, sand-bagged since the war began and discordant with amplified voices from the nest of loudspeakers on the square's stone fountains. Tirzah was not far behind, looking calmer than he felt. It was the afternoon of Tuesday, 2 July 1940, the day of the exhibition's 'private view'. Ravilious frowned momentarily, apprehensive suddenly at what lay ahead. He was reassured by a sparkling smile from a young woman evidently impressed by the artist's uniform – the cut of my jib, he thought – and his eyes followed her as she ran down the steps and headed in the direction of Charing Cross. Ravilious slowly made his way into the gallery, Tirzah's hand by now in his. It was just after two o'clock and the 'private view' would have begun, lines of the great and good filing past his work, separated now from the hand that made them. Private it might be, he thought, but signing his name on the sheet of paper at the open door, it felt dismayingly public.

Strangely, in a gallery where every painting had emerged from the short opening salvoes of the war, the event was reminiscent of peacetime, despite the uniforms and the evident strain etched on some of the faces. People had not lost the art of judging a painting in a moment, shaping compliments, hiding their true feelings, paying court to those with power. It was after all a powerful room: Sir Kenneth Clark himself, of course, all pin-stripe and hair-oil; his fragrant wife, Jane; the Director of the Tate, John Rothenstein; Roger Hinks, whom Clark thought 'one of the most learned and perceptive art historians of his generation' and who had recently been forced to resign as assistant keeper at the British Museum for his alleged part in the inappropriate cleaning of the Elgin Marbles; the architectural historian J.M. Richards; artists – Freeth and Ethel Gabain among them – a critic from the *News Chronicle* ... Gosh! Eric shook hands, smiled, sipped a cheap champagne and, in a sudden sweating moment of doubt, began to count the number of his own paintings on show. Too many by half! It made him feel uncomfortably boyish: he looked across at Tirzah who was absorbed in a conversation, overshadowed by the lordly Kenneth Clark. Eric began to draft a letter in his head: 'I very much enjoyed the exhibition at the National Gallery and it was good to see all those people after such a long time.' Would it be too gauche, he wondered, to say what he really felt – there had been too many Raviliouses for comfort?

'I very much enjoyed the exhibition at the National Gallery and it was good to see all those people after such a long time.' Freedman, Ardizzone, Gross, Clark and Sutherland, amongst others, enjoy conversation, a glass of something and the inevitable cigarette.

★★★

As well as the paintings by Eric Ravilious, some of Edward Ardizzone's work was exhibited in the National Gallery's Spanish Room. At the same time, there was other work – not war-related – lying at the bottom of the Bay of Biscay. In 1938, Ted had been commissioned to produce a set of illustrations for an edition of Shakespeare's *Richard III*: 'a series of beautiful water-colours'. They were produced in Paris and completed on 7 June 1940, the same day Dickey wrote to Ravilious about the exhibition at the National Gallery. The lithographer, M. Fernand Mourlot, managed to flee Paris before the Germans arrived and took with him 'several packing cases containing the reproductions of [Ardizzone's] water-colours'. Such devotion to duty deserved a happy ending, but it was not to be: 'He was able to ship them from Bordeaux … [but] they never reached us. We can only conclude that they are at the bottom of the sea.'[7]

Packing cases of precious Ardizzone watercolours might have been lost at sea, but the artist himself withstood the German blitzkrieg with his usual buoyant optimism. Like other war artists, he set to drawing the results of the German bombing. Anthony Gross, for example, drew air raid shelters, wrecked gas and water mains, and bombed churches. Ardizzone and Felix Topolski were sent into the East End of London to record the extent of the bomb damage. Ted was briefly arrested as a spy while sketching the docks. At night the skies were an evil red as the East End burned: 'Everywhere you looked there was fire … It seemed as if the whole East End docks' were burning.[8] When daylight came, Ardizzone sketched the smoking ruins. In the middle of October 1940, his own house suffered a near miss in a bombing raid. He thanked his stars that the bomb which fell on his own road, Elgin Avenue in Maida Vale, missed by a matter of yards – just five, he claimed. He gingerly salvaged drawings from the 'wreck' of his house which he felt 'might tumble down at any minute'.[9] The month before, Barnett Freedman's house had been hit 'when a bomb blew a heavy paving stone high into the air'.[10] It smashed through the roof and landed on his bed. Fortunately, Freedman was at his club at the time.

As an artist, Ardizzone was stirred by the dramatic acres of damage – naked buildings, twisted girders, blackened bricks – and greatly moved by the manifestations of Londoners' phlegmatic courage. 'People were frightened, but didn't show it – they were marvellous.' In a letter written in 1940, he wrote, 'At the Bank a large bomb has fallen into the middle of

'St Paul's looked almost black in contrast' – Ardizzone, the indefatigable artist, adds a sketch to a letter home.

the tube station, and all there is of it now is a vast hole filling all the road way. They are still digging the bodies out from great tangles of twisted iron and concrete.'[11] The letter included an eloquent sketch: three figures are dwarfed by St Paul's Cathedral, which casts a long shadow over rows of tottering brick walls, the remains of a line of city offices. 'The colour was wonderful. All the bricks had been burnt into magnificent pinks and tawny yellows while St Paul's looked almost black in contrast.' He may have been fascinated by these spectral buildings, but they also moved him to tears. Like Henry Moore, he wandered amongst those sheltering in the underground stations, sketching the stifling confusion of bodies. Ardizzone depicted 'a steaming human throng ... the bustling crowd, the burdened mothers with their endlessly tiresome children. The friendly voices, the smells, the chips, the shelter life.'[12] He thought Moore did it better, but not everyone agreed.

Like Bawden and Freedman, Ardizzone looked back on his experiences in France with mixed feelings. On 4 June he went to see Dickey to put the case for war artists having commissioned status. He had, he said, 'repeatedly been in difficulties in France because of uncertainties about rank.' Over the ensuing months, he toured the country with a sketch pad and pencils at the whim of those charged with deploying him. He also wrote his account of the 1940 campaign, *Baggage to the Enemy*, which he dictated to his sister. His wife he had prevailed on to move out of London – to Montgomeryshire. 'I wouldn't have her here!' he said, looking back decades later. Freedman's family was similarly moved out of London, to Princes Risborough in Buckinghamshire.

Ardizzone's travels took him to Darlington, where he met up with his brother-in-law, Gabriel White, who was in charge of a camouflage school near there. Ardizzone was given a commission which gave him a frisson of anxiety. He wrote to his daughter: 'They want me to do drawings of the squads which remove unexploded bombs. I think I will make my sketches from a place as far away as possible.' He was glad that he could produce a pencilled drawing in perhaps 10 or 15 minutes, since the idea of spending very long on the task 'when they're defusing a bomb at

'I think I will make my sketches from as far away as possible' – Ardizzone draws the bomb squad.

the bottom of a crater' did not appeal to him at all.[13] It was clear to him too that recording the war directly in watercolour was impossible: too time-consuming for the immediacy of the moment.

He traversed the country from the West Country to Scotland. 'I was sent here and there and all over the place' – expenses paid, but travelling third class on slow trains with quixotic timetables. Among his drawings, he faithfully captured the comic opera image of the Home Guard: though decades later he couldn't recall where the drawings were made. 'Bless my soul I wish I could remember!' At one point he was sent to Northern Ireland 'to welcome the American troops'; he was unimpressed with Belfast ('a bloody awful town') but appreciated the warmth of the welcome he got. He was, after all, 'a great charmer with his snuff, his partiality to a pint, and his propensity for eating fish and chips on his homeward walk.'[14] As 1940 turned to autumn, Ardizzone began to suspect that 'they didn't know what to do with me' after France had fallen.[15] It would seem that his intuition was right: by 1941, 'the WAAC was finding it hard to occupy Ardizzone or to give him serious subjects.'[16]

★★★

On 4 July, two days after the war artists' exhibition's private view, Edward Bawden rang the WAAC secretariat from Victoria Station, anxious about the fact that he had been given a first-class ticket, rather than the third he had expected. A few days later, on 7 July 1940, he left the port of Southampton on a Union Castle liner, bound for the Middle East. Early in the voyage his ship passed three burning cargo ships, but that was the most stirring event of a long and uneventful trip. Bawden made no use of the large quantities of artists' paper he had brought with him – there was nothing to draw but boundless ocean. He disembarked at Cape Town, trained to Durban and then took 'an Imperial Airways flying boat to Cairo', a five-day flight from one end of Africa to the other, from one glassy sheet of water to the next, with the pilot flying low enough to spook the game. Bawden stood 'at the big picture window' and gazed at the wildlife teeming below on the African veldt. He was out of uniform, masquerading as a civilian, since the Portuguese in Mozambique were mindful of their neutrality.

Once he reached Cairo, the Public Relations Unit was exercised about what to do with this 'official war artist' and Bawden was soon packed off to a hospital: 'You might find the operating theatre of interest?' Really? Oh, well – Bawden scratched his head, perplexed at the idea that the WAAC would welcome sketches of a profusion of appendix operations. Behind the required mask, he smiled thinly when the tranquillity of the theatre was disturbed by the buzzing of a fly: 'everyone clapped their hands and tried to kill it.'[17] That was it for drama, at least for the moment.

While Bawden stared at the ocean and thought of home, Eric Ravilious was in Portsmouth, staying at Keppel's Hotel. Introduced to the claustrophobic world of submarines, he found the conditions hard, uncomfortably hot when the submarine was under water, with a distinctive and peculiar smell when the craft dived. The absence of rolling movement was a minor, compensatory benefit. On 22 July 1940, he was touched when the Royal Marine band played *Rock of Ages* to celebrate his thirty-seventh birthday. But the senior service was not always so empathetic. Despite his success at the National Gallery exhibition he had unaccountably provoked some official disapproval. He was summoned to Chatham since the 'C-in-C wanted to have a talk about my drawings. I suspect he doesn't like them at all.'[18] The Commander-in-Chief, the Nore, 'read a lecture from his grand mahogany desk with the assurance of the Pope.' Ravilious found it a strange meeting with 'some very funny crosstalk'. He thought that, despite everything, they 'had parted on fairly good terms'.[19] They may have exchanged concluding pleasantries and salutes of varying correctness, but the meeting between Sir Reginald Plunkett-Ernle-Erle-Drax (Admiral) and Eric Ravilious (artist, lithographer and shopkeeper's son) somehow encapsulated a tension between the freedom of art and the stern confines of military life. At all events, Ravilious' links with the Royal Navy were soon to be broken. Instead he turned to the RAF; the beginnings of his doomed love affair with aircraft.

For the present, he turned his attention to the swathe of defences on the south coast, built to repel the anticipated invasion. In mid-September he headed for Newhaven, travelling via London and Eastbourne which, to his horror, brought to mind 'the ruins of Pompeii': the pier was broken in two; the art college had been bombed; people were on the move, anxious to get out of the town and away from the bombs. As Ravilious left London, he stared out of the train window, head leaning against the grubby glass, elbow on the pale chipped wood of the carriage window-frame. His left hand toyed with the leather tongue of the window strap, while his right hand rested on the worn, grey carriage seat with its thin red stripes. The moment stirred a fleeting memory of a pre-war life and a painting from his recent past. Steam drifted past, partly masking the smoking holes in the ground, the coiled hosepipes and the sad, empty bedrooms – curtains flapping and brickwork gone – left exposed by the bombing.

Newhaven, by contrast, despite its proximity to France, seemed more 'solid and naval and reassuring',[20] although it too shook with the noise of guns and bombs. The town was a likely site for a German landing and so he acquired the wherewithal to protect himself. Imagine him in some airless shed: rows of military stores; the clipboard on the counter; the diminutive clerk with the wispy moustache reaching to the shelf behind him for service revolver – 'What a rod,' he wrote of his 'enormous loaded naval pistol' – and tin hat. 'Would you mind signing for these, sir?' The helmet was heavy, a constant reminder of how poorly equipped his skull was to resist Hitler's bombs. It seemed 'to cram my neck into my coat like a tortoise'.[21]

He enjoyed the work, sketching contentedly in fine weather for days on end, on the green cliff tops above the English Channel. In drawing the concrete bulwarks of the coastal defence system, he caught their last-ditch grandeur, their proud resolution. 'It is marvellous on the cliffs this weather, though the wind blows a bit, and bombs fall every afternoon, and sometimes planes.'[22] Flags streamed in the in-rushing westerlies; hilltops were buttressed with concrete and loops of barbed wire; knots of soldiers were dwarfed by guns pointing out to sea; lonely picnic sites were transformed into potential battlefields. 'I draw in perfect peace of mind,' he wrote, 'it is simply wonderful.'[23] The result was seven pictures of Newhaven's coastal defences.

War artists could not expect to remain in one location: the war moved and so must they. Moreover, Ravilious' six-month contract ended on 10 August 1940, as a letter from the WAAC made clear. He left the south coast and returned home, losing his cap as he leaned eagerly out of the train window on the journey from Liverpool Street. He considered the idea of going out to Iceland, imagining painting Royal Marines in 'duffel coats and perhaps those splendid plum skies'. But instead there was just official uncertainty – talk of the WAAC wanting him to produce 'a children's painting book out of [his] submarine pictures to sell at a shilling and print 10,000, so that the rising generation will clamour to go into the navy.' The idea sank without trace ... to Ravilious' satisfaction: 'Submarines aren't suitable for children.'[24]

He was in limbo and grew restless: instead of war painting, he chopped up logs, walked and read. In November he heard that bombs had destroyed the Morley College murals which he and Bawden had done before the war. In addition, fifty-seven local people had died, trying to shelter from the bombs. A bleak letter from the principal described how the mural had 'perished in the ruins'. It seemed to symbolise the darkness of that winter of 1940: heavy frosts, blankets of snow, and little hope that the war would end soon, and certainly not with victory. On 8 November, he heard he had been given a further six-month commission. There was a penny-pinching exchange of memoranda between Dickey and the Deputy Finance Officer in the Ministry of Information, a Mr Crossley, over whether Ravilious should travel first class when on duty. Crossley took the view that, while artists claimed both first class and third, Ravilious was not entitled at his rank to travelling first class. He must travel third, it seemed – until a thunderous Admiralty broadside dismissed the idea. Since the navy's officers had a king's commission, then Captain Ravilious must be able to travel in a first-class carriage. Civilian artists? They can go third.

★★★

'Of special interest will be a series of sketches by Midshipman John Worsley...' Worsley was just twenty when he first went to sea. Within a year he had been torpedoed and sunk twice. His upbringing was of the kind that fosters resilience: expatriate family (growing Kenyan coffee); sent off to school in the UK (prep and public); art school in London. In the summer before the war began he puttered along the south coast in a bull-nosed Fiat, stopping occasionally to paint when the play of light beguiled, or the mood took him. There was no denying the imminence of war, though – his father's newly acquired job title of 'Passive Defence Officer, Plymouth Dockyard' was a constant reminder, and it was through his father that the war caught up with him. 'Have you met my son, old chap? John, this is Captain Vivian, master of the *Laurentic*.'

The ship had been a liner in its former life and, when the war broke out, was undergoing a conversion into a merchant cruiser, armed for convoy defence. She was short of crew members and Worsley enlisted as a Royal Naval Reserve midshipman. After a brief training period, he joined the ship in October 1939, acutely aware of the 'little blue tabs on the lapels' which revealed his status, or lack of it. He derived a certain reassurance from the fact that, if the ship was sunk, he was not necessarily confined to future service in the navy. For the present, however, going to sea offered a heaven-sent opportunity to avoid the army. He had few illusions though about what the war might mean in terms of his pursuing a career in art. 'When one's young like this, you think the world's coming to an end ... Thought I'd never paint again, or I'd be killed or something.'[25]

Through the first autumn of the war, *Laurentic* patrolled the bleak waters between Iceland and Greenland, steadfastly on the lookout for German raiders passing through the Denmark Straits on the way to harry the Atlantic convoys. 'With a top speed of 22 knots, she resembled a block of flats moving slowly across the ocean.'[26] She may have been converted, but there was no denying her vulnerability: she was poorly armed, with 'no anti-aircraft weapons, no anti-submarine gear, and of course no ASDIC or radar.' At first she seemed to be a lucky ship: the first tour of duty was uneventful, while the ship which replaced her, HMS *Rawalpindi*, was sunk in a battle with two German battle cruisers, *Scharnhorst* and *Gneisenau*. *Laurentic* also survived a harrowing air raid on the port of Liverpool. Later, she unmasked a German ship, flying under a Norwegian flag, whose crew then hurriedly abandoned ship before she was emphatically sunk.

In the salty tumult of life on board, Worsley found occasional, fleeting moments when he could sketch and the WAAC was glad to receive work from an artist on active service: the norm was for Admiralty art to consist of uplifting panoramas of busy harbours on a war footing – calm water; pennants flying; blue sky and fluffy clouds. At two guineas a go, Worsley gave them pictures which were truer to the war at sea: fierce winds, cold hands, flurries of sleet, the deep, unremitting roll of waves and the frequent uncertainty about where the grey-green sea and grey-black sky met. For such service Worsley received 5s a day. Then *Laurentic* was torpedoed and sunk.

It happened on 4 November 1940, a night of pitch-black darkness, 300 miles west of the Irish coast. The ship was returning to Liverpool from the waters around Gibraltar in company with HMS *Patrochlus* to resume the treadmill of tedious patrols in icy waters and unforgiving weather.

It was forging east at some 15 knots in a calm sea with a steady swell. Worsley was asleep in his bunk, following a spell when he had been on watch. At 21.50 hours the first torpedo struck the ship on its starboard side, a blow which soon caused the engine room to flood. A second torpedo soon followed and the ship began to list to starboard. There was an unexplained explosion. The German U-boat which had fired the torpedoes was on the surface. Its first torpedo had caused *Laurentic* to list so badly that she was unable to fire her guns at the enemy. One minute Worsley was wrapped in sleep in a silent world; the next, all was noise — explosion, alarms, men shouting. The second torpedo finished the job. Worsley abandoned ship and found himself in a waterlogged cutter which drifted through the dark night. He saw a man stoically waiting at the very topmost peak of the ship as it slowly submerged into the depths, then coolly swimming off at the very last moment before *Laurentic* disappeared. She finally sank at 03.50. Rescue arrived with the morning when a destroyer, *Achates*, materialised through the dawn and took the survivors back to Gourock on the Clyde.

The subsequent inquiry into the loss of the ship was critical: 'the organisation to ensure that signals of vital importance were at once shown to the Captain was not sufficiently rigid.'[27] It took too long for the captain and navigating officer to be told that a German submarine was 'almost directly in the track of HMS *Laurentic*'. The captain, distraught at his ship's loss and disillusioned by the inquiry's findings, sank into a 'profound melancholia [and] ... was invalided and not employed again'. Later Worsley painted the *Laurentic;* fittingly, perhaps, the finished painting was sunk too, en route to South America.

9

No One Can Settle to a Work of Art

Edward Bawden reached Cairo towards the end of that summer of 1940. The war – and the WAAC – had made him a genuine traveller, when once he would have been content with a gentle bicycle ride on the Essex by-roads, on the low rolling hills between Great Bardfield and Castle Hedingham. On 20 October 1940, he wrote to his wife that he would 'like to be home again and able to experience the dangers that [family and friends] are having to face.'[1] Certainly he felt 'completely out of the war' where he was. While he hankered after the comfort and companionship of home, his life would soon become a succession of journeys into the unknown, distant and fly-blown. At first, he was subject to orders given by senior officers in the Public Relations (PR) Unit in Cairo, determined that they 'must get rid of this nuisance'. 'Where can we lose this artist chappie for a while?' 'Why don't we send him to Khartoum?'

Bawden headed south on a Nile paddle-steamer, dreamily watching the paddles turning from the sun-baked deck. It 'was a cousin of the Mississippi showboat, having tiers of decks and a water wheel placed behind.'[2] It was early morning when he arrived at Wadi Haifa, 600 miles south of Cairo; there he took the late afternoon train for Aswan – 'comfortable … [but] dependent on artificial lighting and ventilation':[3] windows had to be closed against the desert dust. Khartoum, when he arrived in the dark of the African night, was a chaos of people and luggage. The following morning he walked beside the Blue Nile, along Kitchener Avenue, watching pelicans cavorting in the coffee-coloured river. Back home, the

Bawden family was contemplating the onset of an English winter, while its breadwinner ruefully shook his head, stirred by the strangeness of it all.

Bawden would regularly walk over the Nile Bridge to Omdurman, where Kitchener had once triumphed, and where now the war artist toiled in the heat, sketching soldiers from the Sudan Defence Force. 'I liked drawing black chaps,' he remembered many years later. He found them 'simply beautiful'. He welcomed the fact that the war had required him to draw people: portraiture hitherto had not been his thing. He was untroubled by the heat, although it proved a challenge technically, since the paint dried so quickly. The sun he fended off with a sketching umbrella which the Ministry of Information had supplied him – and who, in keeping with austere times, insisted on its return when the war finally ended.

Khartoum was a very long way from the Home Counties, but Bawden's odyssey was to become yet more spartan. In the company of the local district commissioner, he spent days at a stretch in the bush, sleeping in the open, surviving on minimal supplies – crusts and water – and revelling in the adventure. Then he caught malaria – the 'malignant tertian' variety, he told his wife in a letter of 22 January 1941. He imagined she would respond with 'Edward, my dear, you must take care of yourself, and not forget to change your socks whenever you have wet feet.'[4] Instead of the gritty outdoor life, he was consigned to a hospital bed, in a ward with no other patients, racked with fever. Once he was past the worst, he began sketching again: a burnt-out Italian aircraft; trees with vast stems and tapering tops. He stayed at the house of the district commissioner, building up his strength. Time seemed to stand still in the African heat, while, beyond the confines of the dark continent, the war rolled on.

★★★

The war was more than a year old by now and with no prospect of it ending. Victory was a mirage; defeat a real threat. For the war artists, late 1940 was a time of anxiety, sudden departures, confusion and separation. Early in 1941, Ravilious was commissioned to draw the bunkers of the Home Security control room, deep under Whitehall. Such contrasts the war was providing him: reluctant submariner in claustrophobic quarters; then sketcher of windswept defences high above south coast beaches, lungs filled with wind from the sea; and then a commission that buried him in the cold heart of wartime planning – unforgiving light, shadowy figures, obscure maps, and a chilling, Orwellian, subterranean existence, where secrecy flourished and the war was everything.

Other artists' lives were hugely disrupted and uncertain: war somehow did not seem conducive to work. Virginia Woolf noted in her diary that 'no one can settle to a work of art'.[5] Henry Moore and his wife fretted about having 'recently bought a new car, a Standard 8, and wished they hadn't'.[6] Moore, like many others, was uneasy about the loss of teaching and the potential difficulty of selling work in wartime. He had turned down an approach from the WAAC early in the war, but a chance tube journey triggered a series of sketches of the thousands living a troglodyte life, sheltering on the platforms and track of the London Underground from the nightly bombing raids. When his studios were bombed in October 1940, Moore moved out of London to Much Hadham in Hertfordshire. The National Gallery itself was damaged by bombs on the 10th of the same month, while at the Ravilious home in Bank House, everyone slept downstairs for fear of the bombing.

Barnett Freedman had an additional worry: he and the War Office were increasingly incompatible. Colin Coote took the view that Freedman was 'cantankerous', even going as far as to remark that it was 'more important to keep out the Germans than to take in Mr Barnett Freedman'.[7] It was a harsh judgement; Christianna Clemence, Edward Ardizzone's daughter, thought him 'enormous fun' who told 'self-deprecating jokes'.[8] Coote, it seemed got his way: at its first meeting of 1941, the WAAC decided that Anthony Gross should replace Freedman who was to be transferred to the Ministry of Information. There was considerable upset about the issue. Just before Christmas 1940, Dickey had written a placatory letter to Freedman: 'I'll see that the powers that be have your letter put before them. You are not the only artist who has been badly treated in this way.'[9]

In early February 1941, Freedman learned that his contract was to be terminated from 10 March: he was very disappointed. He wrote to Kenneth Clark on 8 February: 'I am most sad and upset … I have never had a better job.' A personal letter from Colin Coote expressed his regret that Freedman was leaving his post, but Freedman remained hurt by the decision. He told friends that he had been sacked. 'I do wonder what you mean about getting the sack!' wrote one such friend. 'Have you just worked your time out, or have you been actively naughty?'[10] Freedman was subsequently a war artist working on behalf of the Admiralty, including a period aboard HMS *Repulse*.[11] Later he spent time on the submarine *Tribune*.

Richard Seddon, soon after his dramatic return from France, was diagnosed with tuberculosis and hospitalised ('I'm afraid your army days are over'). While recovering, he received a letter from Edward Bawden, written on 6 July 1940: 'I welcome the opportunity,' Bawden wrote, 'for further adventure, and consider myself undeservedly lucky in being the only painter released from this "island fortress" for service abroad.'[12] He at least seemed to have some certainty about his role. Others were left in limbo. It took time to find a niche or a particular focus with which they were comfortable. For Paul Nash, for example, it was a fascination with aeroplanes: 'I first became interested in the war pictorially when I realised the machines were the real protagonists.'[13] John Piper concentrated on bomb damage 'which allowed him the scope to pursue his interest in buildings and his feeling for 'the spirit of the place'.[14] Vivian Pitchforth's work included 'documenting the rebuilding of the House of Commons';[15] Graham Sutherland was one of three artists commissioned by the Ministry of Information to draw 'pictures of damage which may be caused by enemy action'.[16] Muirhead Bone worked on officer portraits, naval installations, ruins and ships; Richard Eurich produced 'dramatic images of shipwreck survivors'; Eric Kennington concentrated on portraits and was 'fervently devoted to the solidity and heroism of his sitters' – he eventually resigned because he felt not enough was made of the propaganda value of his work; Henry Lamb turned his attention from portraits to 'documenting tank training exercises in South East Command'.[17] Evelyn Dunbar showed a 'particular affinity for the work of the Land Army' – Dunbar was in 'a unique position for a female artist': the only woman 'entrusted with a salaried position'.[18]

The WAAC continued to receive a steady flow of inquiries: Tom Hennell, for example, wrote on Christmas Eve 1939, 'I offer my services in return for food and accommodation only … the work done to remain the property of the Ministry of Information.'[19] He was turned down. But he was not forgotten: in May 1941 the WAAC considered a number of his drawings which they liked but did not buy. Later, on 15 August, he was commissioned to do some harvest drawings: it meant a 15 guinea fee, third-class rail and £1 a day expenses (6s and 8d if he was away for less than 24 hours). The committee 'was charmed' by his watercolours and bought seven of them. His career as a war artist was under way. His involvement – and his innocent charm – are revealed by a note he sent to Dickey on 25 May 1942: 'I cannot visit the National Gallery on Thursday as I am to pack up some bees on that day.'[20]

Albert Richards, his Royal College career abandoned for a temporary life as a sapper with the Royal Engineers, wrote to Dickey on 1 April 1941 to ascertain what work might be available: 'Any information on art in war-time would be very acceptable, and very much appreciated.'[21] He sold his first painting to the committee the following month: *Sappers Erecting Pickets in the Snow* earned him 15 guineas. Anthony Gross was commissioned by the WAAC as a war artist and, in December 1941, found himself sailing from Avonmouth in the troopship *Highland Monarch*. It would take him to Cairo where he would meet up with Bawden. Ardizzone too would find himself in the Middle East, but for now he was sent hither and thither in the UK: to Salisbury at the end of June 1940; to Edinburgh and Glasgow in April 1941 to record the Blitz; to Northern Ireland – content to sketch ruined buildings, well-oiled troops out on the beer, beleaguered Britain.

★★★

Of the hundreds of artists who produced war art for the WAAC, only a relative few got uncomfortably close to action. Whether it was the result of the close-knit nature of the art world, or just the consequence of a quirk of fate, these artists were connected by a web of reassuring and sustaining relationships. The Bawden-Ravilious friendship was long-lasting and profound, while the network of other relationships was extensive, encompassing Paul and John Nash, Henry Moore, Vivian Pitchforth, Thomas Hennell and others. The architectural writer J.M. Richards recalled spending an afternoon at Lords watching cricket with Ravilious, Moore and Vivian Pitchforth, an artist who had lost his hearing in the First World War but, undeterred, worked as an artist in the 1939–1945 conflict.

There were many other connections: Edward Bawden and Eric Ravilious, and their wives, lived together in the early 1930s; Bawden was Richard Seddon's tutor; Albert Richards and John Worsley were the same age (just twenty in 1939); Ravilious, Bawden and Thomas Hennell were all born in 1903, and had been friends since 1931 when Hennell had rented the other half of the Great Bardfield house; Edward Ardizzone, Freedman and Bawden all passed through Arras in 1940; John Worsley and Ardizzone were in Sicily at much the same time in 1943; Ravilious illustrated Hennell's poems; Tom recognised that Ravilious' support and enthusiasm had been invaluable, and that no one had better taste than Bawden; Ravilious wrote to Helen Binyon on a Japanese card which Hennell had given him for Christmas; Ardizzone, Richards, Gross and Hennell were all in Normandy during the invasion; Ardizzone took over Richards' war artist placement in 1945; Hennell had taken over Ravilious' Icelandic posting; Richards and Hennell shared a house in Holland in 1944–45; Hennell was godfather to Edward Bawden's son, Richard Bawden; and so on. They wrote to each other, ate together, shared boozy sessions and looked out for chances to meet, regretting it when they passed like ships in the night.

★★★

Shortly before the loss of the *Laurentic,* John Worsley 'had written to the Committee complaining about his fee, 5 guineas for 3 drawings'.[22] It was as if his work was taken less seriously than that of the others. At least, though, he was alive, having survived his ship's sinking. He took some well-earned leave, then began a period of training at HMS *King Alfred* in Hove in Sussex. Thereafter he joined HMS *Lancaster,* one of a number of old American destroyers acquired in the darkest of days in 1940. They were fast, but had little else to commend them. Big seas made them roll badly and curtailed any semblance of speed, while the crew cursed their ungainly gait, feeling their stomachs churn in the Atlantic's swell. It was convoy duty protecting slow-moving merchant ships from submarines.

The three-weekly turns into the teeth of Atlantic gales were exhausting: 'for three weeks on end they never had their clothes off, and were never able to sleep for longer than three hours at a time.'[23] There was even less opportunity for Worsley to draw, although occasionally he would seize the time and catch a telling moment on whatever paper was to hand. His drawing of the HMS *Lancaster*'s helmsman at work was done on a scrap of a naval signal pad – Worsley's pencil sketched a thickset figure standing feet apart, braced against the ship's capricious movement. Awake himself, he drew exhausted sailors, fully dressed and booted in a mess-room fug, feet up, eyes shut, bodies half stiffened in anticipation of the torpedo's impact.

After six months, HMS *Lancaster* and its crew were battered to breaking point. In dry dock in Hull, the ship's fragile state was all too evident; no more so than when a dock official poked his rolled umbrella clean through the rusted plates on the ship's bottom. Flakes of orange metal fluttered down and meaningful glances were exchanged. This was a ship going nowhere for a while. The crew, however, were not so fortunate and Worsley found himself posted to another aging destroyer, HMS *Wallace*, whose duties involved providing protection to convoys in the 'E-Boat Alley' between Rosyth and Sheerness. The war here was inescapably close, but its dangers were most apparent in darkness: German E-boats tethered to buoys at night and indistinguishable on murky and primitive radar sets; RAF bombers returning from Europe, eyes skinned for the coast, low on petrol and prey to itchy-fingered anti-aircraft gunners on board the navy's ships. Life at sea for John Worsley allowed him to observe a wealth of good material – but little time to sketch.

★★★

Eric Ravilious too was on the move again: by 14 July 1941 he was in Dover, staying at 27 Old Folkestone Road, not far from the Shakespeare Cliff where Henry Moore had spent the first afternoon of the war. Ravilious liked Dover, although drawing was no easy matter, what with persistent shelling, wind and rain. Nonetheless he was keen to get working since, he told Dickey, Essex had been unduly hot. Dover was heavily damaged, both by bombs and by heavy German artillery on the French cliff tops, a score or so miles away. On 6 August he moved from Dover's 'Hell Fire Corner' to Scotland, where he stayed with John Nash, at Crombie Point Cottage, near Dunfermline in Fife. It was 'a very nice house of a solid Scots kind with shutters and two foot walls and there are apple trees and a lane to the beach. You can see the Firth and ships.'[24] Nash's wife thought he looked unwell – thin, pale and careworn. For a time he was based on May Island in the Firth of Forth, landing there from a destroyer and then an RAF launch. He was with five other officers and a few naval ratings on what was a wind-torn scrap of rock in the ocean. There were wrecks and lighthouses, one of which Eric painted, although recognising that it wasn't strictly a war subject, or even a naval one. A November posting to an offshore rock in the North Sea was not a comfortable one: it was bitterly cold – 'I wear all the clothes it is possible to put on and all but burst the uniform'.[25]

He began drawing seaplanes, intrigued by the Walrus – 'comic things with a strong personality like a duck and designed to go slow ... Put your head out of the window and it is no more windy than a train.'[26] Like Edward Bawden, Ravilious never learned to drive a car, but he felt at home in aeroplanes, and savoured the rituals – the flying suit, parachute, Mae West – as well as the novelty of seeing the world from a fresh angle, all towering clouds and the intricate patterns of the fields below.

★★★

Edward Bawden left Juba in style, led by a British officer imperiously astride a white horse. This was Colonel Athill, whose expedition – manned by Ethiopian cadets, with a long train of camels – Bawden had joined, marching perhaps 10 miles a day, avoiding the worst of the heat. They slept under the stars, cocooned in mosquito nets on camp beds. Athill, in his moments of leisure when camp was made for the night, turned from professional soldier to bird watcher, disappearing into the bush with his binoculars. Bawden foraged for flower seeds, optimism fired by the prospect of exotic African blooms flourishing in his precious garden at home. He sent them back to Great Bardfield, but none germinated. When Athill and Bawden returned to camp there were often faced with fierce arguments between the Sudanese and the Ethiopians; the camels raucously joined in.

It was a long, tedious march. The escarpment on the way into Ethiopia was an obstacle that slowed their progress. Camels died en route. Bawden stared in an artist's fascination at the maggots on one camel's corpse: they covered it like a cloak, quivering and shivering with activity. Two men died too and vultures picked their bones dry. Bawden's forensic eye noted the sinew hanging from a corpse's pelvis, but drawing such sights was impossible, since the cavalcade never stopped, a relentless plodding on. He thought Ethiopia 'the most interesting country I have seen' and liked the people, whom he described as 'much maligned'.

Eventually, and with difficulty, they crossed the Blue Nile, its opposite banks separated by a mile of flowing river. The camels struggled with uneven ground, floundering as Athill's force descended into a deep canyon. The men suffered from chigoe fleas in their feet, the discomfort compounded by the fact that the fleas laid eggs under the skin's surface. Removing them was not an easy task, and Bawden was forced on one occasion to climb aboard a camel to avoid a day's marching. The camel rocked like a cross channel steamer, Bawden thought, perched high above the earth.

Finally they reached Addis Ababa: forests of eucalyptus trees and the comforts of Italian food. Established in one place for a time, he could paint again, notably the emperor Haile Selassie – 'Tiger Tim' – in the Menelik Palace. The sitting was hindered by Bawden's lack of French and the emperor's poor English. They communicated by courteous gestures. Soon after, Bawden succumbed to malaria again, this time for six long weeks. The hospital was a low, one-storey building around a courtyard. Bawden was looked after by Italian nuns and South African doctors. Fit again, or at least with the malaria temporarily thwarted, Bawden moved on: to Eritrea in the first instance.[27] He drew more people, revelling in his newfound confidence in drawing figures. The countryside was curiously English, 'like Cambridgeshire', dotted with enormous boulders. At one point he found himself on a fine wide road built by Mussolini in the middle of nowhere. The broad carriageway seemed to symbolise Bawden's thirst for travel: he made his way back to Khartoum, then back to Cairo. At one point he found himself surrounded by a delegation of completely naked young women – 'all 17 or 18 and very beautiful'. They exchanged smiles, while Bawden's companion was oblivious, on the prowl for crocodiles to shoot.

On 16 October 1941 he wrote to Dickey indicating that he would be content if the WAAC were to 'withdraw my appointment in order that I could join the forces as an ordinary soldier'. Coote, when he heard of the proposal, commented that he was 'not physically fit to be a soldier'.[28] Bawden set out into the Western Desert in an attempt to locate the Long Range Desert Group. He and a driver followed the tracks carved in the shifting sand by lines of military trucks, until they faltered, faded – then disappeared altogether, blown away by the prevailing wind. They were now thoroughly lost and, as if that wasn't bad enough, the lorry's wheels floundered, then stuck fast in the sand. A forlorn sign in the middle of nowhere was a godsend: 'Siwa Oasis, 200 kilometres.' After a long drive, churning through the dunes, they arrived at Siwa, whose bare craggy rocks topped by ruins held the artist's attention: naked, pink stone; a wild scattering of boulders; an unpeopled landscape. The way took them through 'a maze of grotesque limestone hillocks which look like something off the moon', then a descent 'between two table-topped hills and (then) a long greeny-blue blur of palm-trees stretched across the desert like a bruise.'[29]

Bawden continued to follow the war in the desert whose progress was marked by rusting and twisted metal on the road to Benghazi and Tobruk. The harbours were studded with sunken ships, lying at stricken angles in the oily water. He grew ever more accustomed to the heat; learned to paint in a more liquid way to compensate for the way the watercolours dried in a trice; and began to think that the tide might be turning in this bitter desert war.

10

Out of the Blue

Through the window, in a pearly thin light, were three Walrus seaplanes, in line and facing into a gentle breeze. Ripples of water drifted inshore, lifting the aircrafts' tails in a slow rhythmic dance. Beyond the neatly aligned Walruses, across the broad spread of the estuary, was the grey smudge of the opposite shore. Eric Ravilious worked undisturbed in the empty hospital ward as he sketched, registering the minimal colour in the view – a red cross on the white flag fluttering in the wind; the delft-blue of the quilted bedspread. He breathed in, smelling the sea, and smiled, thinking of Tirzah and the children. Homesick, yes, but all things being equal, he was happy enough in Scotland. Writing to Dickey at the end of November 1941, he enthused about his stay on HMS *Ambrose* in Dundee; the men he was with (he liked the naval pilots), and the location – the sea and the River Tay – despite the persistent gales. A war artist though could never be truly settled: by Christmas 1941 he had moved on from Scotland, uncertain about where he would go next. 'War Painting is so unpredictable,' he wrote in a letter to Richard Seddon, to whom he also sent a list of the things he liked painting best: lighthouses, rowing boats, beds, beaches, and greenhouses.[1]

★★★

Not only was 'war painting' unpredictable, it also presented technical difficulties, not the least of which was working in uncomfortable – even dangerous – situations. Accepted practice was for artists to make drawings on the spot. That was how Paul Nash operated during the 1914–1918 war: he would make up to twenty sketches a day at the front, and then work them up later in oils, or simply leave them as they were. In the 1939–1945 conflict, he took photographs – as did Edward Bawden – and then, working on a dark paper, sketched a rough outline. He then began to develop the piece, with a hard wax chalk or watercolours in a series of thin washes. Ardizzone sketched on the spot too, having got himself 'a bloody good sketchbook'. Confident in his ability to catch the moment, he usually took a quarter of an hour, perhaps as long as 30 minutes, on a sketch. He also made notes; then worked a painting up later, having found some quiet haven to act as a studio. For example, after Alamein, he hid away in a room in Alexandria – all he needed was 'table, chair and drawing board'. Where his art was concerned he was very self-absorbed: 'Artists aren't interested in other artists' work very much.'[2]

A priority for the war artist was the need to work at speed: Richard Seddon under fire in the Channel, for example, was 'sketching away for dear life' as the guns roared around him. The necessity of working fast made artists more pragmatic and less troubled by uncertainty. Edward Bawden, for example, became less inhibited: 'The meticulous craftsman with all his pens laid out parallel on his desk in the secluded attic studio was already learning to loosen up and extemporise a little.'[3] Where once Bawden had hankered after seclusion when he painted, now he could cope readily with, say, drawing calmly in a burning heat, while policemen with whips kept inquisitive people from pressing too close.

Artists' materials caused some problems. The quality of paper, for example, could be an issue. Occasionally, it prompted Ardizzone to complain that he would have 'to change his technique to suit this bloody paper'. At other times, he might find himself sketching on odd scraps, anything he could get his hands on. When he found 'beautiful paper' in Italy, he was delighted. Richard Seddon was fortunate to have had a large case of paper and a drawing desk with him when he set out for France. He also had a lorry in which to store his materials. Obtaining watercolours was not a major difficulty, but overseas heat could be tricky: sweaty hands were irritating ('sweat dripped like rain on to the paper'),[4] while working in high humidity in a bathroom-like steaminess did unexpected things to paint – colours didn't dry quickly. Anthony Gross had to add water to Indian ink to thin it. He had travelled east with oils, but found they were not easy to use. His preferred method, like many others, was to draw initially in pencil in a sketchbook. Watercolour was the medium that most matched the circumstances of war. It ran counter to received wisdom when, early in January 1942, Tom Hennell wrote to Eric Ravilious urging him to move away from watercolours: 'I wish you would paint in oils on the sheets of the linen scrapbook.'[5] Ravilious duly tried working in oils, but the experiment 'came to nothing – it didn't seem to strike roots at all'.[6]

Ravilious was more preoccupied with where he would be sent next. For a time, it looked as if he was bound for Russia – that was where the WAAC had in mind – to the wing of the RAF stationed there. Dickey wrote to him on 8 January 1942 to that effect, indicating that 'a further tour of duty for six months' should begin as soon as his next mission was confirmed, and that 'all [are] very pleased with your latest work'.[7] The committee was particularly warm towards some artists' work: according to the artist and former Principal of the Royal College, William Rothenstein, it was thought that Barnett Freedman was working well and 'I hear Ravilious, Bawden also much praised, Miss Dunbar too'.[8] As well as a British war artist being sent to Russia, there was a proposal

'Lord W de B is a gent.' Group Captain Lord Willoughby de Broke, at his desk at the Air Ministry. (Imperial War Museum, CH 8811).

to exhibit a range of British war art there. The Russian exhibition was suggested during January 1942, and thought 'excellent' as an idea, but officials soon started worrying about the security of the paintings since their arrival might well coincide with the anticipated German spring offensive. Moreover 'they will be dumped on the quayside at Archangel or Murmansk and from then onwards are to be dealt with by Russians who do not know the meaning of "Fragile" and "This side up with care".'[9] Both the exhibition and Ravilious' trip came to nothing.

So, no Russian adventure. Instead, Eric's newly found love of aeroplanes drew him towards the RAF as a service, and the window it offered into the magical world of Lysanders, Catalinas and Sunderlands. Bomber aircraft, though, repelled him and he had no urge to draw them. He was taken out to a slap-up lunch ('game pie and cake') at Boodles, a gentlemen's club in Pall Mall, by Group Captain Willoughby de Broke, the Air Ministry's man on the WAAC. Dickey was delighted: 'This is grand news. Lord W de B is a gent.'[10]

By late February 1942, he was at RAF Clifton, just outside York, drawing Lysanders. Initially, he stayed at Newitt's Private and Commercial Hotel, number 62, Bootham, within a stone's throw of York's city walls. Thereafter he stayed in Mr and Mrs Orme's at 51 Rawcliffe Lane, Clifton. 'Mr Orme is a beekeeper (the best Yorkshire honey),' he wrote to Tirzah, 'and has a bright red face and is a Mason'.[11] Yorkshire, he thought, was 'an extraordinary place and very large and perfectly flat. The people I like a lot especially the CO who flew me up and down Yorkshire this afternoon and kept pointing out abbeys and ruins.' It was the afternoon of 26 February when he flew with Wing Commander Saunders in a Proctor, taking off at 14.20 and returning 90 minutes later.[12] Saunders apparently promised to take him over Greta Bridge and Richmond next time.[13] 'It was jolly cold, even with two jumpers and a great coat and a warming parachute … It was nice making circles round York Minster on a really fine day – the first bright sun for months.'[14] The weather was bitterly cold, despite that glimpse of sun. Both football and horse racing were off, beaten by the frost. Flying was largely impossible because of the heavy snowfalls. With aircraft confined to the ground, the 'station personnel did excellent work on snow clearance on the streets of York', while the aerodrome was badly waterlogged.[15] Ravilious developed chilblains.

He had anticipated being in York for three weeks but Tirzah's serious illness brought him home after just thirteen nights away. With Harry

Champion singing 'Any Old Iron' on the radio at the top of his voice, Eric wrote to Helen Binyon on 7 March from his office at RAF Clifton: 'This is to tell you that I won't be able to manage a visit to Bath yet as Tirzah is having another and far worse operation and asked me to return at once. I am off in the morning. It is alarming and out of the blue as they said she was all right a week ago.' Soon after, Tirzah had her left breast removed. Ravilious was granted just two weeks' leave. In this middle year of the war, life seemed particularly harsh: his mother had died, while his father was lonely and unhappy. After Tirzah's operation, Eric was posted on 7 April to nearby RAF Debden, Saffron Walden; moving on to RAF Sawbridgeworth on 4 May; and then to Western Zoyland in Somerset. He wrote to Dickey on 15 June, with the exiled Edward Bawden very much in his thoughts. He was keen to see Bawden's latest work. He told Dickey that he had seen a newspaper article recently in which 'there was a wonderful and improbable paragraph about Bawden "helping the Australians keep the pubs open at Tobruk"'.[16]

In Somerset, Ravilious was disturbed by a seaplane crash he had witnessed off the coast. It happened during a training flight and it troubled him that training had just carried on regardless. In London, he attended a farewell dinner to mark the retirement from the WAAC of E.M.

A sketch of Eric Ravilious by his wife, Tirzah.

O'R. Dickey – worth his weight in gold, Ravilious thought. In July, he received an invitation from Barnett Freedman: 'It is suggested that the above five (Sutherland, Moore, Ravillous [sic], Piper, Freedman) join in giving a dinner to Jane and K. Clark. The White Tower, Percy Street, 7.15, Tuesday August 11.'[17] It was a fortnight before Ravilious was due to go to Iceland, a prospect which excited him greatly: the artist Michael Rothenstein remembered that Ravilious had 'had both dreams and fantasies of these hot volcanoes in Iceland'.[18]

A week or so later, Tirzah left hospital. 'The morning before he was due to go,' Tirzah wrote in her autobiography, 'he got up early to make the breakfast and standing in front of the mirror putting on his tie he said, "Shall I not go to Iceland?"' Tirzah knew how much he wanted to go. Her answer was unequivocal: 'No, I shall be all right.'[19] Before he left, he divided in two one of his favourite books (Boswell's *Life of Johnson*), kept one half for himself and gave the other to his wife.

Before heading north, he stayed the night with J.M. Richards at his London flat. Richards thought him 'more tranquil … [with] a sense of resignation …' Ravilious flew to Scotland from London on 25 August. The weather at Prestwick before he flew on to Iceland was calm and windless and he left the Scottish mainland on 28 August. It was an untroubled flight, although Iceland from the air looked like the surface of the moon. He was greeted with a pleasant dinner on arrival. His plan was to stay at the base at Kaldadarnes, on Iceland's south coast, until Christmas.

Kaldadarnes was situated some 25 miles east-south-east of Reykjavik, though the distance stretched to 40 when travelling by the rough, stony track from the capital. It was a lonely spot, a bare plateau with mountains in the far distance. Its isolation caused concern to visiting medical personnel charged with reviewing its amenities and the impact on the state of mind of those based there. One visitor reported on 17 July 1941 that 'amenities are so poor that it is inadvisable for personnel to spend more than 12 months there at a time.'[20] Its atmosphere was 'dull' which combined 'with the short dark days, monotony of surroundings and lack of good recreation facilities' caused 'much boredom with consequent low spirits and lack of enthusiasm for work.' Accommodation was almost invariably in Nissen huts 'banked up at the sides with stones and earth … for warmth and protection against the inclement weather.' The roofs were painted the same muddy colour as the surrounding landscape, for camouflage purposes. Long hours of darkness were a problem too: 'Attention to

A Hudson of 269 Squadron at the RAF base at Kaldadarnes, Iceland. (Imperial War Museum, CS 112).

better illumination is urgently required in Iceland if vision of our person-nel is not to suffer, as much time is spent in reading.' Ravilious may have been keen to see what Iceland was like, but many of those already there were counting the days to get away from the posting.

By now the weather had turned cold, with heavy rain and strong winds. On 1 September it was 'cloudy with continuous rain for most of [the] day.'[21] At dawn on 2 September, three Hudson aircraft from 269 Squadron set out on an air sea rescue mission, looking for a miss-ing aircraft. Ravilious was on board one of the Hudsons. The weather was unremarkable – turning cloudy and wet ('periods of continuous rain and drizzle') towards evening. Visibility was reduced from over 12 miles to less than 4 miles in the rain. A moderate wind sprang up, from the west, in the latter part of the day. It was not, however, bad weather for flying.[22] Nonetheless, Ravilious' aircraft went missing, with no message of any kind once the aircraft had taken off. 'Flight Lt. A. C. Culver, P/O N. J. Graves-Smith, F/Sgt. W. H. R. Day and F/Sgt. C. N. Barnes reported missing from operational trip.'[23] Just under a week later, a solitary wheel was washed ashore. The same day as he disappeared, the WAAC were told for the first time of his mission to Iceland.

Some while later, Tirzah told Michael Rothenstein that soon after Eric arrived at the station, 'there was somebody there he started talking to, one of the pilots, and they got along. I think they had some drinks together. And that was the first contact he made in Iceland. And I think it was the next night, this particular pilot came into their common room, where the bar was, and turned to Ravilious and said, "A fellow's down in the drink. Would you like to come and help me find him?"'[24]

In a last letter, headed 'Care of RAF Iceland', and written on Sunday, 31 August, he mapped out where he might go, and what he might see – Greenland, Icelandic geysers. He sent his love ('Goodbye darling. Take care of yourself.'); and inquired after his father and Edward Bawden … 'Is Edward home yet?'[25] But his good friend was far from home too and soon to be in a situation of great danger, not in the air but at sea.

★★★

War Artists, 1942: Dead Sea

Eric ditched submarines and destroyers, mines and coastal defences, and fell in love with aeroplanes, that beguiling combination of sleek fuselage, intricate struts and rumbling power, and the freedom of the wide blue yonder. His relationship with the senior service had always been equivocal: intense pleasure sailing north to the bleak glories of Norway on the one hand; and, on the other hand, the arcane rituals of saluting, the rigid hierarchies of the officer class, the masonic pink gins and bluster, and the fact that his uniform was khaki when all around him was navy blue. Like the rest of us, he worried about being mistaken for a spy.

There were thirty-seven of us altogether – the full-time salaried artists that is. Thirty-six men and one woman. By the time Eric died, not many had been posted abroad. Instead we concentrated on the narrow canvas that this static war provided – Paul Nash worked for the RAF, but couldn't fly because of his health. In the autumn of 1940 he could be found wandering around a large dump of wrecked German planes near Oxford. What came out of it, his painstaking sketches and photographs, was Totes Meer (Dead Sea), a moonlit chaos of twisted metal, a disembodied wheel here, a Luftwaffe cross there, all in a haunting thin light. At much the same time, Henry Moore was prowling the underground, stepping over the sprawling bodies, sketching with fierce concentration. Ted Ardizzone, meanwhile, was in his element, drawing buxom barmaids resolutely fending off leering NCOs in tartan trousers at Southern Command, Salisbury, or ('very much my cup of tea,' as Ted said) commemorating a day with the Home Guard, engaged in a mock battle for the Bank of England, earnest figures in the shadows of imposing City buildings, while confused civilians emerged from the tunnels of the underground. We painted returning troops from Dunkirk, ruins, evacuees from the East End, the Land Army girls (dear Evelyn Dunbar given a womanly subject!), naval installations, fighting men, life at sea, aircraft and hangars, dockyards, bomb damage. Graham Sutherland, for example, was commissioned to 'make pictures of debris and damage' caused by air raids – at times it was as if the War Artists' Committee were keen to get us to the scenes of bomb damage before the fires burned out. All this frenzy of work seemed, in a way, preoccupied with defence, resistance, the stiffening of morale and what we stood to lose. But why should artists be any different to the rest of the country?

We seemed forever to be on the move, sent here and there all over the place, struggling with equipment, fretting about the blackout, the grindingly slow railways, the uncertainty of the length of contracts, uniforms and rank, expenses (and their slow payment), income tax,[26] the slowness of the post and what the troops thought of us.[27] We worried about our families, those of us who had them. That was a particular concern in the days of invasion fever, and when home lay in the projected path of the German panzers heading for London. Other than our warming correspondence with dear old Dickey, there was little chance to air these anxieties. We felt that we should be better represented on the committee; Muirhead Bone was a good egg, but somehow one of the establishment and we were conscious sometimes of being at the whim of tetchily resolved outcomes from long, tired debates around the National Gallery's polished table. 'Don't we need more paintings of X?' or 'Let's send Y to Scotland to paint Sunderlands taking off in Oban harbour!' For all that, we liked Dickey, Coote too, but we were, at the end of the day, at the mercy of comfortable men jawing their way through a long agenda.

We tried to keep in touch with each other: letters from the similarly rootless followed us around the country, as we drifted from hotel to camp, from camp to digs, that cheerless mockery of home life, trying to sketch in someone else's cold bedroom, or listening to Alvar Lidell reading the news as if he had made it himself. We were alone much of the time: by that I mean that artists usually operated singly; companionship came with our fellow officers who might not necessarily be sympathetic to what we were doing. Ardizzone and Bawden travelled together to France, and paths crossed from time to time ('Well, bless my soul, it's dear old Barnett Freedman!'), but the war artist's journey was, for the most part, a lonely one – have sketchbook, will travel. But you travelled alone and, after all, we weren't all in the first flush of youth. There were moments when that feeling of isolation was kept at bay by shared accommodation, perhaps, or a shared vinous dinner with another artist passing through another foreign city on a journey even further away from home. Ted, for example, hitched up with photographers and journalists, and enjoyed rumbustious evenings in their company in Belgian bars. He was always so positive about the 'magnificent troops', and he seemed able to elicit a reciprocal feeling from them. Eric eyed his Wren driver who was 'extraordinarily nice in a black-eyed way'; Bawden was fussed over by his servant. But for the rest of us, a war artist's work was often a closed dialogue between a blank page, an artist's sharp eye and the mood of some windswept airfield, or city building smouldering in the rain.

Sometimes though it was worth it – being able to work in art at a time when we could have been on the Atlantic convoys, or in the rear gunner's turret of a Lancaster bomber over Berlin. Outdoors in fine spring weather and the work going well, there was nothing to beat it. It was possible to ignore the uncertainty, the suspicious eyes, the gathering storm. And then Eric died, reminding us all that we were in the firing line too, and that the enemy – be it the weather or the Germans – did not distinguish between the artist and the rest of those in uniform. We wondered who would be next, if Eric would be the only artist to die on active service. To disappear as he did, leaving no trace troubled all of us. You couldn't help wondering whether death was more likely for those artists who hankered after being close to the action. Logic suggested it was, despite the dangers of the Blitz. Edward Bawden seemed like an obvious candidate, with his relentless travelling; and then, in the autumn of 1942, he embarked on the long sea passage home when the committee recalled him to the UK.

★★★

Travelling through Africa and the Middle East, Edward Bawden often thought of Ravilious. On 21 February 1942, shortly before Eric went to York, he wrote, declaring that he would 'like to see your work. Charlotte writes enthusiastically about it, and Anthony Gross gives me a skimpy idea of what it is like. It's strange to unseal lips after nineteen months and talk again of paint and painters ... Write again if you can ...'[28] By the time he received the letter, Ravilious only had months to live. Bawden warned his friend not to leave Scotland for Africa, despite the foulness of the Scottish climate. He painted a grim picture of the Middle East: 'there is an awful lot of sand' and at certain times the weather could combine 'rain, an icy wind and a sandstorm'. He reminisced about Essex, 'a landscape painter's paradise' and familiar beauty in the green fields – 'a rabbit flick, the scurry of a stoat, primroses in ditches, or dog roses in hedgerows'.[29]

Bawden was delighted at Anthony Gross' arrival in Cairo – 'It is a godsend' – and he thought him a good choice as a war artist – 'the right temperament and talent'. They were quite dissimilar, but both were lonely and they got on well.' Bawden confessed that he had not met anyone interesting for 20 months.'[30] Despite the quirky weather that he described to Ravilious, Bawden was 'very contented and happy' – and, by the summer of 1942, 'in excellent health' – this despite a bout of sand-fly fever.

However, by the late summer of 1942, Bawden was homeward-bound. He was not entirely happy. His replacement was Edward Ardizzone ('I have taken the news of Ardizzone sedately'), but communications with the WAAC had a flavour of the waspish. On 27 July 1942 he wrote to Dickey: 'Why do you wish to recall me when at the present moment I have not had the opportunity to contract dysentery, bilharzia or hookworm? How unsympathetic of the committee ...' He knew, however, that the committee might not be entirely at ease with his work focus: '"We sent you out to make a record of army life," you will exclaim, "and you choose to get yourself in an area banned to Troops." How true that is.'

Bawden sailed from Cairo on board the SS *Stratheden* and transhipped to the *Laconia* in Durban, leaving there on 27 August 1942, the day before Ravilious flew to Iceland. It was the same month that ninety-six paintings were lost at sea – they included three by Paul Nash, two by Sutherland, a Henry Moore and a John Piper – the ship torpedoed on its way to South America. On 12 September 1942 the *Laconia* was broadly parallel with Lagos, but many miles offshore. Freetown was a few days' sailing time away. To the discomfort of many passengers she was alone: 'It would be nice to have a convoy' was a commonly held perception. Bawden was sitting down for drinks when the first torpedo struck. *Laconia* had been making little progress, almost marking time, it seemed to Bawden, as he contemplated his drink and the languid evening routine on board. This dilatory sailing, alone on a dangerous sea, seemed foolish to him. There was a low hum of engines, desultory conversation, the clink of bottles and glass. It was a night just like any other – and then the explosion shook the boat to its core. The torpedo had 'hit the engine-room; and the mainmast, the wireless transmitter and some of the lifeboats.'[31]

The *Laconia* 'shivered, then stood still; and the air filled with the smell of explosive.'[32] Broken glass was everywhere, crushed further by the rush of feet heading for the deck. Doors had come adrift; woodwork was splintered. Already the ship was listing heavily and the lights had failed. The list was sufficiently great to render the lifeboats on one side unusable and there was an unpleasant swell to the sea. A second torpedo hit the ship, this time in the midst of the Italian prisoners-of-war caged deep below decks.

Bawden remained icily calm: he paused to help someone who had been injured in the initial attack, and then decided to retrace his steps, going below decks again – he had bought his wife a watch when he was in Cape Town and thought, 'I might as well go down with the watch as not.'[33] When he returned to the dark confusion on deck, he allowed a more senior officer to pull rank: 'Major, you go first', and stood back while the man slid down a rope over the side. Moments later there was an ominous splash far below. When Bawden scrambled down the ship's side, hanging on to a rope, his fall into the darkness ended in a lifeboat. It was already full but somehow he found some space. Others were not so lucky: one lifeboat, for example, was 'leaking badly and rapidly filling with water ... [and] crashing against the ship's side.'[34] There were dead bodies in the water and others, still alive, desperately struggling to survive. For days afterwards Bawden would see the corpses of the Italian PoWs who had been freed from the pens down below decks, lifted now by the waves, then falling again as each swell rolled by.

The lifeboat pulled away from the steep side of the *Laconia* – none too soon, since the ship was close to sinking: it reared 'half out of the water, and then, bows first, she sank like a great monster, hissing and roaring.'[35] Her master, Captain Sharp, stayed on the bridge to the end and went down with his ship. Bawden missed the final moments: he was comforting a young girl who had become separated from her mother and brother. For his part, Bawden had lost some drawings, a few exotic hats and his sketching umbrella – all regrettable, but not a matter of life or death. Although his lifeboat was largely manned by merchant seamen, nobody seemed to know where, in the vast sweep of ocean, they were, or in which direction they were drifting. For all that, the survivors in the overcrowded lifeboat, frightened and lost, were better off than the passengers still in the water, swallowing engine oil, buffeted by the waves and torn by barracudas. Things improved further when a young RAF officer climbed on board and rapidly brought some sense of order to the lifeboat. Without him, Bawden, thought, 'We should destroy ourselves'. There was a definite feeling that the merchant seamen left to their own devices 'would have thrown us soldiers out as we were in such a small minority'.[36] Emergency supplies were strictly limited: two biscuits and one drink of water per day.

Bawden feared a descent into chaos and brutality, but he also witnessed the opposite. The German commander of U-156, Captain Hartenstein, having sunk the *Laconia* in what he believed to be a legitimate act of war, took his submarine to the surface and began a rescue operation. He ordered a signal to be sent: 'Sunk British *Laconia* – unfortunately with 1,500 Italian prisoners. 90 rescued so far.'[37] The shipwrecked were taken on board – women and children clustered in every claustrophobic nook and cranny of the submarine – and food and medicine distributed. 'I was picked up by the submarine on Sunday night 13th September,' one survivor wrote, '22 hours after we were torpedoed'. She and others in her boat had survived on 'no water at all, and had kept alive by spoonfuls of "Pemmican" occasionally'.[38] On the submarine, the kindness of the German crew extended to providing hot soup, coffee and rusks with water. They 'really were amazingly good to us'.

Captain Hartenstein and his crew impressed most other survivors: '[they] were of a very fine type. All spoke English perfectly … they expressed admiration for our Air Force and Navy.' Views on the British Army were less positive. One survivor found the German 'very garrulous. Mentioned several ships he was going to torpedo – 'Stratheden', 'Pasteur', 'Ile de France', 'New Amsterdam', 'Duchess of Atholl'. Boasted he was in full possession of shipping movements.' There was no denying, however, the extent of Hartenstein's humanity. He flew a Red Cross flag, solicited help and sought to shepherd the lifeboats together. His pleas for help only produced an aerial attack by an American Liberator operating from Ascension Island. The British were aghast: 'We saw the bomb doors open. Good God, this is it!'[39] The result was the sinking of one of the lifeboats and a rapid change of heart from the Germans, who hustled the rescued out of the submarine, which then took refuge in the wide expanse of the Atlantic Ocean. Hartenstein 'wished us good luck and cut the boats free'. Of the American attack, one of the survivors, Doris Hawkins, wrote that it was 'a most unfortunate incident [which] I am not at liberty to discuss'.

The survivors in the lifeboats had a desperate time: the heat was intense; water was at a premium; sharks surged around the boats. Josephine Pratchett 'put my bum over the side … to spend a penny' and someone had to beat the sharks off with an oar. Some drank their own urine. Gradually people died, one by one. When Doris Hawkins' boat finally came ashore, 60 miles south of Monrovia, they had been at sea for twenty-eight days. Only sixteen of the sixty-eight on that lifeboat survived.

Bawden's lifeboat drifted for five days, under an unforgiving sun. The advent of the French ship *Gloire* was greeted with surprise, then clapping and cheering. The delight was short-lived, since the welcome aboard the Vichy ship was frosty in the extreme. Bawden was given brandy and coffee, but also a Gallic cold shoulder, and then confined in a hot and stuffy room below decks. He was desperate for fresh air. Eventually the men were sorted from the officers and Bawden found himself in another small airless room, this time at deck level. It was so crowded that making one's way through the room at night was virtually impossible. Places at tables were almost fought over. Bawden looked at his fellow prisoners – for so they were – and was reminded of scarecrows. Information was in even shorter supply than food or water. The weather deteriorated and the seas grew mountainous. Bawden found himself wondering when and how the ordeal would end.

They made landfall at Casablanca, where 'the harbour was full of shipping: two destroyers, two submarines and one large battleship.' Bawden and the rest were duly herded on to alcohol-fuelled buses and driven to the internment camp at Mediouna. The journey was at night and involved interminable stretches of waiting in the darkness, moonlight glinting on the tracks. When they reached Mediouna, the camp's boundary was defined by barbed wire. Bawden and the rest were kitted out in French Foreign Legion uniforms: 'silly tunics with round buttons', and given dirty sheets and mattresses.[40] So this was how the adventure ended, in this backwater of the war for its duration it seemed, hating the French, who told them nothing and 'had nothing to do with us'. On 7 October a telegram was sent from the American Consulate in Casablanca to the Admiralty giving an initial list of the survivors. It was almost a further month that a telegram was received: '*To PR3. From PROELICAS, Liverpool. Captain E Bawden. War Artist. Survivor.*'

Yearning for chocolate and clean socks in the squalor of Mediouna camp, Bawden was fed a diet of beans, cabbage soup and coffee substitute. He drew, having scrounged pen and paper from somewhere. Paper was valuable for other reasons too: Bawden never forgot the indignity of a desperate search to locate a scrap of paper for the visit to what were the vilest of latrines: undisinfected and evil-smelling open trenches, abuzz with flies. He resented the disdain and scorn of the French guards, too, remembering what he felt had been the same irritating characteristic in 1940, their evident conviction that the British 'were only amateur soldiers', while they saw themselves as 'the professionals'.[41] Bawden found that profoundly hard to take.

Vichy's days in North Africa were numbered however. In November 1942, the Americans arrived and the thin diet was replaced by 'masses and masses of food'. Some internees made a beeline for the fleshpots of Casablanca, the priority being to have a damned good time, but Bawden stayed put and consequently missed out on an early return home. Instead of home, Bawden found himself on a convoy heading west across the Atlantic, away from Europe, to Norfolk, Virginia. He was still dressed in his ill-fitting French Foreign Legion kit. On US soil, the French tunics were discarded and Bawden was temporarily reinvented as an American GI, causing some consternation with the mismatch between his English accent and his homeland uniform.

On 5 December, Charlotte Bawden, staying at 9 Clarence Square, Cheltenham, received a telegram from her husband which must have come as a great surprise since she had no idea that he was in America. 'RECEIVED MEDIOUNA CABLE SAFE IN AMERICA WILL SEE YOU SOON CHRISTMAS GREETINGS YOURSELF TD AND FAMILY EDWARD BAWDEN.'[42] After a few days in New York – he visited the Museum of Metropolitan Art in Central Park – he sailed for home. Christmas 1942 was spent on board ship, but by the first days of a bitterly cold New Year he was back in England.

★★★

On 5 September 1942 – a week before the *Laconia* was torpedoed – an official at the Admiralty, H.V. Markham, wrote to Tirzah Ravilious informing her that her husband was 'missing'. Details were minimal. In the immediate aftermath she talked constantly about her lost husband: Christine Nash noted in her diary on 20 September that Tirzah was endeavouring to make out that it was for the best that he had died – if indeed he was dead – and that Eric had seemed unhappy about the war, and was troubled by the way his work got disturbed, muddle and children combining to take away a sense of peace. The uncertainty over his death – no body washed up on the Icelandic shore, no coffin or funeral cortege – was hard to bear, made worse by the fact that Tirzah was still recovering from her own serious illness. There were also three young children to care for, the youngest of whom, Anne, was just one year old. Tirzah wrote to Helen Binyon five weeks after the loss of her husband: 'I don't know what if any pension or money I shall get from the War Artists' Committee.'

The authorities seemed less than warm-hearted to the grieving widow, embarking on a lengthy dispute over pension entitlement. The official view at the outset was that 'Ravilious' position in the Royal Marines was an honorary one. There being no pay, there can be no pension.'[43] The correspondence between Mrs Ravilious (writing always as Eileen, not Tirzah) and officialdom in all its forms continued for well over a year.[44] A minor complication was that the WAAC had only been told about the artist's mission to Iceland on 2 September – several days after he had gone there. Moreover, for those civil servants at one remove from the WAAC it raised the thorny question of who exactly these artists were – they weren't fighting troops after all, were they? There was a cold, bureaucratic tone to the official letters, a reluctance to concede an inch: 'His captaincy was an honorary one which means that the normal Service regulations with regard to pensions do not apply.'[45]

By mid-January 1943, Tirzah had lost patience: she wrote a long, impassioned letter to Mr Elmslie Owen at the Ministry of Information. What seems to have provoked it, other than irritation with the grinding slowness of the process, was the fact that she had recently received 'a widow's pension form to fill up for women whose husbands have been killed while acting as air raid wardens.'[46] That was not her only complaint: she had 'so far not received any communication … except the original letter from the Admiralty'; she had not received a 'presumed dead' notice – required for the slow progress to be accelerated – she had not even received his expenses, 'which would normally have been refunded to my husband for the three weeks prior to his death'. Moreover, of his personal effects, she had only received a map of Iceland and a few photographs – not the £50 he had left home with, or his kit. 'I presume there was something else left behind, he wouldn't have taken his pyjamas for instance.' She queried whether she would receive any payment for the pictures she had sent to the ministry, and pointed an accusing finger at the War Artists' Committee: 'I think the committee ought to have given this subject their consideration before an accident of this sort occurred.' She had a point.

Then, finally, having completed the necessary form, she wrote, 'I am enclosing this form which I have filled up so far as I am able … I cannot fill in about the post office as I am travelling round staying with friends, my house is uninhabitable in the winter. I shall in any case have to leave it as I will not be able to afford to live in it.' Her signature at the foot of the letter, *Eileen L Ravilious,* has a shaky, angry look to it.

The passion of Tirzah's letter appears to have cut no ice, nothing that prompted a quick and humane solution to the issue. Officials from different departments sent minutes to each other seeking to avoid setting a precedent and incurring Treasury disapproval. The issue hinged on whether war artists were civilians or combatants, and Ravilious' case became entangled with that of a naval photographer in the RNVR, a Lieutenant Fraser. It was the very issue that Barnett Freedman had foreseen in 1940 when questioning his contractual arrangement with the WAAC – what is the 'compensation if killed?' No one seemed to agree on the issue. For example, Colin Coote wrote to Lord Willoughby de Broke on 7 March 1943, declaring that 'there are more complications than any of us know' and expressing the view that 'the argument that photographers are combatants is stronger than could be made in the case of artists.' He saw the dilemma as being that artists were deemed to be civilians and, therefore, compensation could only be at civilian rates. It would require a change to artists' commissions, from 'honorary or emergency or pro-forma commissions to combatant commissions.' The problem with that would be that the level of compensation would clash with their pay rates (of between £650 and £800) – they would need to be promoted to majors for the level of compensation to match that salary range. For his part, De Broke held that 'there is every justification, therefore for asking for similar relation of rank for our Official Artists.' He suggested that they should 'all speak with one voice on this matter'. Some hope! The following month a minute by H.L. Perkins persisted with the tough line: 'Any artist who was killed in this country even if his death were due to enemy action would get civilian terms only.'[47]

It was all very unedifying: Government officials were all too eager to send artists, in uniform, with official rank, into active war zones, but, when a tragedy occurred, the response was one of prevarication and line-by-line dispute. Before he died, Eric Ravilious had frequently raised concerns about payments and expenses with Dickey among others. Like some of his colleagues, money was a continual preoccupation. It was not the legacy that he had planned to leave behind in the event of his untimely death. Eric's insistence in his will that Tirzah and the children should receive the artist's 'property … and the rest of it as soon as I die' counted for nothing. Instead, there was delay and argument and hardship. Eric Ravilious' 'wealth' at death totalled just £276 10 shillings and 2d.[48]

11

The Lion's Mouth

Edward Bawden was not the only British war artist to travel considerable distances, or cross the Atlantic, in 1942. John Worsley was there before him, transferred from HMS *Wallace*, which had been steadfastly patrolling the North Sea, to HMS *Rampura*, bound for Chesapeake Bay. Once in Baltimore, he was posted to the cruiser HMS *Devonshire* in Norfolk, Virginia, the vast, sprawling naval base, where Bawden would arrive some months later. Worsley found himself slowly steaming down the length of Chesapeake Bay in a pleasure boat, for all the world as if he was on holiday. It was a rare interlude of tranquility. *Devonshire* set sail for the West African port of Freetown in the late spring of 1942, before moving on to Cape Town and the Indian Ocean. The ship was protecting convoys on the Aden to Freemantle run, troopships crammed with Australian soldiers either heading east for home, or west to the fighting in the Middle Eastern desert.

It was very different from convoy work in the north Atlantic: instead of buffeting through grey, white-capped seas, making slow progress and exhorting rust-bucket merchant ships to extract every last drop of speed, these vessels travelled relatively fast under blue skies and light winds. The Japanese were nearby, which added a frisson to the exercise, but there was little sign of action. The exception to the rule was the invasion of Madagascar in May of 1942. A convoy – WS (Winston Special) 17 – had sailed from Glasgow on 23 March and *Devonshire* was deputed to help protect it. Some ships in the convoy took part in Operation Ironclad, whose purpose was 'to seize and hold the Vichy French naval and air base of Diego Suarez at the northern tip of Madagascar and so forestall a possible Japanese landing on the island.'[1] After that brief diversion, it was back to the routine of escort duties for Worsley, beating back and forth along the sea lanes of the east. When they weren't on watch, the crew could relax, even sunbathe on the deck beneath the guns. Men read, wrote letters. Worsley sketched. It was the summer of 1943 before he returned to England when *Devonshire* required a refit. Lieutenant Worsley was also on the verge of a significant alteration in his life.

From the naval yard at Newcastle, Worsley was summoned to report to the Admiralty in London. He travelled south in some trepidation. He had a long time on the slow train journey into King's Cross to reflect on what he had done that was remiss and on whose carpet he might be stranded. He was startled to be interviewed in one of the Admiralty's high-ceilinged, comfortably furnished rooms, with a fire burning in an ornate grate, in front of which a full admiral, one Admiral James, was warming his uniformed backside and rocking to and fro on his heels. 'My boy,' he said, 'you are the youngest war artist we have. You are not to sit on your bottom in the water. Put your head in the lion's mouth!'

The journey into danger began at Northolt Airport in west London. Worsley travelled out of uniform and he left England under cover of darkness in a Liberator aircraft, bound for neutral Spain. On the same flight were three other passengers, all French and all in civilian clothes. Later, they donned uniforms, revealing themselves as generals in the Free French Army. In Morocco, the Liberator was replaced by a Dakota and the newly appointed war artist sat in the cockpit alongside the pilot, looking down on the twisted and sand-blown relics of the recent fighting in the desert. His flight from Tunis to Malta was delayed by the late showing of the other passenger, a 'most boorish and unsociable man'.[2] It was the prime minister's son, Randolph Churchill.

The Mediterranean stretched blue beneath them. Looking at the map, Worsley could see how close Malta was to the boot of Italy. It was even closer to Sicily, where Admiral James was expecting him to begin his encounter with the 'lion's mouth'. The admiral had told Worsley to resist the temptation to 'sit on your bottom on the water'; he would have approved of his young artist crouched low in a landing craft bound for Sicily.

★★★

For Ted Ardizzone, war involved 'long periods of idleness and then short periods of bloodiness'. Be that as it may, he was pleased to leave the UK in the middle of the war. Colin Coote had suggested he be sent to the Middle East to replace Edward Bawden, news which the latter took 'sedately'. The decision about going was left to Ardizzone, who had 'the devil's own job trying to make up my mind.' Eventually he did, unwilling to miss out on the opportunity. 'I have decided to go if they want me.' On 18 March 1942 he wrote to Kenneth Clark: 'The excitement of seeing something new and the additional income (very important with a growing family) have helped very much to decide me ... I have felt for some time I was getting stale and perhaps a new scene will give me the right kick.'[3]

On 6 May he left the UK for the Middle East. The terms of employment were much the same: £650 a year, free of UK income tax; work to be 'vested solely in the crown'; 'rations and accommodation will be provided by the Army where practicable, but will be paid for by the Artist'.[4] He was warmed by the presence of 'lots of pretty ATS's' on the slow boat to Egypt. Conditions on the troopship were very crowded and made work impossible. A period under canvas in South Africa in June 1942 followed. Durban reminded him 'of a Walt Disney cartoon ... I quite expect Pluto peering at me from behind a poinsettia.'

He reached Cairo late on the evening of 1 August 1942, the relative tranquillity of the voyage dispelled by the chaos of the ride in a 'decrepit taxi', accompanied by 'six of the most fearful looking ruffians ... hanging on to the sides'. The drive was punctuated by the ruffians shouting for money. 'I sat in the middle waving my arms and saying go away quite politely.'[5] He tried his best to ignore the hell-for-leather driving of the taxi-driver. After Cairo – where he stayed in a hotel overlooking an open-air cinema – Ted set out for the desert. He wrote to his children Philip and Christianna describing the experience – the 'thousands of flies which are quite maddening'; the food (bully beef stew); the guns; the shot-down 'Jerry plane'; the cool nights when 'I put up my camp bed beside the van and when I am not asleep I lie on my back and look at the stars.'[6]

When he was in Cairo, Ardizzone lived and worked 'in a bare whitewashed room over a garage to get to which I have to climb a small spiral

'I put up my camp bed beside the van and when I am not asleep I lie on my back and look at the stars.' Ardizzone in the Western Desert.

outside staircase.' It was, he admitted, very untidy, 'as my revolver has got muddled up with my shaving things, and on the floor is a nasty litter of boots, dirty clothes, webbing equipment and torn paper.' His servant, Abdul, spoke no English and Ardizzone, no Arabic: 'when I ask for tea and bread and butter he usually comes trotting back with a bright smile, bringing cigarettes – or vice versa.'[7]

In the autumn of 1942 Ardizzone had a ringside seat for the pivotal battle at El Alamein. Until Alamein, the momentum in the desert was not in favour of the British. Indeed, in the streets of Alexandria, Ardizzone had previously seen the local shopkeepers painting up shop signs in German. He watched the struggle unfold from the HQ truck – only 'lying beside a gun' could have been closer, he said. Although he remained a non-combatant, Ardizzone was invariably welcomed by those with guns in their hands: 'Dear Ted, come and stay with us!' Right in the thick of the action he might have been, but it didn't make recording the experience any easier – 'You can't paint shells, draw shell bursts … [or use] watercolours in a battle.'

There were other things he could not draw: the poignant, wonderful sound of 'a bugle [heard] from a great distance', for example, or the haunting bagpipes of a Highland Division. The desert could be beautiful: the astonishing smell of desert flowers after rain; or it could be grim in the extreme: 'Not a drop to drink,' he said of one desert camp, 'the dreariest place I've ever been in!' At times, he wished he had been at the battle of Waterloo a century and more before, where fighting was inescapably visible, rather than caught up in this dashed modern warfare where, after all, there was 'very little to see'. Nevertheless, on that historic morning when the battle began, he watched excitedly as the British tanks edged forward in the dawn, picking their way through minefields in the thin early light. He would never forget that long night of waiting and the expectant dawn before Alamein; nor the dead bodies sprawled in the sand and the troops 'mad for loot', digging like terriers for anything of value.

He watched the battle in the desert unfold, and sensed the change in mood ('Every soldier was smiling,' he recalled), but the real work for him began later, in a sparsely furnished room in Alexandria trying to translate the hot, sprawling battlefield in his head – so much heat and dust – to clean, white paper. Transport back from the fighting had been a hitched lift: 'Anybody going to Cairo?' 'Jump on, dear Ted!'

Alamein changed everything: 8th Army was able to move on from North Africa, exchanging desert for a land with trees. By the summer of 1943, Ardizzone was headed for Europe in a Castle Line troop ship with the Allied invasion force. The target was Sicily: Operation Husky – John Worsley's 'lion's mouth'. Through the night of 10 July, Ted stared into the Sicilian night, its darkness punctuated by flares and gunfire, unable to see the invasion beaches. Troops packed into landing craft suddenly found themselves chest-deep in the Mediterranean and struggling ashore to whatever fate had in store.

First light revealed a sea full of ships, and high mountains to the north. No enemy aircraft, much to the artist's surprise (they came later). He got soaked when his turn to brave the landing craft and the beach came round. His precious new sketchbook he had encased in a French letter to keep it dry and virginal. Once safely on land, he 'acquired a splendid old revolver' – how many war artists were routinely armed like this? – and then settled down to drink wine with some bemused Italian peasants. Suitably fortified, he returned to the beach with his splendidly dry sketchbook and worked through the afternoon, leaving before the Stukas roared in to strafe the invaders. Later, in the lemon grove where camp had been established, he enjoyed a picnic supper in the fading heat of a Mediterranean evening.

Like Ardizzone, John Worsley arrived in Sicily wading ashore from an invasion landing craft. It was a vivid war scene that he had sailed into: 'the battle which raged as Worsley's LCI approached the harbour [of Catania] seemed almost to be for possession of the volcano itself rather than for the town at the foot of its slopes.'[8]

The following day — 11 July — was fraught: Ardizzone bolted lunch (bacon), and was discomforted by the ferocious strafing of low-flying Messchermitts. There were bitter dogfights overhead. Haylofts were searched for desperate Italians — later he would see hayricks burning and anguished peasants watching their few secreted valuables disappearing in plumes of black smoke. Searches of the hay produced few Italians, but frequent bites from voracious fleas.

The lemon grove might have had its bucolic attractions, but a war artist worth his salt had to move with the fighting. On 12 July Ardizzone endured 'a hellish and dusty journey in the back of a 15 cwt. — six in the back, plus our kit'.[9] When he wasn't travelling in a truck through the dust, he wrote letters, took notes, lazed in the sun, watched burning aircraft tumbling from the sky. Later, they journeyed north in a jeep, towards the white plume of Mount Etna. They drove past dead bodies, burnt vehicles and prisoners, and women peering out at them from behind their curtains in deceptively peaceful villages. There were political slogans splashed dramatically on the white cottage walls.

Lunch — white vermouth, bully beef, biscuits and chocolate, polished off with slices of melon — was taken in the shade of an olive tree. Hearing gun fire, Ardizzone went to investigate, only realising after a while that the shooting was still some considerable distance away. He picked some tomatoes instead, before returning to the apparent tranquillity of the olive tree. The following day it emerged that the peaceful lunch stop was 'in the midst of two hundred hidden German parachutists'.[10]

The Sicilian campaign had moments of rare beauty and chilling horror sharply juxtaposed. One day Ted would enjoy a high-noon picnic lunch on a plateau above terraces of orange trees and olives; some feverish sketching; convivial champagne, followed by a recuperative snooze in the sun. Then, all too often, the smell of dead bodies festering in the heat; a tank burning in a stand of almond trees; a barn full of wounded men; disconcerting examples of 'our chaps running away'; hangdog Italian prisoners in open lorries; gaunt, hungry faces; a soldier's severed hand lying in the dust like so much road-kill. Ardizzone was shocked by the horrors he saw: 'such a terrible mess that I find it difficult to draw (don't want to but feel I ought to try)'.[11]

The campaign was physically exhausting: 'Many soldiers lost a pound per day to heat, dehydration and intestinal miseries.'[12] Wounds were slow to heal (it was regarded as the 'Sicilian disease') and mosquitoes – and malaria – were widespread. Noel Coward, who was on the island in August 1943, records meeting a 'chipper little man' in hospital 'who had been shot full of shrapnel and machine-gun bullets [and] was very chatty. I asked him what he thought of Sicily and he said, "The Germans were all right, and the Eyeties were all right but the mosquitoes were bloody awful".'[13]

Ardizzone and a group of war correspondents were heading for Syracuse on Sicily's east coast. It was a simple existence of journeying, eating and sketching, usually in haste. If Ted was lucky, he might get to swim in the sea or some cool reservoir. Nights were characterised by discomfort: on the 16th they holed up close to a gutted farmhouse, blackened by fire; two nights later he slept in a pile of straw where he was feasted on by bugs. Sometimes he slept with his head tucked under the front of the jeep in an attempt to avoid German air attacks. As befits an Englishman in Italy, he was frequently preoccupied with food and wine – lunch might have to be on the move, but Ardizzone's best efforts would be set on making it a decent feast. There might be savage fighting within earshot, but that did not rule out, say, cooking 'a chicken *en casserole* with wine'. He showed a fierce determination to keep up culinary standards.

A priority was ensuring a ready supply of the local wine: 'I find wine in a most disreputable wine shop which was in the process of being put out of bounds by an MP.'[14] At one point, the war correspondents Christopher Buckley and Ronald Monson shared a bottle of 1928 Bollinger with Ardizzone. Buckley remembered that Ted, accompanied by Monson, had bought twelve dozen bottles in Syracuse. '"It's been rather fun," said Ardizzone, "to go up to thirsty-looking front line men and casually offer them a glass of champagne. Their first reaction is an outburst of increased blasphemy coupled with a rooted objection to having their adjectival legs adjectivally pulled".' At which Ardizzone produced a bottle and the troops smiled and held out mugs, shaking their heads in disbelief as the champagne flowed.[15] Eighth Army's Commander General Montgomery would not have approved: 'I advise all of you to leave the Eyetie wine alone. Deadly stuff. Can make you blind, you know.'[16]

Wine sometimes proved easier to find than the Germans. On 20 July, Ardizzone noted in his diary that 'we seem to have lost the war' – he meant the enemy, which had developed the uncanny knack of disappearing, fading into the countryside, their field-grey uniforms lost in dusty roadsides and rocky outcrops. Such moments were characterised by eerie silences and then mounting doubts about whether, after all, they were in territory still held by the Germans. At other times, the enemy became all too visible. A brisk fire-fight might erupt: tanks on fire, the constant rattle of machine-guns, shelling. Ardizzone sometimes found himself in a state of anxiety about the presence of mines. Christopher Buckley felt much the same.[17]

Heading south, through low hills, looking across fields yellow with stubble towards the mountains, they left the battle behind them. There was a stiflingly hot sirocco wind. Where the morning had been memorable through the intensity of combat – picking up 'a man who had his hand blown off and a bad leg wound' – and a fleeting glimpse of Montgomery, the afternoon was a rural idyll, marked by a belated lunch in the cool of a white-washed barn, with a lip-smacking cheese ('of the Caerphilly type') and a 'strong and sharp wine'. Ardizzone warmed to Sicily. He thought it 'an enchanting island' and recognised that it made him feel European. 'It is like coming home,' he wrote in a letter to Tony Gross.[18]

As it had been since the first war artists went to France in 1940, transport was an intense preoccupation. On 31 July Ardizzone began a letter to Colin Coote at the WAAC in London 'telling him of the difficulties of the work without transport'. He might easily have drawn attention to the hazards when transport *was* available: precipitous roads, bone-shaking drives along mountain tracks; detours because of roadblocks, demolished buildings, blown-up bridges; sudden flurries of mortar fire where, moments before, there had seemed no risk. A second, longstanding issue was what constituted an appropriate subject for a war artist to draw. There was something uncomfortable about driving through the most picturesque of countryside, seduced by the colours: 'pale blue sky, pinkish wall, grey green cacti … hill covered with orange trees', alive to its potential for a landscape artist. 'The country looking absolutely divine, one sees a drawing by a master everywhere.'[19] But weren't they supposed to be recording the war? To Coote he wrote that it was 'a maddening war, only the dead and dying stay still for you to draw'. In the

Edward Ardizzone and Geoffrey Keating outside Villa La Scala – the cool Geoffrey and the 'slightly panic stricken' Ted who 'captured the town of Taormina plus a Colonel and four hundred Italian troops', August 1943.

end, he abandoned the letter, preferring instead to describe for Coote what his immediate plans were. Coote was not the sort of man to welcome complaint, or the baring of souls.

On 14 August, Ardizzone and Major Geoffrey Keating of the Army Film and Photographic Unit approached the town of Taormina, 'of all the lovely towns of Sicily … the loveliest of all'.[20] For once they were on foot and unnervingly alone, their spirits partly buoyed by walking arm-in-arm. Ardizzone brandished his walking stick, and instinctively ducked when a gunshot rang out. He 'walked with little steps quite frankly … My God, I've never been so frightened in all my life'.[21] They turned a corner and were confronted by 'half a company of Italian infantry with Spandaus'. This was no time for a shame-faced about-turn. Instead, Ardizzone demanded to see their commanding officer, no doubt with the tone of a disappointed customer asking to see the manager; then he demanded that the officers hand over their revolvers. It was duly done, but grudgingly, and the atmosphere only improved when the Italians realised they were dealing with the British: 'they thought we were Germans. When they discovered that we were English they broke into smiles.' There were cheers, handshakes all round, offers of wine and food – and, thick in the air, 'a frightful smell of shit'. The odour of fear did not, however, spoil 'a cracking good lunch'. Heavy after the midday assault on their stomachs, Captain Ardizzone and Major Keating 'bicycled home having taken Taormina'.[22] Montgomery was furious at the implications of Keating's and Ardizzone's two-man assault on the town, summoning Lieutenant General Oliver Leese of 30 Corps and demanding 'to know why his infantry couldn't do what Keating obviously could.'[23] More than thirty years later, Ardizzone could still chuckle about it, imagining Monty's frustrated fury: 'If Ted and his friend can …'

The stay in Taormina acquired a magical, idyllic quality. The war correspondent, Alan Moorehead, described the villa where he was billeted. It 'straggled up the mountainside and fitted its rooms into each step of each ladder of the rock … through every hour of day and night the light poured in from the garden, a fabulous blinding yellow-white at midday, a theatrical march of sea-greens and rose in the morning and the quick evening, and then the yellow lamps at night.'[24]

'September 3rd, 1939' – Henry Moore (Reproduced by permission of The Henry Moore Foundation).

'Observer's Post' – Eric Ravilious (By the kind permission of the Trustees of Cecil Higgins Art Gallery, Bedford, England).

'Aircraft Runway in course of Construction at Thélus, near Arras, May 1940' – Barnett Freedman (Imperial War Museums (LD 261)).

'An Old Battleground' – Richard Seddon (Imperial War Museums (LD 988)).

'The Bombing of GHQ Boulogne' – Edward Ardizzone (Imperial War Museums (LD 215)).

'Dunkirk: Embarkation of Wounded' – Edward Bawden (Imperial War Museums (LD 177)).

'HMS *Boadicea* shelling German Tanks on the Cliffs near Veulette, 10 June 1940' – Richard Seddon (Imperial War Museums (LD 5988)).

'Dangerous Work at Low Tide' – Eric Ravilious (Courtesy of the Ministry of Defence Art Collection, London).

'Submarine Scenes: Diving Controls, *c.* 1941' – Eric Ravilious (Image courtesy of Towner, Eastbourne).

'The Landing Pier, Freetown, 1941' – Anthony Gross (Imperial War Museums (LD 2093)).

'The Battle of Egypt, 1942, No 5 Ambulance Train' – Anthony Gross (Imperial War Museums (LD 2553)).

'A Convoy in the Pentland Firth' – Thomas Hennell (Imperial War Museums (LD 3657)).

'On the Road South to Taormina' – Edward Ardizzone (Imperial War Museums (LD 3456)).

'The Landing in Normandy' – Barnett Freedman (Imperial War Museums (LD 5816)).

'Gliders Crash-landed' – Albert Richards (Courtesy National Museums Liverpool).

'Calais, 10 November 1944' – Thomas Hennell (Imperial War Museums (LD 4754)).

'Ravenna: Lieutenant-General Sir Richard McCreery decorates Bulow, the Partisan Leader, with the Medaglio d'Oro for conspicuous personal bravery, December 1944' – Edward Bawden (Imperial War Museumss (LD 4966)).

'Naval Officers Filling in a Discovered Escape Tunnel, 1945' – John Worsley (Imperial War Museums (LD 5149)).

'Grand Harbour, Malta, October 1943' – John Worsley (Imperial War Museum (LD 5156)).

'Flooded Maas' – Albert Richards (Courtesy National Museums Liverpool).

Ted shared a villa with Geoffrey Keating. He described it in a letter to Anthony Gross, dated 22 August 1943: 'It is complete with a studio, a large terraced garden with almond, fig and cypress trees, a cellar, now well stocked, an Italian woman cook …' They were, he wrote, 'living like lords'. He was also 'working like mad'.[25] Ardizzone spent a good proportion of time with Keating's unit, enjoying the atmosphere around 8th Army – it was 'almost a family party'. Moorehead described life at Taormina as being akin to a 'summer school' which he, fellow correspondent Alexander Clifford, and Keating had established. It was certainly lively. 'Tomorrow at dinner there are only to be admirals. Yesterday they were infantry and whores. Ted paints in one room, Geoffrey photographs in another, Alex and I write. People start arriving at ten in the morning and keep on arriving until midnight.'[26]

The broadcaster Alan Whicker, who was part of the Film Unit, recalled that Ardizzone found the hills in Taormina a challenge: 'I was surprised poor old Ted could climb the mountainside because he seemed to be overweight and getting on a bit – he was at least 40.'[27] The climb up to the villa from the shore was 800 feet. He might have struggled with steep paths in blistering heat, but Ardizzone revelled in his relative freedom – 'one was so much a freelance'. Nonetheless such freedom did not prevent him from working hard: on 17 August he began 'a large but tentative drawing of troops in the ship's lounge'. Initially he was dissatisfied with it, but fortified by wine ('a white wine called Etna … excellent bouquet of the white burgundy type …'), sustained days of work and some 'bibulous' evenings, he had made appreciable progress. 'Seven drawings in seven days,' he told Anthony Gross.

Evenings in Taormina were dream-like: Sicilian songs sung breathily in the twilight; mandolins and guitars; the Italian family's daughters flirting purposefully; the gramophone churning out its dance music. Alan Whicker noted that the villa's 'garden was heady with the exotic scent of orange blossom, its library equally heady with pornography'.[28] Over the next few weeks, Ardizzone continued to work hard on a number of drawings – troops at Mass; a battle in an orchard; a vinery; troops in Pozzillo … He was not beyond tearing work up when it displeased him.

By now, Ardizzone's time in Sicily was drawing to a close, not least because of the surrender of the Italian Government in early September 1943. The romance of that fleeting time in Taormina was counterbalanced by more disturbing events: the sight, for example, of British troops looting in Reggio – somehow Ted had never imagined that British troops would stoop to such depths, although he had seen the same thing in the Western Desert. Less troubling, but unsettling nonetheless, was the scrutiny his work was subjected to: 'One realises one paints for artists and simpletons only.'[29] Moreover, change was unmistakeably in the air. On 20 September, Geoffrey Keating arrived, bound for Algiers and provoking thoughts about Ardizzone's next move. For his own part, Keating was yet to make his mind up: Cairo? Or the Italian mainland? Overnight, Ardizzone decided to head north, taking the ferry across the Straits of Messina on 23 September.

Once on the mainland, Ardizzone and his driver motored up the toe of Italy, Tyrrhenian Sea on one side, steep terraces of vineyards to the south, and the fields and lanes full of women carrying baskets of grapes. Wine production (thankfully!) didn't stop for the war. They parked the jeep in a lane near Palmi and spent a cold night, kept awake by the autumnal chill and persistent fleas. The next morning the air was heavy with the smell of wine. A contented and deep inhalation of all that fruity promise! Then they continued north, through country whose beauty was marred by the accumulated dust of a long, hot summer. An aching tiredness, and concern as to the whereabouts of the advancing army, both added to the artist's for once jaundiced eye.

The road swung east, away from the coast and climbed on vertiginous mountain roads through beech and oak woods, then swept down through fords and gorges, skirting a soaring mountain wall, before arriving in Francavilla, where they found the army … gone. With the light fading, they stopped in a depressingly stony coastal plain – 'horribly malarial,' Ardizzone surmised. The gloom of the place was worsened by the rumours that the army was already 100 miles further on. They eventually caught up with them between Taranto and Bari, on Italy's heel, and, on 25 September, entered the 'large and rather beastly town' of Bari, whose streets were full of Italian soldiers 'strutting about with revolvers'. Early next morning, Ardizzone woke to find their jeep had been stolen, as well as a bicycle. It put a blight on the day, worsened when it emerged that the culprits were not benighted Italians, but drunken RAF officers who 'had not the grace to apologise or even offer us a drink, the prize shits.'[30]

After three days in a sodden Bari, they set out after lunch on 29 September. The road west – towards the fighting – was 'wild and romantic', turning and twisting through high mountains, small towns rising above collars of cloud, the stony slopes sometimes cloaked with woods of oak trees. The valleys, far below, held rivers strewn with stones. They passed through Salerno, before reaching Pompeii, 'to the forward troops some ten miles from Naples'. Ted heard the familiar sound of mortars and watched troops dig slit trenches while a few tanks and armoured cars prowled.

On arriving in Naples, Ted saw 'a most extraordinary sight'.[31] Opposite the railway station was a brothel where the whores were 'hanging their tits over the balconies' while below in the dust of the street, American troops stood in line waiting their turn. Ted 'would have loved to draw it', but thought better of it, no doubt imagining the admonitions and disapproval of the committee back in London. Did 'war art' encompass a mob of horny GIs hot for the women of the erstwhile enemy? For their part, most Italians had hunger, rather than commercial sex, on their minds. Ardizzone was mobbed by desperate Italians: they needed to be forcibly fended off as they tried to lever off the lid of his ration box with a bayonet. 'People very hungry, any lengths to get food. Women will lie with you for a packet of biscuits.'[32]

He thought Naples 'bloody'. Accommodation was a first floor hotel room over another brothel. 'Girls in kimonos on its balcony and American troops going up and down looking rather sheepish.' Ardizzone could live with that; what exercised him more was the sight of the man walking round his bed with a blowpipe to kill the bedbugs. It was, he thought, 'a bad omen'. He was right – what a night! Bitten by bugs; kept awake by the noise from above (both thunderstorm and brothel); disconcerted by the filth in the streets and the ubiquitous begging. A hospital visit was the last straw: 'A Goyaesque scene of bodies ... headless, armless, clothesless, some in coffins, others on stretchers. Appalling stench, many corpses blackening ...'[33]

Once out of Naples, they drove towards Ravello through the Neapolitan plain, 'dotted with white towns and villages (with) Vesuvius rising up like a giant mole-hill in the middle.' A few days later, he headed for 8th Army, making hurried notes on the colours he was seeing as the jeep headed north (brown roofs, some reddish, greyish white walls, 'occasional patch of blue or pink stucco'). The weather by then was cold enough for battle dress to be adopted, instead of lightweight summer kit, and Ardizzone wondered if they had been rendered soft by the Middle Eastern climate.

Towards the end of October, he began drawing again, the flurry of travelling temporarily over. He was troubled by the paper he was obliged to use, which threatened to disrupt his usual technique. Work started unpromisingly: a 'desultory' attempt and a 'sickly' outcome; 'a day's work with no result', but by 22 October he was more buoyant, with some pleasing drawings despite the 'horrid paper', and he had begun to doodle again, always a good sign.[34] Almost a week later, he completed a drawing of Naples streets and celebrated with a 'spectacular local white wine of 1909' with Alan Moorehead among others.

★★★

Like Ardizzone, the invasion of Sicily had provided John Worsley with a rich vein of subject matter. Through the summer of 1943 he followed the progress of the Allied troops sweeping across Sicily, sketching in Catania (bitter fighting), and Augusta (sunken Italian seaplanes forlornly wallowing in the harbour, like so many broken birds). By early September, he was nearer the fighting than Ardizzone, watching the assault of Reggio on the Italian mainland across the Straits of Messina from a landing craft. Methodically, he set up his artist's paraphernalia on board: easel, palette, paint – as if the subject was some peaceful meadow in rural England where the hazards were aggressive cows, or a sharp shower of autumn rain. Illogically, he believed that as an official war artist somehow he would be safe from the risks of combat. He was to be disabused about that soon enough, ironically by his own ship's guns, whose sudden volley sent his paints, easel and dignity scattering in all directions. From then on, his working method was to draw in pencil on a hand-held board and paint later, using the sketch as a prompt when he was back in safe surroundings. His preliminary drawings would include reminders of colour – 'yellow smoke', or 'gb' for 'green and blue'. Moving on after Reggio, he had 'a dress circle seat' aboard HMS *Roberts* for the attack on Salerno.

Like Ardizzone he found himself slowly heading north, sometimes passing through the same places: both with essentially carte blanche about where they might choose to go. They both passed through Taranto, where Ted had endured 'a nightmare journey along the coast road' on 25 September, and which Worsley reached by sea from Malta; and they both saw 'beastly' Bari at roughly the same time. Thereafter their paths diverged, with Ted cutting back north-west while Worsley, on land for once, forged north toward the beleaguered port of Termoli. It was there he met Major Brian Robb and, as a result, exchanged the conventions of infantry warfare – lines of men

Lieutenant John Worsley, RNVR, at work on an Italian quayside. (Imperial War Museum, A 20824).

marching through heat and dust, tanks and armoured cars grinding past — for a shadier world of saboteurs and guerrillas.

That first meeting with Robb was a strange one: Worsley descending into a gloomy lion's den — the basement of a farmhouse, where the flickering light of candles threw heavy shadows and gave the faces of the Italian partisans a distinctly Goyaesque look. The cellar was crowded with men, all deeply absorbed, not in intense military planning, but in a game of poker. Major Robb took his eyes off his hand of cards just long enough to look the artist up and down.

'And *what* can we do for *you*?' His eyes flicked back to the fan of cards in his hand.

Major Robb, before the war, had been a fashion artist for the *Daily Express*. Now he was responsible for organising saboteurs along the coast as far up as Venice — well behind the German lines. Worsley hesitated, reflecting on the chill provoked by the half-light, the crouched circle of unshaven, thin-faced and gaunt partisans; the shadiness of it all. Partisans were notoriously a law to themselves. Ardizzone, for example, remembered them indulging in a 'jolly game' of catch, lobbing grenades to each other for fun. 'Here. Catch this!' This was not a time for Worsley to talk up his art and minimise his soldiering. He knew he must show he would 'lend a hand whenever'. He spelled out what he needed: to take his sketchbook and pencils on some trips at night by boat up the coast. 'Would that be possible?' He looked round at the faces in the flickering candlelight.

Worsley had entered a world of clandestine operations, many of which took place at night. These included establishing contact with some of the 2,000 British ex-prisoners of the Italians stumbling through the mountains; or depositing saboteurs on some empty beach in the moonlight. He rowed a guerrilla ashore himself on one occasion, when the German transport could be heard rumbling up the coast road, uncomfortably close. The man was disguised as a monk whose cassock concealed 'a whole row of hand grenades', a fact which made jumping clear of the boat no easy task. He duly did so without self-combustion and a relieved Worsley began to row back toward the open sea. Then he heard a desperate plea from out of the darkness coming from the direction of the bogus priest.

'*Momento! Momento!* My bicycle – I must have my bicycle!' There was nothing for it but a return to the beach.

Termoli, where Worsley was based, was quaint: cobbled streets, narrow alleys cloaked in shadows, steep steps and houses cheek by jowl. At this stage of the war it was bristling with 'men with secret jobs plotting beside flickering candles in upstairs rooms, men waging private wars of their own.'[35] The contents of John Worsley's private war included conscience-jogging memories of a well-meaning admiral in a high-ceilinged Admiralty office exhorting him to live dangerously, *do* something. If he wanted risk and danger, there was a surfeit here: hare-brained schemes wacky enough to please the most gung-ho, desk-bound naval officer. Moreover, John Worsley was not a man to shirk adventure. In that sense he was like Guy Morgan. He had met Morgan, a former reporter with the *Daily Express*, on Malta. Peacetime service in Fleet Street over, Morgan was the point of liaison between the navy and the fleet of war correspondents. Neither Worsley nor Morgan could resist a challenge. Faced with the prospect of secret operations and adventure, Worsley took the view that 'You'll kick yourself ever afterwards if you miss it'. [36]

Both Worsley and Morgan, given their roles, could pick and choose the operations they went on. This one was too exotic to resist: the establishment of a forward base on the small island of Lussin Piccolo off the Dalmatian coast. It was part of a scheme to facilitate the rescue of British ex-prisoners, now marooned in the Italian hills, with winter fast approaching. Motor boats would slip on to deserted beaches at night; bloodied and exhausted men would scramble aboard, with a last anxious look back into the hinterland's darkness, and would speed away across the Adriatic under a pale moon, savouring the imminence of freedom. That was the plan anyway.

The small party set out from Termoli on 6 November 1943. It consisted of several partisans and ten assorted 'regular' troops – of an irregular kind – in two Italian fishing boats, the *Lucrezia* and the *Orsini*. It was a grey, gloomy morning. Unnervingly, the decks were stacked with cans of petrol in vivid, highly visible, yellow cans – this on a trip where the sea was persistently patrolled by the enemy. *Lucrezia* and *Orsini* made stately progress, more in keeping with the harvesting of Adriatic sardines than a military operation. An ominous first sign of trouble was the German reconnaissance plane that roared over as they headed out to sea. A barrage of anti-aircraft fire was directed at the lone raider. Then the two boats lost contact with each other in the night. When dawn broke, Guy Morgan on *Orsini* could see no sign of Worsley's ship; instead there was the reassuring sight of 'the jagged dark-blue strip of the Jugo-Slav mountains … on the horizon'.[37] With a recognisable shoreline in sight, they were not entirely lost. That second day of the expedition involved a slow sail up the Dalmatian coast, navigating by sight and instinct, rather than the sardine-stained charts in the wheelhouse.

By the time *Orsini* reached the island there was a storm brewing. The old fort, with its accompanying field guns, loomed over the harbour. A schooner nosed towards them in the gathering gloom, prompting urgent preparations for a welcoming broadside, but, with relief, it was realised that she was *Lucrezia*, with John Worsley aboard. The crew of *Lucrezia* had already made the disquieting acquaintance of the partisans on the island, as well as their prickly commander, whose rank was signalled by the profusion of grenades around his waist. He was 'absolutely festooned with them, round ones, square ones, knobbly ones'.[38] Once both ships were tied up at the island's jetty, the crews could see the partisans' light machine-gun pointing directly at them across the road.

A strange week followed. They were lodged in a millionaire's house, the Villa Mon Désir, in sleek and exotic luxury, but they were never allowed to forget that the partisans were in occupation of the island, and indeed the mansion itself. 'There were rifles in the hat-stand and a tommy-gun lying on the flowery chintz settee.'[39] The sight of two schooners riding at anchor in a blue Adriatic bay, surrounded by pine-clad cliffs and red-roofed villas suggested a lotus-eating idyll, but there was no escaping the long shadow of the war – dark-eyed men with red stars on their shabby uniforms, wielding weapons with the practised air of professional gun-slingers, and exchanging clenched fist salutes at every turn.

Time drifted by. On the fifth day, a group of German aircraft flew over the island, dropping bombs on the fort. It was a precursor of the dawn raid next day, when 500 German soldiers in a dozen landing craft arrived in the bay early enough to achieve near-total surprise. One minute Worsley was stirring in bed, the next he was crouched behind a wall, shooting at the leading barge 'as fast as he could work the bolt of a rifle'.[40] At which point, with every German in that first craft dead, discretion proved the better part of valour, and the heavily outnumbered British 'legged it to the other side [of the island]'.[41] Behind them, the Nazi flag fluttered over the fort, red, black and white against the bluest of skies.

Worsley, Morgan and the rest scrambled aboard an old diesel launch and set a course for the open sea, intent on reaching the mainland. They frequently glanced back to the island, thankful that the German gunfire was falling short. Perhaps luck was on their side? Then two German seaplanes appeared, black against the sky; they were heading straight towards them. There was a 20-minute fire-fight during which Morgan was shot in the arm, and then a pragmatic surrender, hands held high as the boat rocked in the swell. It was 13 November 1943, a week from the day when they had left Termoli.

Guy Morgan was treated by a sympathetic German doctor who, when addressed in Morgan's creaking French, smiled and remarked: 'Better to speak your own language. Is that not what you want the rest of the world to do?' He also had a warning: 'the farther from the fighting, the more the hate.' John Worsley was locked in a bare cell with straw on a concrete floor; no beds, chairs, tables or heating, a prisoner of war. He was a long way from home; beginning a life very different from the excitement of his time in the Adriatic; some distance from the fighting, and closer to hatred, therefore, in the doctor's view. It was to be a harsh test of this war artist's resilience. He had been, to all intents and purposes, just another irregular as they sailed through the Adriatic. Now he was clearly set apart from the rest: hence the isolation in solitary confinement. His priority now was to convince the enemy that a man with a sketchbook and pencils on operations behind the lines was not a spy.

12

'You're Never There When We Need You!'

What was it Guy Morgan's German doctor had said? 'The farther from the fighting, the more you hate'? For the war artist Anthony Gross, distance had a distinct benefit – greater freedom. 'The further away from headquarters, the nicer people became.' It was in such circumstances, he thought, that you were 'freer, more relaxed, more natural'. All those wartime artists' journeys, guarding precious supplies of paper and drawing materials! Soon Gross would stretch connection with home to its very limit.

Tony Gross left the UK in November 1941, bound for the Middle East, on board the *Highland Monarch*. His time in Cairo was less than a pleasure: it was too expensive, and marred further by a botched wisdom tooth extraction which broke his jaw. When Edward Bawden arrived, it cheered him up considerably. Bawden was similarly enthusiastic. 'I was met by a nattily dressed young officer with a thin line of a moustache whose manner suggested that I had better be brief and no nonsense. Can this fellow be a war artist? I wondered. A few words and we were hugging each other with the pleasure of having met.'[1]

In March 1942 Gross set out on a long trek across the Middle East – Transjordan, Beirut, Syria, Persia, Iraq. It was fascinating, but increasingly he longed for home. Prompted by a letter from Coote which hinted at a recall to London, he returned to Cairo, the train journey there from Baghdad taking a week. Coote's letter had given him false hope; however, instead of London, he found himself in the desert. This was in the months preceding Alamein. Gross was 'bitter about Coote's insensitive treatment of him'.[2]

Anthony Gross rolling a cigarette in the desert around the time of the Battle of El Alamein.

Captain Anthony Gross: 'the farther away from headquarters, the nicer people became' – his service as a war artist took him to the Far East. (Imperial War Museum, H 8511).

The desert was to make a strong impression on the war artist: 'The brewing up. The snails in the desert, millions of them. The dung beetles. The dusty dirty sand as against seashore sand. The stones and pebbles. Rock right up to the surface. The dunes and camel thorn … The hazy light all day, fine diffused light for painting …'[3] Later, in Cairo, he shared a studio with Ardizzone in a room over the office of the army magazine *Parade*. The two war artists were to be seen dining regularly in La Crystale, a Cypriot restaurant in Cairo. In November 1942 the two of them held an exhibition of recent work.

Gross contemplated going to Russia – as Ravilious before him had hoped – but they 'had no intention of letting him in'. For a brief moment it seemed that the long arm of London would bring him home: 'Hurry back. You're never there when we need you!' Instead, he found himself transferred to the Indian Army, sailing from Egypt two days before Christmas on an eastbound troopship, slowly chugging past Basra and Baghdad down the Red Sea on a seven or eight week voyage. It was his second successive Christmas on board ship and heading away from home. The sea air cured the last throes of the flu – *'un gros rhume'* – contracted in Cairo. Back in the UK someone would be dealing with his order for '20 tubes of viridian green, 15 tubes of yellow ochre, 12 Chinese white, 10 Vandyke brown …'[4] He would be, he thought, the first war artist to reach India …

Official war artist, that is – Gross found himself treading on the sensitive toes of others, men who were claiming war artist status locally. One such was Anthony Beauchamp, who later became a society photographer and married the Prime Minister's daughter, Sarah Churchill. Beauchamp was, Gross thought, 'a very nice young man'.[5] London's war artist continued east, however, leaving local rivals in his wake; through Karachi, Delhi, Calcutta by train, and on to Arakan in Burma, travelling by paddle-steamer, lorry and sampan. Most of the time he went by water, passing through dense jungle; going by boat was quieter and less observable by Japanese patrols. On reaching Burma, he was startled by the inhabitants' beauty and lulled by the prevailing sense of tranquillity, the reclining figures on sleepy verandas. 'It might have been Hampstead

Anthony Gross in Cairo – 'It was somewhere there among the markets that we were photographed against a background of the Pyramids' (Edward Bawden in a letter of July 1987).

Heath,' he thought, quixotically, since there were screens of bamboo and a 'beautiful Renaissance light'.

The eastern idyll was short-lived, replaced by the unavoidable tension at the front, listening to the alien sound of voices from the Japanese lines and realising that the enemy, in turn, could hear the strange accents of the British, drifting across a green and narrow no-man's-land.

Tony Gross was much admired by Edward Bawden, amongst others: 'Tony always made me feel a country bumpkin whose only interest was in growing spuds. He himself seemed such a man-of-the-world, knowing how foreigners behave and speaking French. I admired him immensely and still do. He was a perfectly lovely friend.'

★★★

Edward Bawden, back in England at the end of 1942, took some leave and then was sent to Dunwich on the Suffolk coast, sketchbook at the ready, to record the earnest sequences of invasion rehearsal, vehicles and troops backed by a grey North Sea. The beach was churned by tanks, pebbles and sand gouged in sweeping, brutal curves. With Eric Ravilious' death still painfully sharp in his memory, he wrote to Tirzah: 'I was really looking forward to seeing Eric again. There was no one whose opinion I valued more highly than his … I can't tell you, or anyone else, or even myself … or how much it is I miss by losing Eric – I find myself in tears.'[6] He hoped he would not be caught weeping by the man clearing the tea things. It was, after all, a time when the stiff upper lip was *de rigeur*. He stood up, blew his nose, brushed crumbs from the khaki, licked the envelope and made himself think where his work might take him next.

At first, it was all a bit run of the mill. He undertook some more desultory commissions in the UK – an 8 foot long watercolour in Aldeburgh ('the longest watercolour I have attempted') in March 1943;[7] a post-mortem in Colchester in May 1943, where the pathologist warned him that the corpse would smell of dead flies; and Polish paratroopers practising jumps in Largo, Fife – equipment-draped men clattering up a metal tower under a stormy sky, watched by a circle of the apprehensive and exiled. From March he had no longer been working for the War Office; instead he was contracted to the Ministry of Information (MOI). Hopes of being sent to Iran or Iraq were dashed. At one point he tried to re-establish contact with Richard Seddon: 'I wonder if your secretary has

Richard Sedden's [sic] address. There is a watercolour of his on view at the National Gallery: he was once a student of mine and I should like to reply to a letter received from him three years ago.'

Then, in August 1943, with his salary confirmed (£800 per annum), Bawden was journeying abroad again, to Cairo, dressed as a naval officer in white shorts, shirt and socks, acutely aware of the potential for ridicule. Before he left he ordered a supply of artists' materials: black pencils, sheets of paper – and '1 sketching umbrella and ground stick' which would be 'recoverable from Captain Bawden in due course'.[8] He reached Cairo on 31 August 1943 and made a favourable impression when he got there: 'He is a shy, but extremely pleasant and agreeable person' was the view of the MOI's Middle Eastern chief, Curteis Ryan.[9] His reception was welcoming, unlike a previous occasion when 'The Army PR with whom I worked in the past shut their doors. The colonel read Coote's letter aloud, "What a waste of paper!" he exclaimed, dropping the letter in the waste paper basket'.

By this stage of the war Cairo had become 'a kind of Crewe or Clapham Junction at which people were continually appearing on their way to somewhere else.'[10] Shepheards Hotel was at the very heart of this itinerary: sit there long enough and some long-lost friend would breeze in, looking oddly different in uniform, face lit up in a smile at the whims of wartime logistics. 'Well, bless my soul, fancy seeing you here of all places!' The architectural writer J.M. Richards bumped into Bawden in just those circumstances. Where they had once socialised in the green peace of rural Essex, here they were on the terrace of Shepheards, in the city's bustle and dust. Richards thought Bawden 'wore his captain's uniform with meticulous correctness' but 'with a consciously satirical air, as though he thought of it as fancy dress.'[11]

True to form, Cairo was just a staging post for Bawden. He travelled further east, enduring the miseries of a slow train to Baghdad, a prolonged meander at snail's pace across the desert. The train's level of comfort was such that he developed crippling haemorrhoids. It was, he wrote plaintively, 'like being impaled on an iron spike'.[12] It was a here today, gone tomorrow existence, criss-crossing the deserts of the Middle East, while the narrative of the war slowly unravelled. In landscapes that you might have thought tediously and monochromatically uniform, he was pleased to find his work changing, less reliant now on the precision of black ink and instead warmed by colour. He regarded them as paintings, rather than tinted drawings. The red rocks in the Iraqi hinterland he saw with a different eye now; he was a long way from the neat hedgerows of rural Essex. Initially he did not warm (if that's the word) to Baghdad – 'too large, and hot, and crowded'[13] – and he missed his wife and home. Excursions into the unknown lands to the north were more enriching. He was stirred by the mountains of Kurdistan, although the weather was cold and rain-sodden. Hunkered down under canvas, writing long letters in the glimmer of a hurricane lamp, he shivered as the wind gusted, billowing the tent like a sail. Thunder reverberated through the hills. Travel by car on tortuous roads was slow and never without anxiety: about punctures, brigands, or wheels stuck fast in unyielding mud. At the oil town of Mosul, he saw pools of the black stuff oozing from the ground in a 'dreadful landscape'.

Later, Bawden ventured into Saudi Arabia, attaching himself to a team working on the destruction of locusts. It made a change from Germans. He wrote to Ardizzone, 'sitting in a salt marsh ... recovering from malaria. Every few minutes I have to wave my arms to keep off the clouds of flies.'[14] He was excited about 'finding good painting subjects' and the pursuit of locusts gave him the opportunity to 'get into a country which normally is practically closed to Europeans'.[15] In the event, the locusts proved elusive – Bawden had suspected that it might prove a wild goose chase – and he soon succumbed to another bout of malaria. The expedition (of 1,000 men and 330 motor vehicles) involved long journeys – across the Red Sea to the Persian Gulf, then Bahrain to Basra and back to Baghdad – bouncing along desert tracks in dust-stained jeeps under a relentless sun in a cruel, blue sky. Bawden hung on to hopes of crossing the path of the legendary King Ibn Saud, but it was not to be and he consoled himself with a period of intense work, while whip-wielding policemen guaranteed his privacy, a lonely figure in the teeming camel market, absorbed in the process of conjuring life from a sheet of white paper. He slept under the stars; marvelled at the absence of water (so rare that thirty-five years later he would remember vividly the trickle of water he fleetingly saw seeping down from low desert hills); saw lizards and miles of sand, but no vegetation, and no great clouds of locusts darkening the sky. Perversely, he was disappointed: he liked insects, after all, even the 4-inch cockroaches with thin antennae he saw at night. He studiously avoided crushing them, reckoning that cockroaches, like artists, did a useful job.

His was a unique view of the war, and he knew it, too – he could be scathing about those who were merely passing through. He was, for example, dismissive of his fellow artist Feliks Topolski, who he thought 'had been in Cairo ten minutes and thought that made him a War Artist'.[16] Bawden's empire stretched wide, well beyond Cairo. Clutching his sketching bag and tin canister of paper, sketching umbrella (that vivid sun's glare on such white sheets!) and a small leather case, he patrolled the extreme corners of the region: the road to Russia across the mountains from Persia; the port of Jeddah; Damascus (which he thought the most lovely town he had seen in the Middle East); Darfur; the Sea of Galilee; Transjordan … He operated alone, took occasional suggestions as to where he might go and what he might draw, but for the most part he 'acted independently'. At one point he harboured hopes of being sent to China: 'I am very pleased about China; indeed I am as wildly excited as it is proper to be at the age of forty.' A letter from E.C. Gregory at the WAAC in August ended that hope: it was now 'highly improbable.' By then he was growing anxious about the future: 'I am worried … will the Committee decide to send me East or West! My wife is worried also.'

In fact, he rarely heard from the WAAC and kept London at arms' length by regularly sending thirty or forty pictures back via the embassy diplomatic bag. That should keep them off my back! Back in London, the paintings would be unfurled, grains of sand spilling on to the polished desk, and smelling of the sun and paint. Through it all, he was 'happily separated from control'.[17]

Happily independent he may have been, but Bawden's Middle Eastern odyssey could be wearisome. He did not feel that he was a natural traveller: 'My upbringing from the lower middle-class gutter has unfitted me for the carefree life of the Bedouin,' he wrote in a letter to 'Dizzy' Ardizzone on 27 April 1944 from Baghdad. A few months later he declared that he was 'a little tired of Baghdad (and) let me confess a trifle homesick'.[18] He was headed for Tehran, he said, remembering a previous visit: 'I haven't been to Persia since that memorable day, two and a half years ago I was handed out of a railway carriage window on a stretcher, quite nude except for a topi resting over my face and a pocket handkerchief held over my privates.' He felt himself lucky that 'there was no Ardizzone present to commemorate the occasion with his bibulous line and a wash of pale ale.' Earlier on Easter Sunday 1944, he described how he had 'crossed this goddam desert from the Red Sea coast to the Persian Gulf.' The artist in him relished the light, the romance, the sense of distance; it was what came with such things that palled – a tedious diet of tinned food and biscuits; eye-stinging, tent-destroying sandstorms; and Arab salesmen persistent enough to pursue a sale even when the prospective client was lavatorially enthroned, inconvenienced at his convenience.

★★★

It may have been a draining existence – and for some a dangerous one – but artists still yearned to be given official status. In June 1943, Thomas Hennell was invited by the Ministry of Information to step into Eric Ravilious' boots: 'to record aspects of the war in Iceland'. It was a three month contract with a salary of £162 10s.[19] Initially worried about drawing paper ('I am using it at the rate of a full sheet per day'), he produced thirty watercolours and filled two sketchbooks.

Another would-be war artist, Albert Richards, was offered a commission by the committee in October 1943. Richards had waited a long time to be accepted as a war artist. It was more than three years since he had been called up, joining the Royal Engineers as a sapper. Over the next three years he was posted to a variety of locations – Suffolk, Northumberland, Wiltshire and back to Suffolk. The work was mundane: helping to build and camouflage pill-boxes; building bridges ('the bane of a sapper's life'); and digging anti-tank ditches. His time for painting was necessarily limited and sappers' work was sometimes uncomfortable, not least because of the cold. There were times when he would be working in thick blankets of snow; cold metal stuck to his fingers; and coastal postings meant bitter tree-bending winds blowing in from the sea. 'At 3 a.m.,' he wrote, 'life in the body has ceased to exist.' He was disillusioned with army life: 'The only subject I see around me is boredom.'

Early in the war Richards had sought information about how he could combine soldiering with painting. He wrote to Dickey at the WAAC on 1 April 1941 asking 'if it is possible to sketch or paint out of doors as I do so much wish to be able to carry on with my work'.[20] A year later, in April 1942, he had written, 'I do hope that one day I shall get a chance to become a War Artist'. Eventually he sold some paintings to the WAAC and succeeded in escaping the tedium of his sapper's life by becoming a parachutist with 591 (Antrim) Parachute Squadron.

The training turned him into a paratrooper, as opposed to a parachutist. The change in his life was stark. Until he joined the paratroopers, he wrote, his 'mind [had been] very blank and I hadn't any desire to paint. Now that my life is more interesting, I haven't the time to paint. But I have the beautiful experience of parachute descents to make up for it.'

A commission as a war artist would give him time to paint and not deny him the thrill of parachuting. On 6 October 1943, he sent a telegram to E.C. Gregory at the National Gallery: 'I WILL ACCEPT THE POSITION COMMITTEE HAS OFFERED ME – RICHARDS.'

★★★

War Artists, 1943: Old Campaigners

It was an unnatural existence, being a war artist far removed from London. We might have been in uniform, but there was an independence there, a freedom, if you were canny enough to exploit it. In practice, we used all the latitude we could find. Bawden got it right when he said, 'We were happily separated from control'! Him most of all possibly. Ted Ardizzone used to say he was as, 'free as air' and certainly Bawden would complain that he could never track his friend down. Ardizzone saw himself as an old campaigner by the middle of the war: 'our value,' he wrote to Tony Gross in August 1943, 'has increased in the sense that we can get about and see things in a way the new boy can never do.'[21] Exactly – all it needed was the use of one's wits. Ted got to Sicily 'extremely unofficially'. He was sure that he would have missed the invasion if he had relied on official channels.

Just as the War Artists' Committee was able to beaver away in its own little enclave, almost as if the military had forgotten all about it, so we acted as if we were own decision makers, answerable to the Public Relations Unit (PR), but easily by-passing it. We could operate alone, not understood by those not privy to the secret. We sometimes wondered whether Churchill even knew of our – or the committee's – existence, but then someone pointed out that he had examples of our work on his walls at home; someone – it may have been Clark – saw them at one of the Prime Minister's garden parties.

And they didn't know what to do with us – at least, not until the Voice of London, in the guise of an official telegram, called us back home. Colin Coote realised it too, and so must the rest of the com-mittee, at least the ones who were awake! Essentially the relationship between the UK and the artist in the field was tenuous at best. There you are, working for PR, behind some desk in a steamy office in downtown Cairo, and an artist turns up, looking flustered by unex-pected heat, and the absence of a proper welcome. What do you do? You shrug and pass the problem on.

Occasionally we would send work back, perhaps in the diplomatic bag. Some of us wrapped paintings in shell cases for safe keeping: the irony appealed to us. If they got paintings fairly regularly back in London, that was enough. Kept them quiet. Anthony Gross wasn't the only one to find the British authorities in Cairo unenthusiastic about his arrival. Ardizzone, for example, always talked about moving around the desert 'in spite of' – that was his phrase – the bods at PR. It's good to think of him smiling knowingly as he kept the necessary few steps ahead of them. The critical thing was to hang on to your transport; without it you were stranded; with it, you were free.

Our duties were pretty minimal: occasionally you might find your-self helping out by censoring letters, reading the men's correspondence home and striking out anything that might make the letter remotely interesting. The travelling though was often slow and tedious, more often by sea than air when first heading away from the UK, but for many of us the experience was unforgettable and one which, during the '30s, we would never have expected to enjoy. Which of us would have contemplated having the opportunity to see Africa and Arabia? Not just see – our senses were assailed on all sides, the cacophony of noise in the streets of Cairo, the barking dogs, the smell of the Nile, or the people's 'nutty aromatic body odour', in Bawden's fastidious words! There were drawbacks of course to our time in the Middle East – heat, flies, sweat, bouts of malaria, acute cases of piles (too much sitting for the two Edwards) – but we experienced a world we would never have touched without the war. And you got used to the heat after a while. Some of us even tried new ways of working, or devel-oped a confidence about some new aspect of work.

The journeying was remarkable, Bawden perhaps most of all. How's this for an odyssey? April 1941: Sudan to Addis Ababa. Then, in August, on to Asmara in Eritrea; then to Khartoum by train, and Cairo. On the move again in November, into the desert and eventually reaching

Benghazi, via Tobruk; then Cairo again, Baghdad, Basra, the ill-fated Laconia, prison camp in North Africa, New York, the UK (Dunwich in Suffolk, Colchester, Scotland, Aldeburgh). In September 1943 he was in Cairo, before travelling to Jeddah, Baghdad, back to Cairo; then the Persian Gulf, Baghdad, Rome, Ravenna and so on. Exhausting.

Anthony Gross was similarly mobile, exploring eastern India, usually by river boat, sometimes ferry, but also on foot or horseback, or mule. It was a remarkably intense experience. At one point he marched some 500 miles on a ridge with valleys 6,000 feet below, pausing occasionally to eat the wild raspberries. He thought the work was desperately lonely, involving what he called the 'endless travelling, [the] endless difficulty'. Such journeying was tiring in the extreme; dangerous too, with poor roads, for example, or in Arabia no roads at all, or rivers come to that, just bruising rides perched on camels. Where there were roads, that could mean a different kind of discomfort or danger: you might find yourself sitting there, eyes averted from the dizzying drop down the mountain side as you are swung around yet another hairpin bend; or hanging on for dear life, horrified at the driver's evident incompetence. Ted told me once about his driver, Gino, whose driving slowly improved, but who still nearly killed him twice in one short return journey.

In the end, for all of us, a kind of travel fatigue set in. Even so, the telegram imposing a change of scene was not always welcome. Bawden, for example, was not entirely thrilled when he was told that he was to be replaced by Ardizzone, making some tart comment in a letter to the committee about the challengingly hot conditions in which he had been working, and how doing so made him lose weight; he noted that he was being replaced by someone 'who can willingly spare some fat in the service of his country.' No doubt, Sir Kenneth shook his head and repeated some comment about Bawden being a tricky customer. For all that there was a fellowship and a camaraderie. We did cheer each other up on those golden moments when our paths coincided: think of those cheering dinners shared by Gross and Ardizzone in Cairo; Bawden and Gross excitedly talking of painting and painters, having been starved of such conversation for many months; or the long lunches Ardizzone had at various times with Henry Carr, Tom Hennell, William Coldstream and Bawden.

Thinking back, it seems odd who ended up where: compare Bawden's global trek in the dusty heat with Ravilious' journeying much nearer home (mundane Grimsby, Sussex, Scotland); even when there was talk about a more distant posting for him – to Russia – the theme was cold winds and blue hands. Norway, Iceland – Ravilious' fate was evidently bound up with a cold climate.

Later, in peacetime, when we returned to a world where travelling was just a bicycle ride down a country lane, or a branch line train rocking its way to the coast, or we took a bracing walk along the beach, we thought back to those war years almost with disbelief: was that us? Did we do that? How lucky we were – those of us who survived, that is.

13

'Please File in Larger Provincial Galleries File'

The war was a time of journeying, of slow movement from one temporary home to another. That was certainly true of those war artists wandering the globe, driven by curiosity, but increasingly travel-weary. At the same time, their paintings of the war were being trundled slowly around the UK's provincial art galleries, travelling by goods train, or lorry when the railways couldn't cope.[1] The exhibitions of war art at the National Gallery in London had proved popular, with long lines of earnest men in uniform or baggy suits and women with bobbed hair and clutch handbags peering intently at the paintings, moved by the representations of this new world which threatened to engulf them. There were some people who demurred: Sir Kenneth Clark wrote gratefully to a George Dunn at RAF Felixstowe, thanking him for his kind words about the exhibition: 'You may have heard that the exhibition had been very much attacked by academic forces, and I am therefore all the more grateful to people who let me know they enjoyed it.'[2]

Some academics might have been guarded in their view of the National Gallery exhibitions and the quality of the art on show, but the initiative had considerable public support and they would continue throughout the rest of the war. Interestingly, exhibitions of war art by German war artists were also being held in Berlin. The London exhibitions were occasionally inconvenienced by air raids and the resulting bomb damage at the gallery. For example, on 10 October 1940, 'the National Gallery roof was damaged by flying paving blocks etc and the

Bomb damage at the National Gallery.

pictures taken down the next day.' Two days later, a bomb hit Gallery XXVI and the floor crashed through to ground level. 'One or two drawings may be under debris.' In November 1940 'the damage [was] terrific … There is a huge gap open to the sky & tons of that coloured marble and fragments of pilasters & cornices are heaped at the bottom'.[3] The air raid sirens sounded with irritating frequency, prompting 'much discussion as to whether people should be obliged to leave the building' during alerts.[4]

After the success of the London exhibition, it was thought important, and good for the morale of the population, to allow the country as a whole to see a substantial selection of war artists' work. E.M. O'R. Dickey began the sensitive task of selecting appropriate drawings, and a substantial correspondence began with the curators of provincial galleries. Dickey's mouth may have tightened momentarily at the insistence of the curator at Norwich to address him as 'Mr Bickey', but his measured, dignified prose showed no sign of any irritation he might have felt. Typically a gallery would receive the exhibition for a three-week spell: the Kelvingrove Gallery in Glasgow, for example, showed it from 22 February 1941 to 15 March 1941. Then the cavalcade

Berlin: Professor Schweitzer-Mjolnir opens an exhibition of work by German official war artists. (Imperial War Museum, HU 39484).

would move on – a complex operation with seventy-two paintings to be shifted safely in a world of blackouts, delayed trains, and air raids – to Aberdeen, Newcastle, Norwich, Leicester, and so on. Sometimes galleries were closed as a result of enemy action; so it was that the exhibitions planned for the Ferens Gallery, Hull, and for Southampton were cancelled. Visitor numbers were high: the Bradford exhibition, for example, had 18,250 visitors in three weeks.

★★★

Dickey cast a weary eye down the list of names on the 'Catalogue of Pictures for Circulation'. He supposed the selected names would do, though he did not doubt that the committee – as was the way with committees – would huff and puff and make more work. He wrote on the draft 'Please file in Larger Provincial Galleries file' and hoped that would be the end of it. It was a sound, safe list, with some real quality. You could rely, for example, on dear Ted: typical Ardizzone humour, portly figures discomforted by war; the artist's energy, humanity and observant eye invariably evident. The work covered a good range – bombing in the east end of London; guns in Belgium; troops on the home front (*Australians in the Grounds of Salisbury Cathedral*), and men caught up in the chaos before the escape from France, smiling despite the uncertainty and fear.

What else? Well, Bawden of course. France again, but a different approach to Ted's. They don't sound terribly exciting, *Constructing a Blockhouse, Halluin,* but he somehow makes you feel as if you were there, seeing things others might miss. Ah, yes, I like this fine portrait of Alan Brooke by Reginald Eves, and the series of paintings by Barnett Freedman works well. He's a fine artist. The Anthony Grosses are also highly capable: tanks, trucks on manoeuvres, signallers practising semaphore. Three works by Eric Ravilious which I like enormously, though I know Sir Kenneth still harbours some reservations. Frankly, I cannot for the life of me see why! *Barrage Balloon at Sea, Midnight Sun,* and *Destroyers at Night.* And one by a serving sailor – Midshipman J. Worsley – a pencil sketch called, let me see, *An Earnest Game,* which shows enormous promise.

Over the piece, it's a strong selection, Dickey thought. The war in paint: phoney war; evacuees harvesting; portraits of the great and good, and the ordinary; gun manufacture; aerodrome runways; tanks rumbling through France; small boats at Dunkirk; fitters crawling over a Spitfire; the white ghost of a Sunderland flying boat barely contained by its hangar (the talented John Nash!); bombers; anti-aircraft defences; and bomb damage, though not too much of that – we all see too much of the real thing.

Dickey leaned back, put the file to one side and moved on to the next item on his agenda: the letter to Sir Kenneth he felt obliged to write. This was the least fulfilling part of his role: it demanded such sensitive drafting skills, and seemed so damned trivial! Where to start? Ah yes, 'referring to Coote's fuss about Ardizzone's two drawings of Staff Officers at Wilton House among naked Venuses and his wish for them to be removed from the National Gallery in case of complaint …' I ask you – you would think a bit of naked flesh would be good for morale!

14

The War Artist's Dummy

John Worsley stood disconsolately near the wire, hands in pockets, eyes fixed on a point beyond the perimeter fence. That was dauntingly high, well over a man's height, with concrete posts at regular intervals. Just as disturbing as the barbed wire was the profusion of stony-faced guards in grey uniforms, each man with a rifle slung loosely from his shoulder, its bayonet pointing to the sky, the metal and the light equally steely. The grass between the single warning wire and the main fence was an unhealthy yellow, the sad colour of sand in the rain.

To Worsley's right was a wooden watchtower, under whose shadowy roof were more guards, crouched over machine-guns, watching him as he stared at the point where freedom began. Step over the line and life, not just the war, is conclusively over for me, Worsley reflected. It was not an original thought: in the months before reaching the PoW camp at Marlag, not far from the north German city of Bremen, he had been kept in solitary confinement in Ljubljana prison; endured persistent interrogation; passed through Berlin during a ferocious night raid by the RAF; suffered bitterly cold, bare prison cells and minimal rations. The first heavy snows of the winter of 1943 tumbling from leaden skies just made the world, and his prospects, seem even bleaker. It didn't get better once he reached Marlag, where his incarceration began with a two-month period of solitary confinement, during which time he was regularly questioned by the Gestapo.

To his interrogators, Worsley's drawings looked suspiciously like the work of a spy, and after all, he had been captured while taking part in a clandestine operation. For the Gestapo the idea of 'war art' was a bizarre concept; these were men whose life centred on illuminating dark corners through pain and humiliation – it was the opposite end of human experience from men who used light and colour to capture truth and feeling. 'Come, come, Lieutenant Worsley, you expect us to believe that you are an artist. You *draw* this war? No, no!!' Worsley shrugged in the face of the relentless questioning, wondering when – if – it would end and how, his artist's eye taking in the scratched table, the curl of blue cigarette smoke, the towering guard by the door and the questioner's bloodless face.

Worsley was suspected of having up-to-date information about secret Royal Navy weapons – 'Tell us what you know about the Hedgehog!' Exasperated, Worsley undertook to draw it and sketched a 'prickly little rodent', enjoying for the moment the chance to draw on virgin white paper, and this minor act of rebellion, not daring to think of the consequences, the fury in the interrogator's voice, the upturned chair, the slammed door; then the sound of boots disappearing up the ill-lit corridor, and a ringing, unnatural silence. The alternative to questioning was a life deprived of everything: 'no music, no books to read, nothing with which to divert [me] except [my] own innermost thoughts.' A flicker of hope came when he earned a commission from one guard, sketching a pornographic picture in exchange for a baked potato. Later, 'he upped his fee to a meal of bacon and eggs'.[1]

Marlag was a camp for Royal Navy officers – the only such camp since sailors, when disaster strikes, either 'get home or get drowned'. Its inmates prowled the perimeter of the camp, deployed pent-up ingenuity in a stubborn battle to improve life (Worsley designed a central heating system using discarded KLIM tins); and plotted escapes. The International Red Cross parcels were a godsend: 'the brown cardboard container, about the size of a tall shoebox, played a part in every major activity that took place in a PoW camp. The string that held it together pulled the trolleys in the catacomb of tunnels under Stalag Luft III, the food tins became the main components for brewing up a cup of tea ... the packaging went towards elaborate stage sets or barrack hut furniture.'[2] For his part, Worsley received brushes, paint (both oil and watercolours) and paper. Canvas, however, was unavailable; when he painted the three Victoria Cross recipients in the camp, he used linen sheets, what had once been the hut curtains. Needs must.

Escape might have been a permanent preoccupation for the inmates of Marlag, but the gap between planning and eventual success was vast. Only one officer, a lieutenant in the RNVR, had successfully made it back to England. Tunnelling was impractical since the water table was very high, and beyond the wire was an enormous ditch. While tunnelling 'was a therapy', much creative energy went into thinking up alternatives. Then Worsley had a brainwave: 'I know! I'll make a dummy.' It was a painstaking job, since 'Albert RN' had to be sufficiently realistic to fool the guards. Worsley constructed the fake officer's head himself, from scraps of cloth, straw, kapok and papier-mâché (pulped from German newspaper). Hair from Worsley's roommates was donated to Albert; his eyes were a divided ping-pong ball; an ingenious method using an old sardine tin was designed to enable the dummy to blink. His skin tone was the product of Red Cross oil paints. His body was a wire cage surrounded by a naval greatcoat, while a clever mechanism allowed the dummy to be supported – carried – by the two men on either side. Finished, with his coat collar turned up, a cigarette drooping from his mouth and a PoW's haunted look, hair poking out from a battered naval cap, Albert looked remarkably convincing. He was truly a work of art. Worsley smiled; Albert blinked back. Worsley winked: one of them knew that the other might just be a passport to freedom.

★★★

The Escape Committee had met; the escaper had been chosen (Lieutenant William 'Blondie' Mewes) and Albert assiduously rehearsed. The dummy was then disassembled and his constituent parts distributed. It was time to test Albert's luck. The guards counted the prisoners – twice, as usual – and then marched them up to the bathhouse. Blondie Mewes winked at Worsley as the steam thickened around them and the noise echoed around the bare wet walls. While the guards weren't looking, Mewes climbed over a low wall and hid in the lavatory. Rations of food and his clothing were passed through to him, and he settled down to wait for darkness, and the second stage of the escape. Meanwhile, the raucous process of getting the men out from the steamy baths and counted in serried rows began, with Albert rapidly assembled and then staunchly supported on either side by his naval comrades. Laconically blinking, Albert passed through two separate 'counts' by the guards, and

'Worsley smiled; Albert blinked
back. Worsley winked: one of them
knew that the other might just be
a passport to freedom.' This replica
of Albert RN can be viewed at the
National Museum of the Royal Navy,
Portsmouth.

then, impersonating Mewes perfectly, he was marched down the hill to
the camp proper, while the man he replaced shivered in the bathhouse
toilet, waiting for the darkness outside to fall.

For five days, Albert stood in the fourth rank of the British officers as
the Germans conducted their regular check of numbers – three times
each day. Mewes got as far as Lübeck on the Baltic Sea. With his heart in
his mouth, he boarded a Swedish cargo vessel, where the response was
an unworthy 'We cannot help you!' He tried another ship whose captain similarly refused to help. Eventually he was caught by the Gestapo
and returned crestfallen to the camp. Albert was 'put in dry dock' for a
while, a wise precaution, though Mewes had not revealed his existence
when interrogated. When a second Albert-inspired escape was initiated,
things started well, but it was 'German bowels not brains that caught him':
a guard was caught short, dashed to the lavatory and there discovered the
would-be escaper. Much to the consternation of everybody, Germans and
PoWs alike, the count now revealed one prisoner too many! The result
was a meticulous search and Albert was finally discovered, his head rolling
noisily and accusingly out of the back of a line of men. The episode ended
with the German commandant haranguing the assembled PoWs:

'You British officers,' he shouted, 'you think that we Germans know fuckin' nothing, but we Germans know fuck all!' Even Albert might have laughed, if he had not already been in pieces.

★★★

War Artists, 1944: Record of the War

The war artists' life was one of mixed emotions: ecstatic moments of laughter and rich experience and comradeship on the one hand, or the opposite: hardship, danger, loneliness, and a treadmill of for-ever moving on. In that sense we were no different from many others caught up in the war. At various times, just to make things worse, we fell ill, sometimes badly enough to be confined to a hospital bed a long way from home. Given the age of many of us, that wasn't surprising. Lumbago, malaria, pneumonia, piles, flu, bronchitis – you name it, we got it. But on our good days we marvelled at the sights before us: the clear light; the desert flowers; the sprawling rivers; the great armies in the desert. We felt foolish sometimes: how can you not when you are required to wear the letters WC (for War Correspondent) on your shoulders as we were in those early days? Cue ribald laughter from one's comrades in arms. We were greeted with acclaim and drenched in bunches of flowers when we swanned into Belgium in 1940, only to be watched with sullen dismay, or worse, as we were booted back across the Channel weeks later. Some of us cemented friendships with the troops on the ground and revelled in the reminders of an earlier bachelor life, the thirsty search for the next bottle, or the freedom to ogle a pretty girl, in uniform or not.

It wasn't all schoolboy fun, far from it. For all of us there was the shocking moment when we first realised what war meant; for some it was the endless lines of refugees and their meagre belongings, or it might be the dismembered and bloody human remains from an air raid, or the evident willingness of German pilots to shoot up the inno-cent on the crowded roads. There were times when you could feel like weeping at the sheer horror of it all, and there were times too when what made us close to tears contained the very stuff that had us itching to draw. Compulsively, we would reach for the trusty sketchbook at the very moment when we most felt sorrow and despair.

We worked damn hard, and fast too, but there will be those who ask themselves 'what sort of "record of the war" did we make?' The committee will have debated that long and hard around the table, and Dickey and others will have faced it when choosing the paintings for the exhibitions which meant so much to some of us. In effect, the 'record' is the sum total of the thousands of sketches and drawings we collectively produced, not just the salaried artists, but also those who submitted work on the off-chance. What did we miss? What gaps are there in the record? Phoney war? Got it. Defeat in France? Some of us were there, although often completely in the dark about what was happening, map-less and lost, but there's a body of work that catches the time well enough. Italy? Yes, from the invasion beaches on Sicily, up the long northward trek through to the Apennines and the winter in the north of the country, the record is detailed. North Africa? More of Arabs, and ancient sites perhaps, but we all struggled to represent the broad canvas of a major battle, with its distant clouds of dust and honey-coloured tanks churning the horizon.

There wasn't much about the Home Front that was missing either, whether it was Paul Nash painting dog-fights in the blue skies of Kent, or Dame Laura Knight recording a blue-uniformed crew struggling with an elephantine barrage balloon on the hills above London. There were artists at Alamein, the invasion of Sicily, Anzio, Dieppe, listening with beating heart to the whispering Japanese on the front line in India, on secret operations in the Adriatic, at sea, in submarines, looking down from the air, staring the length of concreted runways, perched on piles of bricks in the East End of London, sketchbook propped on knee, eyes fixed on yet more debris. The work wasn't always popular: some official at the ministry wrote to Clark that he 'liked' the paintings, but he 'wondered why they were *all* so depressing.' Yes, well, for a long time, it *was* bloody depressing!

But was the record *complete*? Inevitably, each of us had a partial view – and one which was further narrowed by the particular way we saw the world and the way we painted. If you don't believe me, look at the difference between Henry Moore's tube sketches and those done by Ardizzone. Moore's are sombre, bleak and tragic. Symbolic. Ardizzone's have a warmth and empathy and tell an entirely different story of the same event. You feel you recognise and like the people he is drawing. Taken together, they have made the experience of

Londoners sleeping night after night in the subterranean gloom of the underground unforgettable.

The 'record of the war' that Sir Kenneth Clark had in mind even included scenes of PoW life thanks to John Worsley. His reputation grew until 'visiting German admirals came to view his work'. [3] The Admiralty war artist, trapped as he was behind the wire at Marlag, may have imagined how the invasion of France might look, and where and when it would take place, but he would not be there. The role of war artist with the invasion fleet and its aftermath would be left to others, those of us who were lucky enough to be free and not exiled in some desert wilderness. Those were the unlucky ones, too far away to get back to the UK in time. For those of us caught up in the melee of preparation on the south coast of England in that June of 1944, the mood was expectant, tense. We watched the weather with an anxious eye, marvelled at the sheer size of the gathering ships and men, checked that our art materials were ready and complete, the sketchbook potentially waterproof, and wondered what we would see when the armada set sail for France and how well we would record this next great moment of the war.

15

D-Day

Early in 1944, Ardizzone received 'a very laudatory letter from Kenneth Clark' which pleased him greatly. Written on 15 December 1943, Clark was clearly delighted by the paintings of Sicily which would be exhibited, he said, in the coming February. If anything, Clark was even more enthusiastic about the drawings of Naples which arrived on his desk as he was writing to Ardizzone. Lying in his bath, watching a spectacular eruption of Mt. Vesuvius through the window, Ted felt at ease with the world. Within a week, though, he was downcast, feeling ill and not entirely satisfied with his work: 'Patch up drawing of the road to Torino, one of the miserable four I have done in the past six weeks.' The painting, he thought on reflection, might have 'quality though small', but the illness turned into bronchitis and he soon found himself in hospital. Shortly after he came down with an 'acute attack of piles'. Like many people in that fifth year of war, Ardizzone was looking forward to its conclusion with a heavy weariness.

A month or so later, on 14 February 1944, he arrived at Anzio, some 35 miles south of Rome, 'at dawn … pink and white ruins jutting out into the sea'. It disappointed him that he had missed the landings at Anzio − Operation Shingle − but there was no doubting that the war suddenly seemed very close, with shells passing overhead and enemy planes strafing. At one point he was momentarily confronted by a terror-stricken sergeant: Ardizzone 'gave him some sweets' and accompanied them with a crisp 'Don't be silly!' Six days later he flew to Bari − 'a really

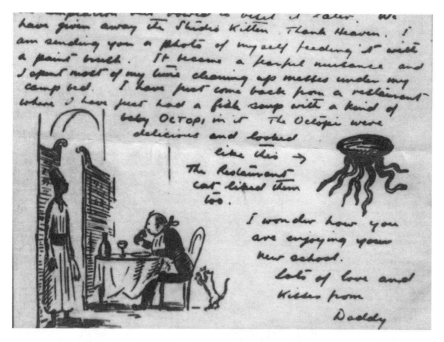

'I have just come back from a restaurant where I have just had a fish soup with a kind of baby octopi in it ...' Ardizzone and the restaurant cat dining in Cairo.

dreadful, bumpy journey' – and then on to Cairo, via a rain-swept Malta. They landed at night on a desert air-strip near Cairo and Ted began what can only be called a social whirl of lunches, dinners and parties whose high and lowlights included a hangover (24 February); a box at the opera (25th); a day at the races (27th); dinners at the Auberge du Turf; and a 'big party ... guest of honour Lord Moyne. Lots of liquor and food'. (10 March).[1] In between times he worked on a number of sketches with varying degrees of satisfaction – on the 11th he spent 'a day working on a very bad drawing'. The next day he received a surprising communication from the War Office – 'I am not to go home'. He was 'dumbfounded', and increasingly angry when he realised that he could well miss the invasion on D-Day.

Still in Cairo, he saw Terence Rattigan's play *Flare Path* and thought it 'a wretched affair', while the oils of artist Feliks Topolski impressed him but also made him 'feel gloomy about my own work'.[2] He sailed for Italy soon after, at the end of March, and arrived at Taranto 'in a flurry of snow and rain' and in the middle of a smallpox scare (all the boat passengers were

Ardizzone being painted by fellow war artist, Henry Carr. (Imperial War Museum, NA 14235).

deemed to be contacts). It meant confinement for a while in an isolation camp and frequent checks of his chest for tell-tale spots. The quarantine period gave time for fellow war artist Henry Carr to paint Ted's portrait. Ted would have been too kind a man to reveal Kenneth Clark's poor opinion of Carr's North African work, which he had confided to Ardizzone in his letter of the previous December.

The date for the invasion of France was drawing closer and Ardizzone was still marooned in Italy. He was shocked by the damage done to Monte Cassino: it was 'so flattened that it looks like a fall of rock'. Then, on 20 April he heard that he was being recalled home 'to join the Navy for a few months'. He thought the prospect 'wonderful'. When he reached the UK on 11 May, there were just three weeks to go before the invasion of France.

★★★

It is the night before D-Day. The war artist and parachutist Captain Albert Richards is killing time with the rest of the men from the British 6th Airborne Division, waiting for the moment when the Dakotas set off for Normandy. The paratroopers are pensive, reflecting on the task ahead. It has the feel of a suicide mission, this storming of the battery at Merville in the small hours before the invasion proper is due to begin. Like the men around him, Richards' face is blackened and he is wearing a camouflage smock and a rimless steel helmet.

Richards is twenty-four, born in the shadow of the First World War. His father, George, had served in France during the Great War and was a wood machinist by trade. His mother, Hannah, worked in a factory.[3] In the early 1920s George Richards was unemployed, like so many survivors of the trenches, before finding work across the Mersey in Wallasey. The family moved there, living latterly at 14 Queensway. Albert Richards studied at the Wallasey School of Art, before winning a scholarship to the Royal College of Art in London.

Shortly before D-Day Richards had written to the WAAC in London, a letter in which his excitement about what lay ahead was palpable: 'I am certain that should I have the good fortune to come through this operation, I will be in a position to send some good paintings to you.'[4] He wanted, he wrote, to 'produce paintings of the war and not preparations for it'. An assault in the summer night on a heavily defended concrete gun battery in occupied France lay ahead. Richards reflected both on his chances of surviving the attack and on how well he could portray the operation on canvas. His letter ended buoyantly: 'Tomorrow,' he wrote, 'I shall be in France. The beginning.'

There had been a weather-induced day's delay: wind and rain lashing the bell tents where the men slept. On the night of 5 June 1944, at RAF Broadwell near Burford, Oxfordshire, each man, in his cumbersome kit, seemed 'as broad and thick as he was tall'.[5] Richards' pockets were weighed down with a paratrooper's paraphernalia: 'drugs and bandages … maps and money and escaping gadgets'. Later, Albert Richards lumbered out to the aircraft that would transport them across the Channel, 'an olive-drab Dakota in the summer evening silence'.[6] He was not carrying the tools of his trade with him: oils and canvas, brushes and paper were left behind. Instead, he was struggling with his paratrooper's clutter, which included a flask of tea and a pack of jam sandwiches (to keep the air sickness at bay).

There was a bright moon over the Berkshire Downs. As the 200 men walked towards the waiting aircraft, other soldiers formed a corridor of honour, cheering and yelling encouragement. Their turn would come later in the morning of 6 June. 'At the airfield,' Richards said later, 'there was no joking. We all had too much on our minds. Our captain-quartermaster who had told us a thousand times that none of us would ever make real soldiers, broke down and wept.'[7] The commanding officer moved through the moonlight wishing his men a spirited 'Happy Landings'. In a matter of hours, the white blooms of parachutes – each individual 'rose of death'[8] – would be tumbling through the night sky, inland slightly from 'Sword' beach on the Normandy coast, near Caen, in what would be the very first moments of the liberation of France.

The Germans were anticipating an invasion, but further north in the Pas-de-Calais. Misguided they may have been about Allied intentions, but they were well dug in and without the need to transport a great army across the English Channel. The 6th Airborne Division's target, the coastal gun battery at Merville, was so positioned that if it remained intact, its guns could wreak havoc on the beaches when the troops struggled ashore from their landing craft. It was a critically important task: 'If the paratroopers … cowered behind hedgerows or hid out in barns rather than [seeking] out the enemy',[9] the invasion would fail.

They climbed on board the Dakotas: fifteen men on Richards' aircraft. Despite his apparent rank, he deferred to the corporal in charge. 'A privilege', Richards thought, aware that the corporal was a veteran of forty-five successful jumps. The aircraft lurched and trundled down the runway and the invasion had begun. The parachutists, and the artist, stared into the darkness, trying not to think about what might lie in store for each of them. The first Allied soldier to be killed by enemy fire that day was a parachutist from 6th Airborne Division.

★★★

Merville was on the coast, to the north-east of Caen. Back in April, the newly promoted Lieutenant Colonel Terence Otway was 'told that the 9th's main D-Day task was a "Grade A stinker of a job"'.[10] He had been driven to the Divisional Intelligence HQ and locked upstairs in a room whose walls were a collage of maps and photographs. On a table in the centre of the room was a model of the Merville Battery, looking ominously impenetrable. Otway rehearsed the attack with his men on Walbury Hill, near Newbury, from the middle of May onwards. With 48 hours to go before the mission, he banned alcohol.

In the Dakotas, heading out across the Channel in vics of three, it was difficult to move. Cigarettes glowed red in the darkness. When the clouds opened for a while, the moonlight shone on the sea below. Just after midnight, Richards and the others began their preparations. The French coast was suddenly visible about 700 feet below and, as well as the line of white breaking waves, they could see bursts of flame from German guns. Suddenly, the red light in the Dakota turned green, and the paratroopers began to jump through the hatch, one after the other as quickly as possible. Captain Richards fell into the slipstream, his heart thumping furiously before it was calmed by the sudden silence. There followed the characteristic, tinny sound of the static lines clattering against the side of the aircraft. He pulled the parachute's toggle and above him, despite the darkness, he could see the globe of the canopy opening. The overriding impression as he fell through the night was of a furious and relentless storm of flak; it was as if the sky was alight. He continued to fall, swaying slightly in the wind, looking down at his own artificial bulk and beyond, to where the ground was coming up fast to meet him. It was the beginning he had imagined for many days past.

They landed in an area of marshy ground which added to the confusion of men trying to rendezvous in the darkness. Once untangled from his parachute, Richards edged forward cautiously, waiting for a sudden curtain of gunfire, alert to the dangers in the boggy terrain, and momentarily startled by the arrival of another glider 'wheeling silently above the objective like a gigantic hawk'. It came down 50 metres from the battery. There was a fierce fire-fight and then a series of desperate hand-to-hand struggles, to the accompaniment of exploding grenades. 'Things were so hot that Richards had to drop sketchbook and pencil and fight.'[11] It was all over in 15 minutes with prisoners taken and the Merville guns destroyed.

★★★

The fighting in the aftermath of D-Day was intense: at Le Plein, Albert Richards sketched earnestly as British paratroops, attacking a tree-shadowed

War artist and paratrooper, Captain
Albert Richards.

farm building, came under persistent sniper fire. He watched anxiously —
but kept drawing — as two men sheltered behind a wall, occasionally taking
a cautious look through a loophole where the stones had crumbled. Later,
that sketch safely done, Richards found himself on the road from St Aubin
to Benouville. This was the main supply route to the troops on the east side
of the River Orne. It was under constant heavy shell fire from the German
guns in and around Caen. Rumbling along the straight road, Richards
was thinking about his 'gallant airborne friends' — the losses on the raid on
Merville were the first time he had seen 'death in this crude form', and he
could not put the picture out of his mind.

His eye was caught by the sight of a soldier's broken body lying on the
ground, on his back amidst a confusion of debris. His eyes stared, open
but unblinking. Richards was acutely alive to the landscape through
which he was travelling. On both sides of the road, he could see damaged Horsa gliders, zebra stripes on wings and fuselage, lying broken and
twisted on the ground. The wings were still largely intact, but the main-
frames were shattered; one wing was twisted as far back as the glider's
tail. In the borrowed jeep's rear-view mirror he could see plumes of
black smoke filling the sky. Little colour, he thought, mostly black, no
people, confusion all round.

Momentarily he smiled at the irony of the rubble strewed around, since that was the very thing that was needed to repair the damage caused by the wear and tear on the roads from tanks and armoured vehicles. The whole of the beachhead was a vast car park, after all. He had recently sketched men crushing iron ore near the Colombelles Factory. As ever, the figures were dwarfed by the surroundings: men at work on a mound of red rock in a bleak yard, while a conveyor system turned and turned. This was close to the heart of Richards' subject matter – looming skies, thundering transport, rubble and dirt, men dwarfed by the war itself.

For days on end, Richards sketched in Caen, before returning to camp in the evenings to work up his drawings. There was much for a war artist to draw: Caen was at the sharp end of the invasion. The bombing was relentless: 'some 800 people died in Caen as a result of the bombing and naval bombardments of the first two days.'[12] Its population over this period fell from 60,000 to 17,000. When Anthony Gross passed through the city in mid-July he 'was appalled by the scale of destruction and by the flies and stench of dead bodies beneath the ruins.'[13] Richards worked at speed, recording the coils of barbed wire, dusty rubble, the beleaguered Hotel de Ville with its yellow walls and blue roof surrounded by shell-holes and wire, a solitary tree the only thing left untouched beneath an ominous, troubled sky. That drawn, Richards turned his attention to the rooftops and spires of the town, which he saw as cowering beneath the onslaught. Ten miles north of Caen, at La Délivrande, he halted at a farm which had been turned into a military camp. There were army trucks in the farmyard, while the sky bloomed with smoke and fire.

Those who met Albert Richards at this time remembered him vividly: early in the invasion he 'had worked hard alongside the medics, collecting wounded and also the bodies of the dead.'[14] Lieutenant Henry Thompson of the Army Film and Photographic Unit thought Richards a 'tremendous enthusiast' and taught him to drive a jeep – the artist had been much exercised by his inability to drive. Soon after, Thompson recalled, he 'took off with his jeep and we never saw him again'.[15] Lieutenant Alan Jefferson, who shared rooms with him in camp, thought him an 'extraordinary man'. Anthony Gross met him briefly at this time too and recalled 'a nice young chap' who was 'a good young artist'. Geoffrey Keating described Richards in a letter to Edward Ardizzone on 30 November 1944, describing his boyishness and undoubted talent.

As that summer of 1944 passed, Richards slowly moved north through France. During the advance, he maintained his prodigious output: his eye entranced by what the war did to people and landscape. He looked out from his jeep as he headed north, slowly passing four burnt-out oil tankers abandoned in the woods. He noted their rust-red decay, the gaunt, charred trees, with a sombre green patch of woodland in the background. At Rouen, he drove over the Marmalade Bridge crossing the Seine. It had come under heavy attack by RAF Mosquitoes on D-Day and had slowly subsided to river level. He watched a strange cavalcade making its contorted way over the twisted metal: a man with a handcart, a lone cyclist, then grinding army transports, tyres wet from the river water. Overhead the girders were skewed, fragile now, on the verge of collapse.

He drove on, past more fire-blackened trucks in the forest; wrecked gliders; a boy on a ladder stretching to tie a French flag to a line of iron railings; two young women swinging their legs from an upstairs window looking down on the street; dead horses; upturned vehicles; ambulances alongside a walled garden that retained the air of a sanctuary; bridges snapped in the middle and forlornly dangling in the water; coils of wire; and everywhere, the dust of broken masonry. Just once, he indulged himself: drawing a full-length seated nude wearing a headscarf, not a hint of the war anywhere.

Briefly he went back to England before returning via a stormy Channel crossing. He wrote to the secretary of the WAAC: 'At present I'm on my way back to France. I shall spend a couple of weeks finishing off the work with the "Airborne", then I am following up the land-forces'.[16] He was anxious about his work, aware that circumstances had required haste: 'I was in a rather dazed condition when I painted them.' This, despite the fact that he could see the power of the material. 'I have always felt that if the subject was good enough, it would still be as fresh months after seeing it.' He told Gregory at the WAAC that he was thinking of coming back to England again 'with the wounded on the cross-channel planes'. The French summer was glorious and he was able to keep working until 11.00 p.m. at night, on beautiful evenings with the 'countryside bathed in soft hues of pink and blue'. He was pleased that Tom Hennell, 'who lives in the same house as myself, has returned here safely from England' – and he hoped that the committee would extend his six-month contract …

With winter on its way, Richards left France behind. He spent time in the Ardennes with his old comrades from the 6th Airborne Division. In the company of Ian Struthers from Paramount News, he visited Bande, where evidence was emerging of the Germans having murdered thirty-four villagers. He 'made notes on the bodies and the scene of the bodies being put into the coffins'. It was slow progress towards the German border and Holland, in particular, was bitterly cold: one drawing he labelled 'The land of central heating with one pound of coal per person per week'. He drew collaborators, more ruins, German prisoners in a bombed sports stadium, its roof torn away. At Geleen, he stood and watched a group of men from the 52nd (Lowland) Division watching a flamethrower belch fire, shocked at the vast stab of flame amidst a bleak thicket of trees, the fires elsewhere in the distance and a sky the colour of blood. Near Tilburg, he drew an 88mm gun rendered harmless outside a bomb-damaged farmhouse, its roof gone, surrounded by bare trees. It was the family in the foreground looking at the ruin that he could not erase from his memory.

16

Foxholes and Calvados

Edward Ardizzone landed in Normandy on 12 June 1944, getting his feet wet in the process; then dallied on the beach, sketching 'barbed wire, prisoners ... dumps, vehicles and marching men', all to an accompaniment of thunderous gunfire. A Scottish officer abruptly demanded: 'What are you doing there?' and imperiously pointed him to a slit trench in the sand.[1] It had no supports and so he spent that first night on French soil in a foxhole which was 'very deep and cold as the grave', and which finally caved on him when a bomb fell nearby.[2] Throughout the night he felt dribbles of wet sand on his face and neck. The next morning he walked along the beach and explored the nearby village; he even tried to catch up on lost sleep by having an afternoon nap in a grove of trees, but rolling gunfire kept him awake. The weather was gloomy: flurries of rain, scudding clouds, not at all the holiday France of golden summers. He caught the greyness on the page in a series of sketches of muddled beaches: churned sand, gaping craters, wind-whipped flags, olive-green trucks, and shifting dunes.

Three days later on the 15th he passed through La Délivrande, but missed seeing Albert Richards at work with his sketchbook. The next day, however, he did bump into another war artist. It was a cold, wet Friday: '[Tom] Hennel [sic] turns up and lunches with us. Seems very excited and wants to stay in France beyond his contract.'[3] Ted noted the 'string in his shoulder straps, his shy manner and moral courage'. By now Ardizzone was a grizzled old hand, with four years' experience of the war, and he watched Hennell's boyish enthusiasm – that latecomer's anxiety to catch up on what had been missed – with an avuncular eye.

The weather improved in the afternoon and Ardizzone sat in the sun, jotting notes and sketching, reasonably content. At night, though, there was a lot of activity in the air, much of it low and directly overhead, and that meant more disturbed sleep. It was to be, however, a brief posting to France. It was all rather bloody, the return home. It began with a grumpy confrontation with a cantankerous Highland Division colonel who sent the war artist packing with a flea in his ear when he was trying to arrange a crossing. Ted was not impressed: they were, he thought, a 'rude lot of bastards'.[4] Worse, when he sailed for England on the 18th on the coaster *Ability*, he had to climb aboard by rope-net, not something which men with a comfortable girth and of a certain age should have to suffer. Once on the coaster's deck, puffing and cursing, he settled down to enjoy the captain's hospitality: private cabin, cigarettes, a long bath and several warming whiskies. It would be August before he left the country for the war again, for a return to Italy.

Anthony Gross, like Albert Richards, hit the Normandy beaches on D-Day itself. He had spent the months leading up to the invasion in various locations in East Anglia, shivering through one 'of the coldest winters of my life', billeted in large, rambling country houses which had been stripped of carpets and curtains, with icy winds blowing through the cracks in the window frames and army boots echoing on the wooden floors. The day before D-Day he had been disconcerted to see a tank intended for the invasion beaches out of action because of the bird's nest on it. The crossing on a landing craft was rough – the gusty tail-end of that summer storm which had threatened the invasion's timing. Sailing past the Needles, Gross looked round awestruck at the thousands of ships all heading for France. He spent the morning sketching the men scrambling ashore; he drew a grey wash of sky; ant-like figures scurrying through colourless sand; festoons of coiled wire; and an ominous sign proclaiming the widespread threat of mines.

For two hours or so, Gross's boat beat up and down the coast, too far away for him to draw the detail of the action. Then, at 2.00 p.m., he jumped ashore at Arromanches, having watched two unpopular sergeants leap in too soon and drown in deep water. Gross waded ashore with his watercolours and paper held high over his head away from the sea water. He began drawing soon after; preoccupied with that, and what he would

Barnett Freedman at work in his
makeshift studio in Normandy, 1944.
(Imperial War Museum, A 24517).

eat (eggs bought from an entrepreneurial farmer; 'frightful American
sardines'; vegetables), and where he might be able to bed down for the
night. He had to dig his own trench. He was deeply moved to be back on
French soil. Later, on 24 July, he wrote to the committee: 'I had a fairly
peaceful landing even though it was distinctly wet ... [I spent] the first
evening in a grand Normandy farm with walls built in grey like a castle
and of similar dimensions. We knocked back glasses of cider and calvados
"à la Victoire"... and rolled over sound asleep.'[5] The effort of carrying his
heavy pack and drawing materials, coupled with the celebratory toasts to
victory, were the guarantees of a good night's sleep.

Richards, Ardizzone, Gross – they all savoured those early days of
invasion, when the Channel was thronged with ships, exiled Frenchmen
returned and kissed the earth, tricolours fluttered in the stiff west wind,
and troops and transports lumbered and lurched away from the choked
beaches. Barnett Freedman, however, missed the invasion, having been
taken ill and hospitalised. Edward Bawden missed it too, holed up in distant Baghdad, a city steamy with heat and thick with mosquitoes. As the
Allies laboriously broke clear from the Normandy beachhead, he was
revisiting the Marsh Arabs of the Euphrates with Richard Wyndham,

a journalist with the *News of the World*. He felt far from home again, as he had before when he met Gross in Cairo: '[We] agreed that artists like them have the worst sort of job in wartime being quite rootless, lonely, never settled for long enough to make friends, and with no one interested in what they were doing.'[6]

For his part, Ardizzone was in Europe, but aboard a ship bound for the Mediterranean. It was 'all rather a bore,' he wrote to his daughter Christianna at the end of August 1944. There were 'hordes of officers on board [and] … not enough chairs to go round'. At one point, 'a Salvation Army lass (rather long in the tooth) who is looking hard at my letter' provoked him into drawing 'her face and see what she makes of it – no response – she looks on calmly and steadily without batting an eyelid.'[7] He reached Naples on 4 September and then headed north for Rome, arriving on the 7th.

★★★

In August 1944 Edward Bawden was summoned back to England by the War Artists' Committee. A telegram announced that his 'commission terminates 11th August'; he was instructed to 'return here with a view to reemployment nearer home'. Around the committee room table there had been some doubts. There were concerns as to the military relevance of some of his work and there was a view that he should be working closer to the centre of the action. His keenly anticipated trip to China would now never happen. Instead of such grandiose plans he was now being pestered about his sketching umbrella: 'I have also been asked by our Finance Department to enquire what has happened to the sketching umbrella and ground stick which was loaned to you.' (He returned it on 16 October 1944.)[8] He liked Iraq, its 'sand and palm trees, turtles, terrapins and watersnakes, lizards and geckos', but his time in 'shoddy, drab old Baghdad' – a city of which he had grown fond – was soon to be over.[9] The call from London came and, disgruntled, he flew back via Gibraltar. He was soon in Southampton. After the heat of the Middle East he found himself faced with an English autumn; the chill of austerity was almost palpable.

Worse than the cool greyness of a country exhausted by war was the sudden war artist's block which loomed up unexpectedly: what on earth to draw? It was a strange feeling for a prolific artist after five years of war. In Baghdad, or Persia, or in the desert, he had never seemed short of subject matter. Now, in this drab world where sunlight too seemed rationed, he struggled – what to draw here, for God's sake! He was staying in a Merchant Seamens' Hostel. He wrote to Ted describing the room: 'My bed and bible was bequeathed by Miss Peck, the late Miss Peck of the Richmond and Twickenham Ladies Guild, in perpetuity for sea-faring and bible-reading mariners. The memorial plaque over my head, together with a framed copy of the Lord's Prayer is, with the exception of a mirror, the only things of an ornamental nature on the hot chocolate-painted walls.'[10]

Gloomily he watched lines of the wounded being stretchered off the boats from France; turned a jaundiced eye to the tall cranes leaning over the holds of rusty ships and the oil-tinged stretch of Southampton Water. Not for me; he shook his head. Frankly, I would rather be anywhere but here. By 12 October he had made a decision: 'I have decided to return to London tomorrow … I have felt no enthusiasm for boats which come in one day and are gone the next … the confusion, large scale and rapid movement cause a feeling of distress, anyway the important thing is lacking – that something which ought to touch the imagination.'[11] He felt ashamed, recognising a kind of defeat.

By the middle of November Bawden had joined Ardizzone in Italy. It had been a glum autumn: toothache, influenza (or was it another bout of malaria?) and anxiety over 'the awful mess' of his income tax which had him 'entangled like a kitten with a ball of wool'.[12] He 'had two nights and one day of memorable awfulness' in Naples and reached Rome by 18 November, although his kit was still somewhere in transit from Baghdad. It left him feeling stranded: 'without a bed or mackintosh exploration must be of a limited nature.' As ever, transport was a problem. He was keen for Ted to visit him, mixing compliment with exhortation: 'I have never found yr. good nature at fault; don't disappoint me.' He confessed to feeling 'lousy' and drew Ted a map of where to find his 'palazzo … 10 minutes from the British Embassy'.[13]

Bawden's 'lousiness' turned into something more serious. On Sunday 26 November Ardizzone visited him at the 48th General Hospital. Ted 'thought he looked wretchedly ill'. It was more than four long years since Bawden had been required to minister to his lumbago-plagued friend in that damp attic room in Arras, before the collapse of France. Now, the roles were reversed: Ted was startled by Bawden's evident ill-health. The illness, however, didn't stop him enjoying lengthy three-bottle lunches with Ardizzone and the war artist William Coldstream.[14] Bawden led sight-seeing expeditions: 'Guiding Ted is like persuading a large bluebottle to take a certain course across a window pane … he sometimes gives a wild stare, pulls himself up with a start. Stares again in a defiant manner and declares that he doesn't really like it.'[15] He had Ted to thank, however, for learning to work from memory and the notes that he had made – the method that Ardizzone had confidently relied on from the start.

The two men saw much of each other in this period: lunches were shared, bottles of port too. Bawden wrote again on 8 December from Cesena, following a 14-hour journey across Italy which was 'hellish'. It was made more diabolical by the loss of his sketching bag, which contained 'the drawing board and miscellaneous odds and ends, a tin mug, mess tin, razor strop, writing materials and free issue of cigarettes'. How it disappeared he could not imagine, but it left him anguished by the loss.[16]

Early in 1945, the two war artists met for lunch in Ravenna. Ted took 'a look at his work, good – fills me with gloom about my own'. For his part, Bawden commented that Ardizzone resembled a country clergyman. Ted felt isolated in Italy: 'marooned in this bloody place while fantastic things [are] going on elsewhere'. It made work difficult through that Italian winter and he was delighted when he was told to leave for France. It was 30 March 1945.

Bawden (far left) in Rome, with, amongst others, the artist John Aldridge.

17

The Last Winter of the War

It was a vertiginous spot, perched on the terracotta tiles of a building high above the square – the Piazza Garibaldi – in Ravenna. There was a brilliant blue sky, although in the far distance there seemed to be snow in the clouds over the mountains. The altitude added to the wintry feel of the eyrie where the artist had placed himself. Bawden found the vertigo easier to manage than the cold. The figures in the square below were dwarfed by the square's municipal splendour. He leaned warily over the parapet. The sun might be bright but it was low in the sky and the square was already largely in shadow; it fell across the statue of a mounted Garibaldi whose white stone was thrown into relief by the pale yellow of the building behind, on the other side of the square, with its high windows under curved arches.

Soft colours, Bawden thought, trying hard to memorise the scene: sorry Ted, I hear what you say, but this is not a spot to make notes, he thought, and a momentary smile faded as he slipped slightly on the tiled roof. It would not help the dignity of the ceremony to have it disturbed by a tumbling Englishman. What else to see? Lines of partisans (those red bandannas and pea-green uniforms!) A VIP party sporting a British general. Townsfolk, liberated and chattering like sparrows. A military band, now still after an upbeat entrance to the piazza. Yes, Bawden thought, I can paint this.

★★★

It was another harsh winter, that winter of 1944 – deep snow in the Apennines – and a sense of an ending that was taking too long to arrive. The bitter cold made work difficult. Ardizzone found that his 'shaving brush and face flannel were solid blocks of ice most mornings.' Bawden wrote to the committee in London: 'All the drawings you will receive have been done with cold fingers. Sometimes … I pee'd into my cold enamelled mug & then cupped my hands around it to try & receive back some of the heat I had lost.'[1] It had amused him that Tom Hennell had 'painted an especially lovely sky in Iceland with his own water'. The more jaundiced committee members will have looked at the fog and frost of London, far removed from an imagined Italian sun and frowned … did Bawden protest too much?

It was undeniably cold. Bawden could only work by adopting a steady routine of one hour's work followed by an hour's brisk walking. He slept fully dressed. There were fleeting moments of celebration: the party to hail the advent of 1945, when Ardizzone 'bobbed' like a 'Rural Dean', and the pleasure of the best Christmas for six years. But it was more often a treadmill of journeying. An exception was a nostalgic trip to Florence. 'Florence has been lovely these past two days, sunny and warm and full of charm – but then, I've had a nostalgic hangover for Florence since I saw it first during my impressionable years.'[2] The norm, however, during these last months of the war was for the most part a succession of bug-infested rooms (Coldstream and he were obliged to sleep on the floor);[3] grime-coated baths in dingy hotels; and reminders of what the war had done to Europe. The worst such reminder was the heart-rending sight of thousands of Italians slave-workers shivering in their striped pyjamas; they were thin and broken, bewildered and cold, bemused by their release from German concentration camps.

As the war ended, Bawden went to Greece – he had been keen to get to Yugoslavia – but he had long since had enough of travelling 'and the waste of time it entails'. He wanted 'to get home and get some work done – work too of a peacetime character'. He told his wife that he never wanted to travel again once the war was over. The war seemed to have exhausted everybody, making them quick to take offence. A Mrs Ruthven-Murray in the Balkans Section of the Foreign Office wrote a sharply worded minute about Bawden's perception of the conditions in Yugoslavia: 'Evidently Bawden's open ear was too ready to receive the mischievous tattle of knaves and fools which his open mind should have rejected.' She liked his work, she wrote, but seemed unforgiving nonetheless: 'If the War Artists Commission should ever turn into a Peace Artists Commission I should like to get Graham Sutherland to the Balkans. At least he has no illusions about "the band of ferocious brigands".'[4]

Edward Bawden reached the UK in July 1945, arriving by sea. On 27 July he wrote, 'I landed at Liverpool on Monday, an auspicious occasion as a taxi man told me it was the first fine day for a month. I would not doubt his word as it has been raining ever since'. Welcome home. You survived.

★★★

Bawden's friendship with Tom Hennell went back fifteen years – they first met in the Great Bardfield kitchen, with Eric Ravilious, one early morning. In September 1944, Bawden wrote to Ardizzone from Southampton, pleased that Hennell and Ardizzone had become acquainted. Bawden thought very highly of Hennell: 'he is an extraordinary man; the only person who gives me a feeling that he has a wonderful genius. He is a scholar, poet, painter and writer. His watercolours done in Iceland are incomparably the best items on show at Trafalgar Square – they are in the great English tradition, just as your own work is, my dear. He is of course exceptionally spartan, and thinks no more of physical discomfort than a polar bear.'[5]

★★★

Tom Hennell's fingers throbbed with the cold as he watched the fishermen on the quay lifting boxes of fish. Which was tougher, trying to hold a pencil in this icy climate, or lug a crate of herring? He smiled grimly at the thought and the way the arctic chill made the fishermen, anonymous in their shapeless oilskins, lean forward into a non-existent wind. He began to sketch the first figure as he walked in front of the trawler. Diminutive figure dwarfed by the boat's bulk: yes, like that. Hennell wanted the sketch to capture that brittle, painful cold and the sharp smell of fish and diesel. Oh, and then there was that vast and lovely sky! He noted the variations of colour, the way it somehow signalled that the weather would change sooner than you would want. Pools of frozen oily water glinted in the sun. A small boy was sitting alongside him on a wall, staring fixedly at Hennell's drawing as it all too slowly took shape. Mountains behind the trawler, Hennell thought, tawny slopes like animal skin. That must be snow on that high, north-facing slope. Just … there. The small boy said nothing at all, just watched, and the artist was too absorbed to want to throw a question or a smile in his direction. Better simply to savour the moment: this sea, those hills, this window of peace in wartime.

★★★

Twelve months after Ravilious had been reported missing, Tom Hennell found himself in Iceland as Eric's replacement. He had been offered a commission for three months on 21 June 1943 'to record aspects of the war in Iceland'. There was a brief delay before taking up the post 'owing to certain Security reasons', but by the middle of August he was in the Island Hotel, Reykjavik.[6] The climate was challenging: he was snow-bound in Akureyri for twelve days in October ('we had blizzards and Arctic effects'). The air was thick with dust and grit, while the glaring light hurt his eyes. It was not to be a long posting, however; he returned to the UK at the end of November, disconcerted when all his Iceland paintings were confiscated on arrival at Leith. They reached the Admiralty and the WAAC later, after the harbour officials had had their brief moment of power. Clark was very excited by Hennell's paintings of Iceland, despite

Lieutenant T. Hennell in RNVR uniform.

their not being overtly warlike.[7] He went home to Kent; was frustrated by bad weather on Tyneside, where he had travelled to paint fishing boats. At one point, he travelled from Yorkshire to Stamford down the A1 by lorry, to give a 'lantern lecture' at Kingswood School, Uppingham. The weather, at the end of February, was grim – 'NE gales for most of last week' – and heavy snow made cycling 'almost impracticable'.[8]

In March 1944, he was in Grimsby, another place that Ravilious had been before him. He was more positive about the town, or at least its subject matter: 'I have been here since Tuesday last and find good material to draw. Grimsby docks are rich in subjects, really grand timber vessels being built with adze and caulking hammers.'[9] He happily drew trawlers unloading: it was warmer than Reykjavik, after all! The fierce winds, smell and the horrors of the Royal Hotel which had so troubled Eric Ravilious did not seem to bother him. The following month he received a further three-month commission with the same fee of £162 10s.

In May there was the prospect of a posting to Malta. Spring in the Mediterranean – nice! But it wasn't to be. Instead, Portsmouth. On 29 May he began a three-month commission as an honorary lieutenant in the RNVR, attached to the Press Division, Admiralty. 'Ardizzone is here,' he wrote in a letter to Kenneth Clark, 'and finds subjects ready for him, but to me it is a vast, intensely complicated scene – lovely in form, light and colour.' He felt 'clumsy, feeble and inept'.[10] It was the D-Day preparations that they were drawing. Hennell reached Normandy on 11 June, the day before Ardizzone, and D+5. It was five days too late, Hennell thought. On the 15th, he wrote, 'My main subjects are to be found along the beaches: they are splendid and varied, but alas! Why didn't they let us come on D Day? The doors have opened and shut and we are still in the ante-room.'

There was no problem now in identifying what to draw. There were 'fine subjects,' he thought, throughout Normandy: 'inland camps under orchards and villages with grand Norman buildings almost unscathed.' He drew 'seaside villas' which 'make rather deplorable undignified wrecks'. He was disturbed by the outcome of a massive air raid on Caen: 'We saw the great air attack … two nights ago from a point near the coast … when it was dusk we saw a red glow: but the bombing produced a dust storm that darkened and obscured everything.'[11] Two weeks later he began sharing a small house with Albert Richards, who 'secludes himself daily in intense concentration.' Hennell was provided with a bicycle by

Thomas Hennell painting in the ruins of Caen.

his commanding officer, and some high-quality watercolour paper, and pedalled eagerly through the French countryside, eyes bright with the glory of French summer, at least where it wasn't scarred by the war.

Back in London, the final secretary of the WAAC, E.C. Gregory, liked his pictures: 'You are basking in glory,' he wrote on 15 July. 'I am interested to hear you are sharing quarters with Richards: give him my love.'[12] Hennell's work made Gregory 'long for Normandy again'.[13] Gregory evidently had fond memories of long lunches in the shade of apple orchards, sun glistening on glasses of cider, and ripe cheeses spreading across a plate. Such warm nostalgia perhaps lay behind his reassuring advice to Hennell: 'We must leave you to choose the subjects you find most suitable in France … use your discretion as an artist.' The artist needed little encouragement to follow his instincts about subject matter. He sought to set Gregory right about Norman cheese and cider: 'Normandy cheese is OK – cider is poor quality and in short supply.' He travelled back to Kent at the end of July, working up a series of his French sketches, but he was keen to return as soon as possible. By the end of August he had returned to Normandy. On the 24th he wrote: 'I go to join Richards today … We have suffered from mosquitoes and stomach ache but are still happy and well.'

Like Richards – and the invading armies – he slowly headed north and east as the autumn approached. He drew German prisoners of war, killing time behind wire; ominous and gloomy missile launching sites; and war-torn landscapes, often towns reduced to rubble as the war raged around and through them. His commission was extended by a further three months and he left the Canadian unit he had been with to re-join the navy. Working in a Europe on the move did not get easier. On 15 November he wrote to Gregory: 'I write to you in trouble for I find my work completely obstructed. One of the other war artists who was here had produced a SHAEF pass signed "By Command of General Eisenhower"… and nothing less will now satisfy them [the Security Police]'. At the end of the year, he heard that he would be posted to the RAF from 1 April; the letter ended with 'Every possible good wish for 1945'.[14]

In the event it was 31 January 1945 when he was appointed an Air Ministry Official war artist. However, as well as the difficulty with military bureaucracy, the weather had turned foul and his health was not good. At the end of February 1945 he went into the Naval Hospital, Chatham for a hernia operation. He was on sick leave until 13 April but the spring found him working intensively in Holland – crisp snow-scapes, army trucks, whitened windmills, clean light. Four days after the war in Europe ended he set off for South East Asia. The trip was preceded by a visit home. His friend, the artist Vincent Lines, watched him stride off. 'My last impression was of his tall striking figure in naval uniform, folio under his arm, making his way down the Victoria platform to catch the train for his native Kent.' On a spring day in a London railway station, with the war in Europe over and people's minds beginning to wonder when demobilisation might come, he did not look like a man walking into danger.

★★★

This was flat, dead country in the bleakest of winters. Albert Richards wrote to his parents in Wallasey that he was painting in watercolour because the cold made it impossible to squeeze oil from his tubes of paint. West of Eindhoven he shivered as he sketched a bare field in various shades of brown and black, sodden debris, emaciated trees, a lone tank. Between Heerlen and Aachen he stood overlooking the remains of the Siegfried line: ruins, shell holes, damaged pill-boxes. The Germans counterattacked at Meijel and columns of British troops marched below him along a country lane towards the front line, as he stood on a slight rise in this shapeless country. There was an ominous pall of fire and smoke in the sky. It all had a nightmare quality: once a horse reared up in the moonlight in a land surrounded by rubble. Winter tightened its grip: Richards' hands were frozen as he drew British transports crossing the flooded River Maas.

In February 1945 at the Forward Press Camp at Cuijk in Holland he met a South African war artist and correspondent, Barbara Loxton. She thought him shy and introverted, but he evidently took to her, driving her round in his jeep while she looked for subjects to sketch. By 19 February Richards was close to the German border: he and Barbara Loxton set out for Goch in the jeep and soon stopped at the ruined village of Asperden, close to the Siegfried Line. They came under heavy shellfire and were encouraged to take shelter in a cellar. Barbara Loxton wrote in a letter to her parents about the sanctuary provided by the crowded cellar, 'amongst the men jammed tight in it, while the shells positively rained down, and the walls shook and the lamp flickered. Maybe I exaggerate but not very much. I admit I was deeply shaken, not to say frightened, and wondered how in heaven's name I was ever going to get away. Albert was worried about the jeep, but nothing hit it fortunately. I remember that he didn't like the shelling, and winced when they fell. In the cellar the men joked and discussed football, and I drew a bit, not showing any fright.'[15]

With spring in the air the battleground became a flooded landscape, with warfare requiring a kind of island hopping. The drive into Germany was in bottom gear. The muddy roads held things up and made the artist impatient. 'I'm not very good at waiting in traffic hold-ups which I suppose are inevitable, and I've developed the bad habit of trying to find a new road.' To Richards' regret, he kept failing to make contact with Tom Hennell. Spring it may have been, but the fighting had a bitter, wintry feel to it: 'To me, the fighting seems to be the hardest we have met in this war. Perhaps it is the end.'[16]

He was right. One spring day in 1945, Anthony Gross met a group of engineers sitting by the roadside. They were in charge of a minefield. To Gross's dismay they had been witnesses to Albert Richards' final, impatient search for an alternative route. At nightfall Richards had driven up in his jeep. He had stopped, leaned out of the window, smiled.

'In the cellar the men joked and discussed football, and I drew a bit, not showing any fright.'
The picture by 'paintbrush reporter' Barbara Loxton of the cellar where she and Albert
Richards sheltered from German shelling, February 1945.

There was a brief exchange of conversation – cup of char? Any sign
of Jerry? All clear ahead? – and then Richards revved his jeep, keen to
move on. 'Good night!' he said, letting the handbrake off. He heard a
concerned 'Be careful!' as he drove off, before leaning out of the window.
'I'll be all right,' he shouted.

The explosion followed soon after as the artist's jeep struck a mine. It
was 5 March 1945. The engineers, in wintry darkness, could do nothing
to help. They could hear the artist moaning in pain through the night,
reminding each of them how, in wartime, the line between life and death
was desperately thin.[17]

Richards died a slow death, alone and lost. Some days later Edward
Ardizzone wrote home to his wife Catherine: 'I hear that poor Albert
Richards … has been killed. I go to take his place.'

★★★

It was a glorious day for flying – for being alive – blue sky and sea; white-capped mountains below them on the flight from Rome to Marseilles; artists' light up the Rhône valley. Ted Ardizzone reached Paris at 6.30 in the evening of 5 April 1945, his aircraft descending through a blanket of north-European grey cloud. For all that, the cherry trees in the French capital were in blossom and the bars were full of American troops, pinching themselves that they were alive, and in Paris in the spring. Ardizzone though was too tired to enjoy it – constant travelling had taken its toll. Rome and Paris on the 5th, then Brussels the following day. He finally reached Main Army Group on Saturday 7 April. He exchanged an Avro Anson for a jeep the next day, setting out to the sound of church bells, and driving through flat, green countryside and cascades of white blossom. They drove for 8 hours, crossing the Rhine by pontoon bridge. The day ended with a game of poker.

The next day he was given a revolver for his own protection. It was unwelcome – 'the bane of my life,' he thought, unsettled by the feeling of acute self-consciousness it induced. With Geoffrey Keating and a group of correspondents he set out for Bremen. En route he noted the profusion of white flags in windows and the sullen faces of the defeated. On the 11th, he joined a tank crew and sat on the top, hanging on for dear life as the tank 'called *Hyperion*' ground its way east in convoy, through rolling pine woods, the long column sending up plumes of dust. He felt that he was 'regarded as an extra on the strength' and he certainly shared in the crew's discomfort, sleeping, or at least trying to sleep, under a makeshift tent, comprising a tarpaulin draped between gloomy, dripping trees and *Hyperion*.

The war might be in its closing phase, but Germany that spring was a disturbing place to be. To begin with, there was the extent of the damage caused by the Allied bombing. Ardizzone was appalled as they drove through towns which had been simply erased, flattened. The roads were crowded with the displaced, the lost, the homeless, the rapacious. It was all very unsettling. Later, Ardizzone would recall: 'The bloody Black Forest frightened the life out of me … You couldn't get out of your tank to do a pee because you'd probably be shot by some bloody boy behind a tree.'[18] Being Ardizzone, he faced each day with hope and tried as far as possible to balance the unpleasantness of the relentless advance east with lengthy lunches and damn good dinners. He invariably 'dined' rather than simply 'ate'; dinners were 'bibulous' (3 April);

'pleasant ... with Geoffrey' (9th); 'a bottle of champagne each' (14th); 'white table-cloth, glasses, claret and champagne' (22nd – when an air raid interrupted the meal); 'we drink Mouton d'Armailhac 24 ... from a jeroboam, a most delicious wine (24th – good choice for a 1924 wine); a party on the 25th – and so on.

Ardizzone, as ever, was splendidly defiant in making the best of things, but there were some grim moments still to come. On 15 April his tank was shot at by a German with a panzerfaust – 'Thank God he missed' – and, later that day, he found himself in the middle of a fire-fight. 'We seemed to be ringed with fires ... distant explosions as bridges are blown up ... mushrooms of smoke.' The next day, a Monday, they arrived at Stalag 257, a newly liberated PoW camp. They were the first British troops to arrive at the camp, with its 15,000 prisoners who were 'almost crazy with delight'; Ardizzone noticed however that some of them found it hard to tear themselves away from the 'protection' of the camp's wire. Old habits die hard, he thought. After four or five years of imprisonment, wouldn't you cling to what you knew? Hurriedly, he drew the barbed wire fence, the clusters of men, the low buildings, the coils of wire, scribbling notes on the paper – the colours all variations of grey. A few days later, he saw 'an extraordinary and moving sight. Burning buildings, cherry trees in blossom and black fir trees against early morning light.'

★★★

The road was narrow and shadowed by trees, so that although the day was sunny and the sky a bright blue, there was a distinct chill in the air. Beyond the bend in the road, there was sunlight, but not here. The jeep's driver had slowed, as if to savour the moment, and Ardizzone could readily turn to look back and begin to sketch. To one side, in the darkest shadow, there were two German soldiers, one wounded, doubled up in pain, while the other was curled up at his feet, somehow a picture of despair. On the other side of the road were a straggling double line of German troops, all pretence of soldiering gone – field-grey uniforms torn and bloodied; some men on crutches; several towing handcarts with forlorn collections of possessions; every man leaning forward as if into the most ferocious of winds. This was the mighty Wehrmacht reduced to the ragamuffin. Ardizzone finished the sketch, noted colours (thin green, a shabby grey, washed out yellow, a deep blue sky, a near black for the shadows). 'Okay, old chap, you can drive on. I've got enough.'

★★★

War Artists, 1945: The Governmental Magic Carpet

It is a slim book with a sand-coloured, drab cover, *War Through Artists' Eyes*, published by John Murray in austerity wartime paper and written, so the introduction said, as 'our armies are gathering along the frontiers of Germany'. At that point in time, early 1945, only one of us had died, although John Worsley remained a prisoner. One of the things we liked about the book was that it seemed to signal the imminent ending of the war – that we would soon be home, teaching again perhaps, or more importantly, free to paint what we liked whenever we liked. No more looking round for 'war subjects' and worrying if we were at risk of disappointing the committee by focusing on subject matter too far removed from 'recording the war'.

We are all in the book, along with a mix of other artists, some of them commissioned; some employed short-term to produce specific pictures; and the rest, what you might call amateurs, who had been serving in the forces and submitted work off their own bat. There are forty-two artists in the book altogether, an introduction by the well-respected art historian Eric Newton, and well over 100 images of wartime paintings – these somewhat marred by the fact that the colours are distorted, wartime austerity restricting the printers' best efforts to remain true to the originals. *War Through Artists' Eyes* was printed at the dear old Curwen Press in the East End of London. That seems fitting given the firm's longstanding, pre-war connections with Ardizzone, Bawden and Ravilious, amongst others. It was good to see German bombs hadn't silenced the printing machines.

So what did we contribute to the book, and more widely, to the collective picture of the war? Dizzy Ardizzone appears early in the book – we can imagine him smiling at the sight of the bumbling comic confusion of the Local Defence Volunteers (not yet Home Guard) under a soft English sky, or the leery troops in Salisbury cosily wrapped round plump girls, all hips and willingness. We get views of the war in Europe from him too: cookhouse fatigues and scruffy soldiers festooned in camouflage; children begging for biscuits in an Italian square, a white campanile towering over a jeep; exhausted soldiers lying by the roadside with trees casting shadows over their sprawled bodies.

Some paintings by Bawden are reproduced alongside the Ardizzones and the difference is stark: few if any figures, instead guns, thin trees and sunken ships in an alien landscape. Palaces and angled roofs under a brooding sky. When he does do figures they are small, dwarfed by the surroundings – a gym being used as a hospital, or the Sudan Defence Force marching in a maze of military buildings near Omdurman. Figures lost in a landscape of heat and dust. Bawden always felt that Ted 'should give [his] feeling for landscape more play', and followed that in a letter of February 1945 by wondering if that was 'an impertinent suggestion', recognising that 'you might retort that it would be better if I studied figures more carefully and troubled less with the landscape litter around them.' He would've made Ted smile with what followed: 'even our doodles reveal a basic divergence, your pen curls around skirts and breasts and bottoms whilst mine takes its recreation in formal geometric rectitude!' He was confident that Ted would agree about doing more large drawings since 'we agree as closely as twins who have come out of the same paint-box!'[19]

Anthony Gross' sketches illustrate detailed yet anonymous figures caught up in the battle of Arakan, for example; gunners buried in deep fronds of grass, pinpointing Japanese positions. There are two of his paintings, side by side: one of the arrival at Lofoten in Norway in 1940: snowbound wooden quay, lots of khaki in boats, and men beginning to climb up ladders to dry land; a sense of expectation and hope; and the aftermath, fires burning, sky heavy with snow, red Norwegian flags flying stiffly in a wind that casts a pall of smoke over the town. The British troops are leaving in an undignified hurry, crammed into landing craft, watched from the quayside by the townsfolk whose stillness contrasts with the whirl of confusion in the boat below.

There's a series of works by Ravilious: a submariner looking at a flying boat through a periscope; a submarine's ward room (men dozing, a sense of tight enclosure); broadsides from one aircraft carrier, and another in Arctic waters, cold blue sea, a wintry sun and a flurry of aircraft in a troubled sky. His Norway is even bleaker than Gross': snow, icy fjord, a sunken ship, heavy cloud, no sign of life. Other work includes ships heading out to sea, a Fairey Battle on a runway in a winter landscape, three flying boats on a Scottish loch.

Richard Seddon is there with one of his sketches from the time when he drove towards the Maginot Line in 1940, passing the detritus from the last war: corrugated iron, wire, rotting wooden fence-posts. There's a couple of works by John Worsley, a ship's crew in voluminous waterproofs watching smoke on the horizon intently through binoculars and two sailors off watch in hammocks slung from hooks.

Poignantly, there are three paintings by Albert Richards: two from his pre-paratroop days (a searchlight battery on the Mersey, and sappers building a hutted camp in Essex). The very last picture in the book is by him: he is in France; there is a barn burning, trees in full foliage, a wall with a breach in it, and two soldiers hugging the ground, all too conscious of the danger of enemy snipers. It is a fine painting which tells you much about what we lost when the mine exploded under Richards' jeep that March night, as the Allies edged into Germany.

The book is a narrow selection from thousands of images from six years of war. It makes you wonder where these paintings will end up – where will they hang? Will they, sixty years from now, end up in some forgotten gallery store gathering dust? Will anyone ever seek to replicate one of the National Gallery exhibitions, painting by painting? Or perhaps there might be an exhibition which comprised just the paintings from *War Through Artists' Eyes*. Better still, a representative selection from the artists of this story, carefully avoiding Ravilious' anxiety about his being over-represented. The Sketchbook War Exhibition would begin in the same rooms at the National Gallery, have a preview which the descendants of that first preview in 1940 would attend, and then it would travel the country, following the same itinerary as its predecessor, perhaps by slow goods train. There would be long queues outside and people would shake their heads at the range of work, the hardship – the 'tension and strain' as Eric Newton put it in the book's introduction – we all went through that in those hard times. It would pay a tribute to the years of our lives that we gave up, the sacrifice of losing control over our choice of subject matter, not to mention the privations, the loneliness, the exile. It would also be an appropriate remembrance of those who died.

For we survivors, though, we knew what rare opportunities we had gained, what learning. Tony Gross spoke for all of us when he wrote to the WAAC in 1946: he wanted to thank the committee and tell them 'how much [he] enjoyed working as a War Artist and what a terrific experience it was ... Seldom could an artist, tied down to his studio, to his habits, his regular haunts of landscapes and holidays imagine himself transported by a governmental magic carpet all over the world.'[20]

★★★

By 25 April Ted had reached the outskirts of Bremen. Not far away, John Worsley was sketching the vapour trails of aircraft in the skies above Marlag camp. Ardizzone found Bremen to be a desperate, dead place, ruins everywhere. The shops were being looted by Russians and other displaced men. He saw a Dutchman drunk and staggering in the street. An elderly German begged the British troops with Ardizzone to stop the looting and looked desperate when it was made clear that they couldn't do so. Hamburg on 4 May was even worse: 'Another dead city given over to tanks and guns. It must have been beautiful once with its canals and lakes. I hadn't the heart to draw it, beside ruins have been done so much.'[21]

With peace imminent, Ardizzone left Germany for Copenhagen. He spent the first day of peace (7 May) in the Danish capital enjoying a party which went on through the night. He drew a sketch of himself standing, arms aloft, on a table in some unremembered bar, with below him a scrum of glass-waving, bleary celebrants, heading for that first peacetime hangover. The war was over at last. On 15 May, he went to Belsen concentration camp, noting in his diary that the visit was 'fruitless ... Nothing to see there'. A month before, when the 11th Armoured Division arrived at the camp, they had been confronted by '60,000 emaciated, disease-ridden inmates, along with 10,000 unburied corpses.'[22] They soon burned the camp down to prevent the spread of typhus. Ardizzone saw little but charred remains.

Driving away, the oak and chestnut trees in full blossom helped to hold at bay the chill in his heart, and in a welcome diversion – a reminder of the comfort of ordinary life – he won £5 at poker that night. Seeing Tony Gross was an additional delight. Typically, Gross had pursued an independent line in the last period of the war: he had been in the Pyrenees with the *maquis* (according to Geoffrey Keating, he had acquired a vehicle from 30 Corps to 'swan around' in); been in Paris for the liberation; and he was present at Torgau on the River Elbe when, on 26 April 1945, the Russians and American forces met – Kenneth Clark described it as 'the barbarians from the East meeting the barbarians from the West.'²³

With the war in Europe conclusively over, the way was now clear for Ardizzone to resume his life: back to Brussels first, then Croydon Airport. It was 5.30 in the afternoon of 18 May 1945 when his flight touched down. Five years had passed since he had first set out for France, wondering then quite what it was that a war artist should be and do. Now, of course, he knew.

★★★

Behind the wire at Marlag, John Worsley waited for the end. He continued to teach drawing and painting to the other prisoners and read the aeroplane trails in the sky as evidence of how the war was progressing. The high-altitude lines of spreading white vapour, cotton wool in the distant blue, marked the path of heavy bombers. A Mosquito pilot flew over one day in a flurry of triumphant bravura, before departing with a final curtain-call – a fusillade of gunfire at a cart approaching the camp. It was the camp's bread cart and, in consequence, the prisoners went hungry for a week. Worsley was keen to do some drawings in Milag Nord where the merchant seamen were imprisoned. Condemned by the Red Cross 'as unfit and insanitary', it comprised 'the most derelict collection of huts I had ever set eyes on'.²⁴ It required a cunning plan for the war artist to gain access to the camp; not just cunning, painful – since he needed a convincing medical reason for the move. He opted for a circumcision.

Minor op over, and presumably walking with some caution and a limp, he began to draw a series of sketches which caught the 'free for all' nature of the place. It was a PoWs' Liberty Hall: 'there were huts in which to get a haircut and a shoe-shine, and huts which were sort-of pubs, and a hut which housed a [male] brothel. There was a considerable range of shops.'²⁵ Worsley drew the illicit alcohol stills; gambling dens; prisoners tending their imprisoned rabbits; a cricket match between the two camps; the would-be escaper, Lieutenant 'Blondie' Mewes, resignedly decorating a Christmas tree; and a morose party of PoWs filling in an escape tunnel with sand, while the guards stood by. A notice in English warned: 'DANGER! WARNING WIRE. There will be shooting without challenge.'

Then, suddenly, the routine of Marlag changed and the prisoners were marched out of the camp by their German guards. The intention was to march them 80 miles to the north, to Lübeck, the idea being to use the PoWs as bargaining counters when peace finally came. There was a brief moment when the prisoners could consider what to take with them. Worsley would always regret having to leave behind one of the paintings he had done on a hut ceiling board. The wise move, of course, was to travel light. He took some sketches curled up in canisters and began the long march.

They walked for two weeks, sleeping at night in fields and ditches and, once, in a pig sty. By day, they trudged north along muddy paths, the guards and their dogs sullenly shepherding the motley collection of limping prisoners burdened with their rucksacks, pushing prams, and, in Worsley's case, carrying rolled-up tubes of artwork. Prisoners deliberately dragged their heels to confound the guards, and both sides were constantly casting anxious glances at the sky. That was where the danger came from now: trigger-happy Allied pilots, hounding what they saw as the enemy, spreading confusion and fear. Six prisoners were killed by a Typhoon pilot who roared in despite the clearly visible White Ensign.

Eventually the prisoners were herded into a large military barracks near Lübeck, and even nearer to an anti-aircraft post. More waiting. Then on 2 May 1945, in a 20 minute flurry of action, it was all over: first, the flak post obliterated by RAF fighter-bombers, and then a wonderfully uplifting sight – a lone tank with a figure scanning the autobahn ahead through field glasses. It was the lead-out tank for the British 11th Armoured Division. The German soldiers simply put down their guns and walked away.

After a free man's tour of what was left of Lübeck – and a chance meeting with Anthony Gross – Worsley was taken home, flying in a Lancaster bomber, each of the twenty-five released PoWs taking it in turns to sit on the aircraft's bomb sight. When it started to rain John knew he was home; ah, England! They landed in the Midlands but there was no hero's welcome. Instead they were confronted by 'a battery of very formidable ladies in nurses' uniforms each armed with a can of anti-nit powder.' It was a cue for a visit to the pub. He 'had never imagined that beer could taste so good'.[26] Worsley was soon sent to Portsmouth where he was issued with a new Royal Navy battledress; the WAAC gave him a new six-month contract with a brief to paint a series of military VIPs.

One such commission took him back to Germany where he arrived at Montgomery's HQ at Schloss Ostenwalde in Hanover …

★★★

Worsley coughed and saluted, disconcerted by the whippet-like officer in front of him. 'I've, er, come to paint your portrait, sir.' The field marshal looked exasperated. 'Right, I can sit for you on Monday and Tuesday. On Wednesday one of my aides will substitute for me, wearing my uniform.' Fine, sir, I'll just get on with it, should I?

He painted Monty sitting on a patterned grey chesterfield, its reassuring domesticity contrasting with the field marshal's pent-up energy, as if he was itching to get away and give vent to the series of orders inside him. Once Worsley asked him if he had done any painting himself. 'Never had the time!' Montgomery snapped, as if all that was necessary for a war artist to draw the war was unfilled hours and an empty diary. Talent? Phooey! You don't know how lucky you chaps are. Some of us actually had to do some fighting in this war after all! With the picture done, Worsley stood back and looked critically at the canvas: he had caught Monty's sharp profile; that stiff posture; the sidelong look of disdain; the spartan, empty feel of the room. There was little colour other than a dull military green, just a gaudy splash of medal ribbons, and that quirky dash of yellow from the caged canary over the field marshal's right shoulder. At first, Worsley had thought the bird hinted at the soldier's hidden humanity. An aide of Montgomery's soon disillusioned him: 'No! He only keeps those to test for gas!' Yes, thought Worsley, the picture has that in it too. Job done.

18

The File Marked 'Hennell'

The ceiling fan whirred, disturbing the room's heavy, tropical heat. His hands stuck to the sheets of paper on the desk. Bloody London, they have no idea how chaotic the situation is out here. Just because the war is over! Outside the window he could hear shouts – you usually could – and although the sprinkler on the long lawn pulsed water in a soothing rhythm, and there was ice in the gin on the desk, he could not get his irritation under control. He opened the file marked 'Hennell'. Gaunt, nervy looking chap judging by the photograph. War artist? What's one of those for God's sake? What do they *do* all day?! Nice work if you can get it. He sighed, then slurped some consolatory gin. The trouble with London is they will want chapter and verse, and I hate knocking this sort of stuff into shape. It's one thing to write a letter of condolence; quite another to come up with a thorough, detailed account to satisfy a government committee. And the Air Ministry does seem surprisingly keen to get to the bottom of this odd business.

So what have I got? He picked up a pen and began to make notes on the file, underlining what could be trusted as fact. Here goes … Lieutenant Thomas Hennell flew out of the UK on 12 May 1945, no doubt thrilled to have survived the war. Pause for a wry smile. The file held a copy of a letter he had written the day he left. 'Today is my D-Day,' Hennell had written. An impatient shake of the head; he looked up from the desk and stared into the blue afternoon. Hmm. A month goes by. By June the fifteenth he's in Rangoon. According to the briefing note

from the WAAC, the artist had completed a picture of Mountbatten at
a Victory Parade in the city. Splendid topic! Ah, I see, stationed with an
RAF unit 15 miles outside Rangoon. Burma eh? I can remember some
other war artist complaining about damp, sticky Burma: 'mushrooms in
my boots … and my watercolours all coated with fungus'.¹ Yes, that's the
Burma I remember! It seems Hennell tried to get the war artist Frank
Wootton commissioned without luck, but he did succeed in getting his
painting umbrella sent out. A bloody painting umbrella, I ask you!

He read on … bout of lumbago, then two of amoebic dysentery; spell
in hospital; sent back seventeen pictures to London, neatly protected
by bamboo. What on earth did he paint? 'Magnificent stuff,' it says here.
Painting Indians building an airstrip in the jungle – magnificent? Oh
well. He was there with this other war artist Leslie Cole. *He* should be
interviewed clearly, if he hasn't been already. He scribbled a marginal
note, initialled it, and wrote a Churchillian 'Action This Day' beside it.
No one will take a blind bit of notice, he thought.

Good lord, this is a veritable Cook's Tour! The file held a copy of
Hennell's movement order to Ceylon: boat to Calcutta; then a sweaty,
protracted journey by rail to southern India. 'Sweltering and deadly'
– I'll bet it was! Then a boat to Colombo. When did he hear about the
bombs dropped on Hiroshima and Nagasaki, I wonder? Anyway, he was
on Ceylon for VJ Day. Somehow I don't imagine him indulging in wild
celebration, too earnest looking for that, too cerebral. Is that the word?
Anyway, he didn't stay long there either. Never keeps still, this chap. There's
a witness statement from a Group Captain Dodds who seems to have wangled a passage for him aboard the aircraft carrier HMS *Hunter*. He sailed
in her from Ceylon to Penang; then completed the journey to Singapore
by flying boat. He sent another fourteen paintings back to the UK from
Singapore in September. There's a receipt on file relating to that.

And this is where it all begins to have a sense of inevitability about
it. He picked up the copy of one of Hennell's letters and walked to the
window. The gardeners were busy, despite the heat, and far below he
could see two warships in the bay, grey war paint in a background of
deep green trees, white buildings and blue-green sea. The letter was to
the secretary of the WAAC: 'I am very fit and willing to go on as long as
the committee wishes.' Well, good for you – evidently a glutton for pun-
ishment. Ah, there's a reference to this Leslie Cole again … what does
it say? Ah, yes, he had lost some drawings, Cole that is, and our Hennell

was doing the decent thing. 'I have enough paper & materials to keep us both going for the time.'

Where next? Now this is where he comes here for the first time. Java, a flight over the Java Sea and he would surely have known that there was an element of risk. What sort of briefing did these chaps get? It might not be common knowledge in London, but here we're right in the middle of the Indonesian push for independence pitted against a Dutch refusal to accept any such thing. And so there are casualties caught in the middle, Mr Hennell. He will have felt a long way from home, not least because the mail was so uncertain. I empathise.

Anyway, he seeks instructions from London. 'What do you want me to do?' he asks. Return home via India? Or cover Borneo, Hong Kong and Tokyo and then come home via Australia, 'taking such opportunities for work as come my way?' Quite the intrepid traveller! 'I shan't try to send you any drawings at least till I get back to Singapore and if I return direct I shall carry them with me.' And that is the last London, or anyone, hears of him. Emphatically missing.

Damn it all! Where does that leave me? What can I say? There *is* evidence of a sort, but it's a mish-mash of witness statements, none of it definitive. We know he was in a requisitioned planter's house and that there was a crowd of 100 or more Indonesians outside the perimeter …

He reached for his glass of gin, frowning when he saw the ice had already melted.

★★★

Tom Hennell can hear the furious noise beyond the peace of the garden, even see faces pressed up against the perimeter wire. It is very hot, but neither that nor the noise can divert his attention away from the insects and the garden's lush planting. He sketches a few leaf shapes into his notebook, watches a large beetle scurry past his sandal, wipes beads of sweat from his forehead. The noise of the mob grows louder and he looks up to see the wire toppling, then being trampled underfoot and figures running towards him over the grass. Some of them are waving clubs. Too late, he looks around for help. There is no one, just figures looking down from an upstairs window. He hears gunfire and realises that someone on the first floor is firing over the heads of the rioters. 'Hennell, for God's sake!' a voice shouts and a Sten gun is dropped into the soft earth near his feet. 'Use the bloody thing!' He shakes his head, looks up and sees a man in uniform in an upstairs window, his arm in the final movement of throwing the gun. Hennell picks it up, but it is too late – not that he would have used it anyway. This war artist does not fight! Moments later, he is overwhelmed, kicked and punched, until a last blow knocks him unconscious. Rough hands pick him up, and carry him like a sacrifice out of the garden, through the shadows of high hedges and into the sun-blasted street. Later, he wakes, hears questions that he cannot understand or answer. Feels blood in his mouth, spits teeth on to the dusty floor, and finally understands what is to happen to him, as a bearded man with a gun walks slowly, irresistibly, towards him. So, this is how it will end …

★★★

Impossible to know really if that's the way it was, he thought. I can add the interview notes and witness statements as an appendix, but predictably they all conflict. So here goes with my letter to the Air Ministry…

> Dear Blackborow, Herewith my report on the disappearance and presumed death of Lieutenant Hennell. It follows extensive work over here and the cooperation of the local police…

A few weeks later, on 11 November 1945, the Air Ministry's A. Blackborow looked round the room where the WAAC was meeting. 'I have sad news,' he said. 'I have now received further news regarding Hennell, although there is, I am afraid, nothing definite. It appears that he was last seen on Monday, 5th November with a Sten gun in Surabaya Hotel where there was trouble with the Indonese. He became separated from the other members of the party and has not been since. This information was brought back by a War Correspondent who returned to Singapore last Thursday.' There was a moment's silence, heads bowed, and then the meeting resumed to deal with its unconscionably long agenda. It was left to Lord Willoughby de Broke to tell Hennell's mother: Tom was the second of her sons to die. Subsequently Leslie Cole wrote to the WAAC about the disappearance of his fellow war artist: 'The whole thing puzzles me because it's so out of character – Tom was unwarlike.'[2]

19

By Way of Goodbye

By the time of the WAAC's final meeting, on 28 December 1945, the National Gallery's Boardroom had a tired look about it, and so, in truth, did everyone around the table. It was an exhaustion shared by the nation. Admittedly, the Ministry of Works had redecorated the rooms where the war artist exhibitions had been held and Sir Kenneth Clark had been quick to ensure the return of some of the gallery's great masters in place of their temporary, uniformed replacements. There was, however, a grimly austere feel to this post-war world and change was in the air, symbolised by Churchill's shock defeat in the 1945 General Election. Clark, who had been Director of the National Gallery for thirteen turbulent years, was also facing the need to move on. He 'did not like institutions and would have been sorry to become one myself'.[1] When he finally offered his resignation, it was all too readily accepted. 'My successor, who had been appointed solely on my recommendation, refused to come and see me.' It was December 1945 when Clark was replaced by Philip Hendy.

When he looked back over the years of the committee's work, Clark would have dwelt on a series of vivid images, not least that first fortuitous after-lunch discussion in the Berkshire countryside in the first month of the war, when Betjeman, the Eshers and the Clarks had plotted how best to save the nation's artists. He thought often of the fears artists had had about a world where the art industry had dried up and prospects were confined to camouflage work at best, and a return to the fields of Flanders at worst. That was the starting point for the whole war artists scheme; in Clark's mind, it was very largely to prevent the nation's artists from being killed.

Then there were the people he had worked with: dear old Dickey, what a jewel! No one better at smoothing artists' feathers. He had great respect for O'R. Dickey who was an art lover and a painter in his own right. Thoroughly good chap – equable, indefatigable, very kind and supportive, admirable at meetings. Just what a chairman needed. He had worked with some first-rate men all in all. Coote of course: very intelligent, another lover of art. And the divine Lord Willoughby de Broke. Such a nice man, clever and witty. There were some of course who were less than perfect, Gleadowe for one! Clark was less than impressed with his contribution. The same with Dickey's first replacement, Arnold Palmer, whose family made biscuits, Clark recalled. He had taken over for a few months in 1942 and while he was charming, Clark thought, he was also fairly lazy.

His views about the artists were predictably strongly held; Clark knew what he liked. Ardizzone? 'Adorable man … jolly, wonderful and loved life. Loved food of course, loved food and drink. But he loved life in all its aspects.'[2] He thought it came out in Ardizzone's work. He was inordinately fond of dear Ted. Saw him constantly through the war years – when he wasn't off on his travels of course.

Antony Gross? 'Very good … adventurous. He liked travelling … Burma suited him perfectly.' He remembered the recent discussion around the table caused by the artist's request for a paraffin heater. He had been fretting about the cold weather towards the end of the war: 'It is essential for my work as in rainy and cold weather my watercolours will not dry on the paper.' Made a change from endless discussions about sketching umbrellas! But Gross was 'really awfully good. He gave a very lively record, a true record and a lively record.' And Paul Nash. Those objections to his work – 'Bad propaganda point to paint crashed aircraft!' Air Commodore Peake had said. Those RAF wallahs had never warmed to him. He remembered too the extended discussions about what a war artist should paint – one of them had said to him early on: 'We'd like to draw the war, but how the heck are we going to draw it?' He had always taken the view that the bombing was a bonus because it gave wonderful subjects.

He was less sure of Bawden: 'I found it very hard to employ him. Didn't know what to make him do … He may have had lots of enthusiasms but he concealed them … He wasn't keen on anything, you know.'

Sutherland? 'Wonderful'. About Ravilious he was more equivocal; the committee liked his work very much, and admired him greatly, but at the time Clark had question marks about his quality. Much later, reviewing the work, he thought 'they look very well'.

Many years after the war, Clark was asked about Albert Richards. 'I don't know what's happened to him,' he said. His interviewer told him he was killed at the end of the war. 'Oh, was he really?' Then he commented on the Liverpool artist's work: 'He was a discovery. Nobody had ever heard of him and the best of his work is awfully good I think and a lot of feeling too ... I'd forgotten he'd been killed ... I started this scheme very largely to prevent artists from being killed and I hadn't any success in that at all.' His voice betrayed a hint of regret for what might have been. What gave him some compensating comfort was his belief that whatever success the committee had had was because the bureaucrats had forgotten they had given permission for it to exist.

★★★

After the war an art sub-committee was formed, under the chairmanship of Muirhead Bone. It was given a small grant, available until 31 March 1946, to close the whole scheme down. Sir Kenneth Clark did not sit on that sub-committee, but he was chairman of another, responsible to the Treasury, and charged with the task of distributing the thousands of war artists' pictures. The Allocations Committee distinguished between artists' work which was deemed 'art' and that which was simply a 'record'; the former had more value and status. So far as the art was concerned, the Tate Gallery was accorded the greatest priority; the British Council was second in line, while the Imperial War Museum acquired both 'art' and 'record' works. For example, the IWM took 337 works by Anthony Gross under its wing. Claims were made for the works more widely and pictures were distributed to galleries, regiments, embassies, libraries and town halls. Some went abroad, from Sudan to New Zealand. The work of the Allocations Committee was approved by parliament on 25 March 1947 and distribution began of the 5,570 works 'accumulated by the WAAC at an estimated cost to the nation of £96,000'.[3]

The war took six long years out of the war artists' lives. For those born early in the century, it took away that period in their thirties when a career is often shaped and set in stone. Ted Ardizzone, for example, was thirty-eight when the war began and forty-five when it ended, the heart of middle age. He saw himself as an illustrator and took the view that the war hadn't fundamentally changed his work. He still liked drawing pubs and tarts, as he said years later. To him the work of the war artist was not one of propaganda. 'I wasn't preaching about anything.' Above all, he was interested in people and, although he wanted to be in the thick of the action, his work 'wasn't at all warlike'. Bawden looked back on his work as a war artist as being 'entirely beneficial' since 'it forced [him] to do things he wouldn't have chosen'. He had once lacked confidence in his abilities as a draughtsman, but the war conquered his doubts and gave him greater confidence. Now he knew he could draw people. He never regretted what he thought of as a marvellous opportunity. Anthony Gross's perception was that his work as a war artist was just 'a record of what I see ... I had no philosophy to put into it'. For John Worsley, the time was one which made one 'less precious'; it made his mind 'uncommon clear' so that he 'discarded essentials'. For all of the war artists who survived the war, it had been a life-changing experience and one that they would not have wanted to miss – or repeat.

★★★

Richard Seddon stood in the university cloister, looking across green lawns, faded red brick buildings and warmed by the prospect of high summer. In his hand he had a letter from Paul Nash that had brought back memories – of Kenneth Clark standing on a chair at one of the National Gallery war artists' exhibitions to make a speech. 'If we are going to pickle the war,' Clark had said, 'it should be well pickled.' Seddon found himself remembering his convoy of trucks slowly grinding its way east in 1940 – it had been a case of coming through the same country to fight the same battles. He had been proud to have been 'a real soldier' first and foremost and 'was very proud of not being a war artist'. He had not received a WAAC commission. He took a jaundiced view of the work of many war artists: too little action, too far behind the lines. Too many ruined buildings or troops peeling potatoes and too few works seeking to capture what the war was really like when the bullets flew. Looking back, Seddon remained disappointed that there was so little war action in the work generally. The trick, he thought, was 'to get it right and at the same time, intensify it.'

Looking back on the war: Edward Bawden, photographed in 1946.

The receipt for the return of Ardizzone's pistol, September 1945.

He remembered meeting Edward Bawden for lunch near Trafalgar Square soon after he had returned from the western desert. Bawden was in uniform and had a train to catch later that afternoon. He described how he had lost more than seventy paintings when the *Laconia* went down. They sat over the remains of lunch while Bawden showed snapshots of them; he had dealt them out on the table-top like playing cards. Seddon thought Bawden had solved the problem of what war artists should draw by 'ignoring the war altogether and going off and painting the Arabs'.

Edward Bawden looked out at the rain sweeping in, relentless and cold. In his mind's eye he could transport himself back to Persia and to an existence where, despite the nature of service life, he had felt free. He hadn't liked army people much, but the life was such that he had had little difficulty in getting away from them whenever he could. Now there were children to look after, responsibilities beyond his mere survival, and worrying where the next tranche of paper and paint might come from. He really should get back to work and earn some money again.

Ted Ardizzone was warm and snug in one of his favourite locals: muted light, the smell of beer and the subdued talk of the regulars. He had returned his revolver in September 1945 – an act that seemed to symbolise somehow the end of his wartime adventure. It began to feel as if a new life had begun. He put the receipt back into his wallet. The future! With satisfaction Ted recalled Bawden's encouraging view of Ardizzone's plans for 'post-war reconstruction.' He had anticipated 'tight little nudes in cosy bedrooms with a pair of striped pants on the bed-rail for a spot of tone'. He smiled at dear Edward's way with words, his references to 'Ardizzone's tenderness' and 'his humanity'. It was pouring outside and the streets were slick with rain, but the thought did not deter his most immediate plans: a slow walk home after perhaps one more drink, and a stop for some fish and chips on the way. Bliss.

John Worsley walked out of the depot gates at Portsmouth into Civvy Street. He had a new set of civilian clothes and a travel warrant. Next stop, London, then home. There were so many possibilities ahead and he had no intention of turning work down. 'If someone says will you paint a white mouse, I'll paint a white mouse!' He smiled – that's the spirit! – only to assume a false seriousness as the trilby-hatted spiv approached. He had been warned that this is what happened when you left the service: you could sell your new civilian suit for hard cash. John Worsley was equal to the challenge and his reply was succinct. He wasn't in the business of shady deals.

Antony Gross returned to his cottage near Paris, wondering in what state the Germans who had installed themselves there had left it. The pram had gone – they had used it to transport their luggage – but the house was relatively unscathed given the circumstances.

Barnett Freedman looked out of his study window, trying to set to one side his worries about income tax. It was April 1947 and he was writing to the former Prime Minister, Winston Churchill: 'May I respectfully ask if you would care to see a large ten foot oil painting of the Mulberry at Arromanches ...' Probably nothing will come of it, but one never knows. There were other things in the pipeline: lithographs for J. Lyons and Co., the possibility of designing a set of National Insurance stamps, an exhibition in Cairo, some more book illustrations. Enough to keep the taxman at bay ...

There were three official war artists who did not live to see the war's end: Albert Richards, Tom Hennell and Eric Ravilious. Albert Richards

Thomas Hennell remembered, one of the 18,000 names at the Chatham Naval Memorial.

is buried at Millsbeek War Cemetery, Holland, one of 210 graves. Tom Hennell's death is marked thus at the Ash-next-Ridley war memorial in Kent:

> Thomas Barclay Hennell aged forty-two, son of Rev. Harold Barclay Hennell former vicar of Ash and Ethel Hennell, was granted a Temporary Commission as a lieutenant in the Royal Naval Volunteer Reserve Unit on becoming a war artist in 1944. He visited Cherbourg Harbour amongst other places following the Allied Invasion of France. He then went to the Far East as a war artist covering the campaign against the Japanese and was killed by terrorists in Indonesia on 5 November 1945 soon after the end of the Second World War.[4]

Eric Ravilious, like Hennell, is commemorated at the Royal Navy Memorial, Chatham, the naval town to which Ravilious had been posted in 1940. The site is a windswept and lonely one, high above the River Medway, sufficiently out of the way to have a problem with vandalism.

Richards, Ravilious and Hennell were not the only artists who died: there were fatal casualties among men serving in the forces who were not 'official' artists: for example, Rex Whistler had decided that 'he would rather join a fighting battalion'.[5] He was killed in the battle of Caen in 1944 when 'a mortar bomb … fell at this feet'; he had got out of his tank to investigate problems with another tank. Clive Branson was another who had been killed in action, in February 1944 on the Arakan Front in Burma.

Captain Eric Ravilious' name on the Chatham memorial.

***

Early in the autumn of 1939 Henry Moore had spoken for many artists when he described his attitude to the war: 'However when the time comes that I'm asked, or have got to do something in this war, I hope it will be something less destructive than taking part in the actual fighting and killing. There ought to be ways of being used even as a sculptor, in making of splints etc, or jobs connected with plastic surgery – though the most likely thing I suppose is camouflage work. But until I'm prevented from doing so, my idea is to go on working just as I am, for as long as it's possible, or our finances last out.'[6] He spoke for many other artists facing the prospect of war.

***

On a summer's morning in Hertfordshire, the sunlight streamed into Moore's studio, reflecting back off the white emulsioned brick. The window was behind the artist and the light was perfect at that time in the morning. So was the peace of the space. Once a stable, it now smelled of paint and wood and oil. There were carved half-finished pieces of stone and wood scattered around the room, and sawdust and stone fragments littered the floor. There was a deep silence too. Moore sat leaning forward on a low chair, brush in one hand. The easel was close to him and he found himself looking lovingly at the sketch of two family groups, mother sitting, man standing; children clutched close, one child's fist on the broad spread of the man's chest; the woman holding the infant up to her husband. Nothing could separate them, in this world at least. They were entirely at peace. The war was not forgotten but nor was it any longer a preoccupation or a duty. There was life to be lived and, for the surviving artists, a different kind of work to be done.

20

Starting Over

People's lives restarted after the war. The six years from 1939 to 1945 had been a remarkable and gruelling interlude, but the hard-won peace was time to pick up the reins of a normal life. The participants in this story were no different. For a long time, the war had dictated how lives must be lived. For the war artists who had put on uniform, careers had been put on hold – although the WAAC had provided a stable market for their work. In 1945, the survivors had to begin again.

Post-war Britain was kind to some of the people in *The Sketchbook War*, but not all. Henry Moore was one of the lucky ones – he became an internationally recognised figure whose sculptures in particular commanded huge sums of money. He was arguably the greatest sculptor of the century. He died in August 1986 aged eighty-eight at his home in Much Hadham, Hertfordshire.

Sir Kenneth Clark – who kept a Henry Moore painting in one of his bathrooms – left the National Gallery and took up a post as Slade Professor of Fine Art at Oxford. He was Chairman of the Arts Council of Great Britain from 1955 to 1960. In 1969 he wrote and presented *Civilisation* for BBC television, a series on the history of Western civilisation as seen through its art. It proved enormously successful. He became Baron Clark of Saltwood in the County of Kent and died aged seventy-nine in Hythe after a short illness in 1983. He was the father of the Conservative cabinet minister and diarist/historian Alan Clark.

E.M. O'R. Dickey, whom Sir Kenneth Clark had valued so highly, died in 1977. Sir William Hildred, who was the early RAF representative on the WAAC and whom Clark suspected of being unduly ambitious and keen to pursue a career beyond the workings of the committee, became the first Director of the International Air Travel Authority and a Minister for Civil Aviation in the UK. Colin Coote, the army's man on the committee, became Editor of the *Daily Telegraph* between 1950 and 1964. Knighted in 1962, he died aged eighty-five in 1979. Gleadowe, who had irked Clark during the WAAC's lifetime, died a year before hostilities ceased.

Paul Nash died of pneumonia aged just fifty-seven in July 1946. Eric Ravilious' widow, Tirzah, who had married again in 1946 and resumed her own artistic career, died of cancer in 1951. The captain of the U-boat which sank the *Laconia*, Captain Werner Hartenstein, died when his submarine was sunk on 8 March 1943, a matter of months after the *Laconia* incident.

Edward Bawden's career flourished after the war and included success at the 1951 Festival of Britain. His wife Charlotte died in 1970 and he moved out of the house at Great Bardfield and moved to the nearby town of Saffron Walden. He returned to the Royal College of Art to teach. He died in 1989.

Edward Ardizzone's career went from strength to strength. He became much in demand and highly respected as an illustrator and writer of children's books, winning the Kate Greenaway Medal in 1956 for his book *Tim All Alone*. He was awarded the CBE in 1971 and received the accolade of being interviewed by Roy Plomley on *Desert Island Discs* the year after. He died of a heart attack in November 1979.

Anthony Gross lived for most of his post-war career in France, having bought a house in the south-west of the country. He routinely returned to London each winter. He was a very successful painter and printmaker and became a Royal Academician in 1980. He died four years later.

The effervescent Barnett Freedman was awarded the CBE in 1947, despite his capacity for annoying some of the powers-that-be at the WAAC. He pursued a successful career in design and as a painter, but died young, at the age of fifty-six in January 1958.

Another to die young was Guy Morgan, who had been captured with John Worsley in the Adriatic. He became a highly successful screenwriter whose credits included episodes of *No Hiding Place* and *Doctor Finlay's Casebook*. He co-wrote the script of the 1953 film *Albert RN*, about the

Albert Richards' jeep in Brussels.

escape from Marlag. It starred Jack Hawkins and Anthony Steel. He died in 1964, in East Grinstead, Surrey, aged fifty-five.

John Worsley was another who sustained a successful career in art after the war: he was credited with work as varied as drawing the comic strip *PC49*; painting portraits of various military and political leaders, including the former Prime Minister, Edward Heath; and sketching as a police artist for Scotland Yard. He died in 2000. Albert RN survives – or at least his doppelganger does – and can be seen at the Royal Naval Museum, Portsmouth.

Richard Seddon, following his doctorate in art at Reading University (1946), became a highly respected artist and writer. He was appointed Director of Sheffield's City Art Galleries in 1948 and held the post for sixteen years. He was an art critic on *The Yorkshire Post* and, in 1995, President of the Royal Watercolour Society. 'Richard had the air of a senior civil servant – and yet a civil servant who beneath his long Lowry-esque raincoat invariably wore a jaunty hand-tied bow tie to go with his well-cut suit.'[1] He died in 2003.

A retrospective exhibition of Thomas Hennell's work was organised by the Arts Council and ran from July 1948 to June 1949. Each watercolour was insured for £15.

Mrs Hannah Richards was devastated when her son Albert died. Each room of the house in Wallasey had been full of his work during the war years. In the aftermath of his tragic death, George and Hannah Richards sold the collection to a dealer in Stockport, and so the walls of the Richards' home were no longer a constant reminder of what the young artist's future might have been if not for the war. Richards was twenty-five when he died; Hennell forty-two; and Ravilious thirty-nine. There is no knowing, of course, what they might have achieved, given but time.

Notes

Chapter 2

1 *The Life of Henry Moore* by Roger Berthoud, page 168.
2 *The Other Half* by Kenneth Clark, page 1. Later, in mid-1940, there would be talk of despatching them to Canada; Clark disapproved and elicited the Prime Minister's backing. Churchill was typically forthright: 'Bury them in the bowels of the earth, but not a picture shall leave this island, WSC.'
3 Ibid., page 5; also recorded interview, Imperial War Museum (IWM) Sound Archives, 4778/02.
4 *The National Gallery's Role and its Influence on Regional Museums in World War 2* by Catherine Pearson, page 1.
5 Clark, page 10.
6 *The Plot to Save Artists* by Lionel Esher, in *The Times* Literary Supplement, 2 January 1987.
7 Clark, page 22.

Chapter 3

1 Recorded interview, IWM Sound Archives, 4778/02.
2 National Archives, AIR 2/6140.
3 Ibid.
4 From an interview by Richard Nelson of the artist George Jardine, a contemporary of Albert Richards. Walker Art Gallery, National Museums, Liverpool.
5 The pay was half what he had originally thought.
6 *Eric Ravilious – Memoir of an Artist* by Helen Binyon, page 112.
7 'The Artist in Wartime' by Sir Kenneth Clark in *The Listener*, 6 October 1939.
8 *Edward Bawden and His Circle* by Malcolm Yorke, page 21.
9 Ibid., page 15.
10 *Edward Bawden* by Douglas Percy Bliss, page 19.

11 Ibid, page 22.
12 Ibid., page 56.
13 Yorke, page 114.
14 *Ravilious at War*, ed. Anne Ullman, page 31.
15 Yorke, page 30.
16 *Memoirs of an Unjust Fella* by J.M. Richards, page 95.
17 Yorke, page 30.
18 Richards, page 95.
19 Ullmann, page 190. The diary entry was for 17 November 1941.
20 From the Barnett Freedman Archive at Manchester Metropolitan University Special Collections.
21 Bliss, page 72.
22 *Thomas Hennell* by Michael MacLeod, page 20.
23 Ibid., page 19.
24 Ibid., page 30.
25 Ibid., page 35.
26 Ibid., page 74.
27 Letter dated 9 September 1939 from Bawden to Eric Ravilious – see Binyon, page 112.
28 MacLeod, page 74.
29 *Edward Ardizzone's World* by Nicholas Ardizzone, page 8.
30 When Ardizzone appeared on 'Desert Island Discs' (on 5 August 1992), his chosen luxuries were malt whisky and drawing paper.
31 *The Young Ardizzone* by Edward Ardizzone, page 151.
32 'Something Always Turned Up' by Huon Mallalieu in *Slightly Foxed* magazine, No.28, Winter 2010, page 17.

Chapter 4

1   *East is West* by Freya Stark, page 1.
2   Ullmann, page 19. 'Restless and uneasy' was the view of his friend, J.M. Richards.
3   *A Hand Uplifted* by Richard Seddon, page 33.
4   Recorded interview, IWM Sound Archives, 960.
5   Seddon, page 35.
6   Ibid., pages 34–35.
7   Ibid., page 35.
8   Ibid., page 38.
9   Ibid., page 35.
10 He was not, however, commissioned as a war artist by the WAAC. He was a soldier who had been given licence to paint; not an artist put into uniform.
11 Binyon, page 111.
12 Ullmann, page 23; letter dated 9 September 1939.
13 Binyon, page 112.
14 Ullmann, pages 25-26. Letter to Diana Tuely, 10 September 1939.

15 *Editorial: the Memoirs of Colin R Coote*, by Colin Coote, page 213.

16 In a letter to Lord Esher. See Esher, *The Plot to Save Artists* op.cit.

17 Ullmann, page 34.

18 Ibid., page 32, letter dated 29 October 1939.

19 Ibid., page 41.

20 Gleadowe subsequently designed the Sword of Stalingrad which Winston Churchill presented to Stalin.

21 National Archives, AIR 2/6140.

22 Richards, page 105.

23 The contemporary is the author and designer Robert Harling. See *Ravilious in Pictures – the War Paintings* by James Russell, page 6.

24 IWM, War Artists Archive (GP/55/14).

25 Letter to his mother, dated 3 March 1940. See *Edward Bawden – War Artist'* ed. Ruari McLean, page 19.

26 Ardizzone family archive, courtesy of Christianna Clemence.

27 'Of all places' Ardizzone recalled with a laugh, looking back at the events of 1939 at the age of sevety-seven. Recorded interview, IWM Sound Archives, 4525.

28 IWM, War Artists Archive (GP/55/10).

29 Ardizzone kept the document and it remains in the family archive.

30 From the Barnett Freedman archive at Manchester Metropolitan University Special Collections.

31 *Anthony Gross* edited by Mary and Peter Gross, page 77.

32 From the Barnett Freedman archive at Manchester Metropolitan University Special Collections.

Chapter 5

1 IWM, War Artists Archive (GP/55/6).

2 Ibid., minute dated 29 January 1940.

3 Ibid.

4 Ullmann, page 58; letter to Tirzah Ravilious, 12 February 1940.

5 Binyon, page 115.

6 Ullmann, page 64; letter to Tirzah Ravilious, 18 February, 1940.

7 Ravilious in a letter to Dickey, IWM, War Artists Archive (GP/55/6).

8 Ullmann, page 69.

9 Binyon, page 117.

10 From the Barnett Freedman archive at Manchester Metropolitan University Special Collections. Letter dated 26 April, 1940.

11 *War Diaries 1939–1945* by Field Marshall Lord Alanbrooke, page 55; the entry is for 23 April 1940.

12 Interviewed many years later, Ardizzone remembered going to France with Barnett Freedman and struggled to recall being with Bawden. Recorded interview, IWM Sound Archives, 4525.

13 National Archives, AIR 2/6140. Dated 3 January 1940, the note was drafted

by William Hildred.

14 Seddon, page 167.

15 *Baggage to the Enemy,* by Edward Ardizzone, page 7.

16 Michael Rothenstein interviewed by Mel Gooding, *Artists' Lives,* July 1990, British Library Sound and Moving Image Archive Catalogue reference C466/02, transcript page 11 © The British Library. Interview accessed online via sounds.bl.uk.

17 Ardizzone, page 8.

18 Letter of 12 April 1940. IWM War Artists Archive (GP/55/6).

19 Ullmann, page 88.

20 Esher, op.cit., pages 12–13.

21 Alanbrooke, page 54.

22 *Artists and Authors at War* by Henry Buckton, page 47.

23 Seddon, page 59.

24 IWM War Artists Archive (GP/55/34).

Chapter 6

1 *Dunkirk* by Hugh Sebag-Montefiore, page 60.

2 Ibid., page 60.

3 Alanbrooke, page 60.

4 Alanbrooke, page 62.

5 Ardizzone, page 36.

6 Ibid., page 48.

7 Ibid., pages 49–50.

8 Ibid., page 71.

Chapter 7

1 Letter to Helen Binyon, 30 May 1940.

2 *The Second World War* by Anthony Beevor, page 105.

3 Sebag-Montefiore, page 189.

4 IWM, War Artists Archive (GP/55/14).

5 Yorke, page 120.

6 From the Barnett Freedman archive at Manchester Metropolitan University Special Collections.

7 Seddon, page 66.

8 Ibid., page 67.

9 Ibid., page 69.

10 Seddon, page 103.

11 Most of the 51st were captured by the Germans. See *Dunkirk: The Men They Left Behind* by Sean Longden.

12 Seddon, page 122.

13 Ibid., pages 139–140.

14 Ibid., page 147.

15 Ibid., page 151.

16 Beevor, page 114.
17 IWM War Artists Archive (GP/55/34).
18 From the Barnett Freedman archive at Manchester Metropolitan University Special Collections.
19 Ibid.
20 Ibid.
21 *The War Artists* by Meirion and Susie Harries, page 215.

Chapter 8

1 IWM War Artists Archive (GP/55/6).
2 In IWM War Artists Archive (GP/55/6) there is a list of the paintings selected by Ravilious. Written on HMS *Highlander* notepaper, with the ship's name crossed out, some fifteen titles are listed.
3 IWM War Artists Archive (GP/46/24).
4 Recorded interview, IWM Sound Archives, 960.
5 Seddon, page 71.
6 IWM War Artists Archive (GP/46/24).
7 *Edward Ardizzone – A Bibliographic Commentary* by Brian Alderson, page 46.
8 *The Blitz* by Juliet Gardiner, pages 16–17. She is quoting the AFS dispatch rider, Stan Durling.
9 IWM War Artists Archive (GP/55/10).
10 *Barnett Freedman – the Graphic Art* by Ian Rogerson, page 141.
11 *Sketches for Friends* by Edward Ardizzone, page 19. The original letter is in the Ardizzone family archive.
12 Gardiner, page 158. The comment was made by fellow artist, and conscientious objector, Keith Vaughan.
13 Recorded interview, IWM Sound Archives, 4525. The letter to Ardizzone's daughter Christianna is in the family archive.
14 Alderson, page 43. The 'homeward walk' is from his printers in Plaistow to Elgin Avenue, Maida Vale.
15 Recorded interview, IWM Sound Archives, 4525.
16 *To War with Paper and Brush* by Malcolm Yorke, page 58.
17 Recorded interview, IWM Sound Archives, 4622.
18 Letter to Helen Binyon, dated 6 August 1940.
19 Binyon, page 122; letter dated 18 August 1940.
20 Russell, page 26.
21 Ibid., page 26.
22 Letter to E.M. O'R. Dickey, 29 September 1940. IWM War Artists Archive (GP/55/6).
23 Binyon, page 123.
24 Ibid., page 123.
25 Recorded interview, IWM Sound Archives, 3173.
26 *John Worsley's War* by John Worsley and Kenneth Giggal, page 10.
27 National Archives, ADM 1/11215.

Chapter 9

1 McLean, page 24.
2 Ibid., page 24.
3 Ibid., page 25.
4 Ibid., page 32.
5 *House of Exile* by Evelyn Juers, page 261.
6 Berthoud, page 168.
7 *Colours of War* by Alan Ross, page 62.
8 Interview with the author, 4 August 2012.
9 From the Barnett Freedman archive at Manchester Metropolitan University Special Collections.
10 Ibid. Freedman's correspondent is unknown: the signature appears to read 'HJ'.
11 *Repulse* was sunk in the Far East in December 1941.
12 Seddon, page 167.
13 *War Painting: a No-Man's Land Between History and Reportage* by Sarah Griffiths, Leeds Arts Calendar, no. 78, page 24.
14 Ibid., page 30.
15 *The Artist at War* by Angela Summerfield, page 15.
16 Ibid., pages 23–24.
17 For details on Bone, Eurich, Kennington, and Lamb, see *War Paint* by Brian Foss, pages 196–202.
18 *Women War Artists* by Kathleen Palmer, pages 2 and 35.
19 McLeod, page 75.
20 IWM, War Artists Archive (GP/55/123).
21 *The Rose of Death*, Paintings and Drawings by Captain Albert Richards, page 29.
22 Ross, page 173.
23 Worsley and Giggal, page 22.
24 Letter to Helen Binyon dated 10 October, 1941. Ullmann, page 183.
25 Letter to Dickey, 15 November, 1941. IWM War Artists Archive (GP/55/6).
26 Binyon, page 132.
27 Both in Ethiopia and Eritrea he struggled with the high altitude which 'produced unpleasant nervous symptoms.' IWM, War Artists Archive (GP/55/14).
28 Letter of 12 December 1941.
29 *Three Against Rommel* by Alexander Clifford, page 239.

Chapter 10

1 Ullmann, page 207.
2 Recorded interview, IWM Sound Archives, 4525.
3 Yorke, page 120.
4 Bliss, page 84.
5 Ullmann, page 204.

6 Letter to Helen Binyon, 27 March, 1942. Ullmann, page 222.

7 IWM, War Artists Archive (GP/55/6).

8 From the Barnett Freedman archive at Manchester Metropolitan University Special Collections.

9 National Archives, FO 371/32968.

10 Ullmann, page 207; letter dated 19 January 1942.

11 Ibid., page 213.

12 National Archives, AIR 27/48.

13 Greta Bridge had been the subject of a painting by John Sell Cotman (1782–1842), an artist whom Ravilious greatly admired.

14 Letter to Tirzah, 26 February 1942.

15 National Archives, AIR 27/1556.

16 Letter of 15 June 1942.

17 From the Barnett Freedman archive at Manchester Metropolitan University Special Collections.

18 Michael Rothenstein interviewed by Mel Gooding, *Artists' Lives*, July 1990, British Library Sound and Moving Image Archive Catalogue reference C466/02, transcript page 5 © The British Library. Interview accessed online via sounds.bl.uk.

19 Ullmann, page 258.

20 National Archives, AIR 49/15.

21 National Archives, AIR 27/1566.

22 National Archives, AIR 27/1566.

23 Ibid. There is, however, no specific reference to Eric Ravilious being on board that aircraft.

24 Michael Rothenstein interviewed by Mel Gooding, *Artists' Lives*, July 1990, British Library Sound and Moving Image Archive Catalogue reference C466/02, transcript pages 5–6 © The British Library. Interview accessed online via sounds.bl.uk.

25 Binyon, pages 138–139.

26 There was a long running dispute about income tax – whether artists abroad should pay it or not (Ardizzone, for example, was explicitly told that he would not be required to pay when abroad). The issue caused Edward Bawden and Barnett Freedman considerable heartache. Predictably, perhaps, the rules were changed during the war.

27 Edward Bawden, for example, sent a letter from the Middle East on 16 October 1941 which arrived in London in mid-December.

28 Binyon, page 133.

29 Letter to Eric Ravilious, 21 February 1942.

30 M and P Gross, page 84.

31 *Atlantic Torpedo* by Doris M Hawkins, page 8.

32 Ibid., page 7.

33 Recorded interview, IWM Sound Archives, 4622. Yorke, page 127.

34 Hawkins, pages 8–9.

35 Ibid., page 9.
36 Yorke, page 127.
37 *U Boats to the Rescue – The Laconia Incident* by Léonce Peillard, page 90. The actual figure of Italian PoWs was 1,800.
38 The survivor was Doris Hawkins. See National Archives, WO 361/190.
39 Josephine Pratchett, survivor, on the BBC2 TV programme *The Sinking of the Laconia* first broadcast in January 2011.
40 Recorded interview, IWM Sound Archives, 4622.
41 Ibid.
42 IWM War Artists Archive (GP/55/14).
43 IWM War Artists Archive (GP/55/6).
44 There were some seventy-five letters written over a fourteen-month period, involving the WAAC, Ministry of Information, Ministry of Pensions, Air Ministry, Admiralty and the Treasury.
45 Letter dated 17 January 1943.
46 Letter dated 14 January 1943.
47 National Archives, ADM 1/12722.
48 Oxford Dictionary of National Biography.

Chapter 11

1   *The Winston Specials* by Archie Munro, page 268.
2   Worsley and Giggal, page 48.
3   Ross, page 138.
4   Official War Artists with the Middle East Forces, Conditions of Service. From the Ardizzone papers, courtesy of Christianna Clemence.
5   Letter to Christianna Clemence, dated 2 August 1942.
6   Letter dated 16 August 1942.
7   Letter to Christianna dated 2 October 1942.
8   Worsley and Giggal, page 49.
9   *Diary of a War Artist* by Edward Ardizzone, page 6.
10 Ibid., page 10.
11 Ibid., page 15.
12 *The Day of Battle* by Rick Atkinson, page 144.
13 *Middle East Diary* by Noel Coward, page 37.
14 Ardizzone, page 28.
15 *Road to Rome* by Christopher Buckley, page 69.
16 Atkinson, page 123.
17 Buckley was later killed in Korea when his jeep hit a mine.
18 Letter dated 22 August 1943. From the Ardizzone papers.
19 Ardizzone, page 23.
20 *Eclipse* by Alan Moorehead, page 2.
21 Recorded interview, IWM Sound Archives, 4525.
22 The cameraman Billy Jordan of AFPU referred to the incident in his memoirs *(A Cameraman for All Reasons)*, but Ted's part in the escapade went unremarked: 'I heard later that Geoffrey Keating went into Taormina and

captured 400 Italians single-handed. Sounded like Keating to me!' See *The History of the British Army Film and Photographic Unit in the Second World War* by Dr Fred McGlade, page 101.

23 *Bitter Victory* by Carlo D'Este, page 531.
24 Moorehead, page 6.
25 Letter dated 22 August 1943. From the Ardizzone papers.
26 *Alan Moorehead* by Tom Pocock, page 173.
27 *Whicker's War* by Alan Whicker, page 66. Ardizzone was approaching 43. Whicker was just 18.
28 Ibid., page 66.
29 Ardizzone, page 55.
30 Ibid., page 60.
31 Recorded interview, IWM Sound Archives, 4525.
32 Ardizzone, page 63.
33 Ibid., page 64.
34 A former student of Ardizzone's remembers that he never stopped drawing.
35 *Only Ghosts Can Live* by Guy Morgan, pages 21-22.
36 Ibid., page 22.
37 Ibid., page 23.
38 Ibid., page 25.
39 Ibid., page 26.
40 Worsley and Giggal, page 67.
41 Recorded interview, IWM Sound Archives, 3173.

Chapter 12

1 From a letter written on 26 July 1987 by Edward Bawden to Anthony Gross's daughter Mary. Bawden remembered both Gross and Ardizzone with great affection.
2 M and P Gross, page 88.
3 Ibid., page 88.
4 Ross, page 152.
5 Recorded interview, IWM Sound Archives, 4621/02. The diarist, James Lees-Milne dined with Beauchamp and Mrs Churchill in December 1948 and noted that he was 'a dark gigolo with a scar.' *Diaries 1942–1954*, page 373.
6 The letter is dated 17 March 1943. See Yorke, page 130.
7 He was with B Company, 5th Royal Berkshire Regiment.
8 The sketching umbrella saga rankled with Bawden years after the war was over, with good reason. Listening to his interview recorded decades later it is not clear whether there were *two* such umbrellas, one of which went down with the *Laconia*, or just this one he ordered in 1943. Either way, while it might have been an invaluable thing in the heat of the Middle East ('the greatest blessing'), it was also a cause of irritation for London-based civil servants (who regularly asked questions about it), and for Bawden himself (who was exasperated by those very questions!)

9 In a letter to Miss E. Monroe. IWM, War Artists Archive (GP/55/14).

10 J.M. Richards, page 180.

11 Ibid., page 181.

12 Yorke, page 131.

13 Letter dated 17 September 1943. McLean, page 82.

14 Letter to Edward Ardizzone dated 27 February 1944.

15 Seddon, pages 186–187.

16 Yorke, page 132.

17 Recorded interview, IWM Sound Archives, 4721/02.

18 Letter to Edward Ardizzone from Baghdad, dated 18 July 1944.

19 MacLeod, page 77.

20 Captain A. Richards, page 29.

21 From the Ardizzone papers. Letter from Taormina, Sicily, dated 22 August 1943.

Chapter 13

1 In 1941, for example, the exhibition was sent by lorry from Middlesbrough to Edinburgh since 'the railways are impossible'. IWM, War Artists Archive (GP/46/24/2/1a).

2 IWM, War Artists Archive (GP/46/24/2A-B). Clark's enthusiasm was not sufficiently great, however, for him to agree to opening an exhibition in Edinburgh in April 1941. 'April 12 is quite impossible for me, not only because it is my Easter holiday, but because it is my son's birthday and my family would never forgive me.'

3 *Wartime Britain 1939–1945* by Juliet Gardiner, page 398. She is quoting the artist Percy Horton.

4 *The National Gallery in Wartime* by Suzanne Bosman, page 99.

Chapter 14

1 Worsley and Giggal, page 75.

2 *The Barbed Wire University* by Midge Gillies, page 30.

3 Gillies, page 93.

Chapter 15

1 Lord Moyne, the British Minister of State in the Middle East, was assassinated in Cairo eight months later.

2 Ardizzone, page 106.

3 Albert Richards' cousin, Bruce Beatty, remembers George as being a kind man who made Bruce and his brother a sledge during one winter of the war. Hannah he recalled as being 'a proud lady'. Telephone interview, 31 July 2012.

4 Capt. A. Richards, page 36.

5 *D-Day* ed. Jon E. Lewis, page 63.

6 *Overlord,* by Max Hastings, page 75.

7 Walker Art Gallery, National Museums Liverpool, Albert Richards object history file.

8 The 'Rose of Death' as an image for the parachute stems from the Spanish Civil War. See Capt. A. Richards page 2.

9 *D-Day* by Stephen E Ambrose, page 25.

10 *The Day the Devils Dropped In* by Neil Barber, page 23.

11 Walker Art Gallery, National Museums Liverpool, Albert Richards object history file.

12 *D-Day* by Anthony Beevor, page 147.

13 M & P Gross, page 103.

14 Barber, page 195.

15 Recorded interview, IWM Sound Archives, 3952.

16 Capt. A. Richards, page 37.

Chapter 16

1 'Scots were always rude to me,' Ardizzone thought. Recorded interview, IWM Sound Archives, 4525.

2 Ardizzone, page 126.

3 Ibid., page 128.

4 Ibid., page 129.

5 M and P Gross, page 101.

6 Bliss, page 86.

7 Letter to Christianna, dated 29 August 1944.

8 Finance reported it as 'in quite good condition except for fair wear and tear.' A year later he was badgered for it again when he attended a private view at the National Gallery!

9 Yorke, page 135.

10 Letter dated 30 September 1944.

11 Ross, page 143. Letter to E.C. Gregory, dated 12 October 1944.

12 IWM, War Artists Archive, (GP/55/14 B).

13 Letter from Edward Bawden to Ardizzone dated 18 November 1944, from 5 Via Romagna, Rome.

14 Coldstream thought his war artist career constituted 'a highly privileged time'. He believed that the troops thought he was 'in some sort of secret service.' Recorded interview, IWM, Sound Archives, 3184.

15 McLean, page 90.

16 Letter from Edward Bawden to Ardizzone dated 8 December 1944, from P.R. Camp, Cesena.

Chapter 17

1 IWM War Artists Archive, (GP/55/14 B).

2 Letter to Edward Ardizzone, dated 20 February 1945.

3 Bawden was used to such hazards: for example, he reported in a letter of 3 February 1945 that 'bed bugs met me in the best hotels of Cairo.'

4 Minute dated 10 August 1945; IWM, War Artists Archive (GP/55/14B).

5 Letter to Ardizzone, dated 30 September 1944.

6 IWM, War Artists Archive, (GP/55/123).
7 He told Ardizzone so in a letter written on 15 December 1943.
8 IWM, War Artists Archive (GP/55/123).
9 MacLeod, page 80.
10 Ibid., page 81.
11 Ibid., page 83.
12 IWM, War Artists Archive (GP/55/123).
13 E.C. (Peter) Gregory became secretary on 5 July 1943.
14 IWM, War Artists Archive (GP/55/123).
15 I am grateful to Polly Loxton for allowing me to quote from her mother's letter. Barbara Loxton's story is told in Polly Loxton's book *Barbara Loxton: Paintbrush Reporter 1944–1945*.
16 Captain A. Richards, page 40.
17 Recorded interview, IWM Sound Archives, 4621/02.
18 Recorded interview, IWM Sound Archives, 4525.
19 The letter was dated 20 February 1945, and written from Rome.
20 M and P Gross, page 107.
21 Ardizzone, page 209.
22 McGlade, page 140.
23 M and S Harries, page 256.
24 *The Last Escape* by John Nichol and Tony Rennell, page 82.
25 Worsley and Giggal, page 106.
26 Worsley and Giggal, page 112.

Chapter 18

1 The artist was Leslie Cole.
2 M & S Harries, page 261.

Chapter 19

1 Clark, page 76.
2 The quoted sections here are taken from a recorded interview, IWM Sound Archives, 4778/02.
3 M and S Harries, page 274.
4 His younger brother David who died on 6 June 1943 is also commemorated there.
5 See Buckton, page 12.
6 Collection IWM: IWM 16597 2 a–b; letter from Henry Moore to Arthur Sale, 8 October 1939.

Chapter 20

1 So described by another Past President of the Society, Maurice Sheppard. The quotation is taken from an obituary of Seddon written by Simon Fenwick and is contained in the files of the Royal Watercolour Society, to whom I am grateful.

Appendix A

Bibliography

War Diaries, Alanbrooke, Lord, Weidenfeld & Nicolson, 2001
Edward Ardizzone – A Bibliographic Commentary, Brian Alderson, Oak Knoll Press, 2003
D-Day, Stephen E. Ambrose, Simon & Schuster, 1994
Edward Ardizzone's World, Nicholas Ardizzone, Unicorn Press, 2000
Sketches for Friends, Edward Ardizzone, David R. Godine, 2002
The Young Ardizzone, Edward Ardizzone, Studio Vista, 1970
Baggage to the Enemy, Edward Ardizzone, John Murray, 1941
Diary of a War Artist, Edward Ardizzone, The Bodley Head ,1974
The Day of Battle, Rick Atkinson, Henry Holt, 2007
The Day the Devils Dropped In, Neil Barber, Leo Cooper, 2002
D-Day, Anthony Beevor, Viking, 2009
The Second World War, Anthony Beevor, Weidenfeld & Nicolson, 2012
The Life Of Henry Moore, Roger Berthoud, Faber & Faber, 1987
Eric Ravilious, Memoir of an Artist, Helen Binyon, The Lutterworth Press, 1983
Edward Bawden, Douglas Percy Bliss, Pendomer Press
The National Gallery in Wartime, Suzanne Bosman, The National Gallery, 2008
Road to Rome, Christopher Buckley, Hodder & Stoughton, 1945
Artists and Authors at War, Henry Buckton, Leo Cooper, 1999
The Other Half, Kenneth Clark, John Murray, 1977
Three Against Rommel, Alexander Clifford, Harrap, 1943
Editorial, Colin R. Coote, Eyre & Spottiswoode, 1975
Middle East Diary, Noel Coward, Heinemann, 1944
Bitter Victory, Carlo D'Este, Collins, 1988
War Paint, Brian Foss, Yale, 2007
The Blitz, Juliet Gardiner, Harper Press, 2010

Wartime Britain 1939–1945, Juliet Gardiner, Headline, 2004
The Barbed Wire University, Midge Gillies, Aurum, 2011
Anthony Gross, ed. M. and P. Gross, Scolar Press, 1992
House of Exile, Evelyn Juers, Allen Lane, 2011
The War Artists, M. and S. Harries, Michael Joseph, 1983
Overlord, Max Hastings, Michael Joseph, 1984
Atlantic Torpedo, Doris M. Hawkins, Victor Gollancz, 1943
Diaries 1942–1954, James Lees-Milne, John Murray, 2006
D-Day, ed. Jon E. Lewis, Robinson, 1994
Dunkirk: the Men They Left Behind, Sean Longden, Constable, 2008
Thomas Hennell, Michael Macleod, Cambridge, 1988
Edward Bawden – War Artist, ed. Ruari McLean, Scolar, 1989
The History of the British Army Film & Photographic Unit in the Second World War,
    Dr Fred McGlade, Helion, 2010
Eclipse, Alan Moorehead, Hamish Hamilton, 1945
Only Ghosts Can Live, Guy Morgan, Crosby
The Winston Specials, Archie Munro, 2006
War Through Artists' Eyes, ed. E. Newton, John Murray, 1945
The Last Escape, J. Nichol & T. Rennell, Viking, 2007
Women War Artists, Kathleen Palmer, Tate, 2011
U-Boats to the Rescue, Léonce Peillard, Jonathan Cape, 1963
Alan Moorehead, Tom Pocock, The Bodley Head, 1990
The Rose of Death, Albert Richards, Arts Council, 1977
Memoirs of an Unjust Fella, J.M. Richards, Weidenfeld & Nicolson, 1980
Barnett Freedman – the Graphic Art, Ian Rogerson, The Fleece Press, 2006
Colours of War, Alan Ross, Jonathan Cape, 1983
Ravilious in Pictures – The War, James Russell, Mainstone Press, 2010
Dunkirk, H. Sebag-Montefiore, Viking, 2006
A Hand Uplifted, Richard Seddon, Muller, 1963
East is West, Freya Stark, John Murray, 1945
The Artist at War, Angela Summerfield, Walker Art Gallery, 1990
Ravilious at War, ed. Anne Ullmann, The Fleece Press, 2002
Whicker's War, Alan Whicker, Harper, 2005
John Worsley's War, Worsley & Giggal, Airlife, 1993
Edward Bawden & His Circle, Malcolm Yorke, The Fleece Press, 2005
To War with Paper and Brush, Malcolm Yorke, The Fleece Press, 2007

Appendix B

Locations of the War Artists in *The Sketchbook War*

	1939	1940	1941
Edward Ardizzone	Anti-Aircraft Battery, Clapham Common, Woolwich, Little Hope.	France (March). Home via Boulogne (May), London, Salisbury (June), other locations in the UK.	Edinburgh & Glasgow (April 1941) & other locations in the UK.
Edward Bawden	Great Bardfield, Essex.	France (March). Home via Dunkirk. Ship to Middle East (July), Cairo (late summer), Omdurman.	Khartoum, Various locations: Middle East and Africa.
Anthony Gross	Paris, London.	Caterham, Catterick, France, Bordeaux to Glasgow (July), London.	Dover, Shoeburyness. On board *Highland Monarch* (November).

1942	1943	1944	1945
Convoy to Cairo, leaving May; Durban (June), Cairo (August), Alamein.	Sicily (July), Taormina (August), Italian mainland (September), Bari, Naples.	Anzio (February), Cairo, UK (May), Normandy (June), UK (June), Naples, Rome, (September).	Ravenna, France (March), Paris (April), Brussels (April), Bremen (April), Hamburg (May), Copenhagen (May), Belsen (May), UK (May).
Middle East and Africa. *Laconia* (torpedoed September), Casablanca, PoW camp North Africa, New York (winter).	UK: Dunwich (Suffolk), Colchester, Aldeburgh, Fife, Cairo (August), Baghdad, Saudi Arabia.	Middle East. Recalled to UK (August), Southampton, London, Rome (November), Ravenna, Cesena (December).	Ravenna, Florence, Greece, Liverpool (July).
N. Atlantic & Indian Ocean, Cairo, Transjordan (March), Lebanon, Syria, Persia, Iraq, Cairo and Alamein, boat to India (December).	Karachi, Delhi, Calcutta, Arakan Burma, Tunis. Home via Cairo, Algiers and Fez.	Normandy (D-Day).	France, Germany.

	1939	1940	1941
Barnett Freedman	London.	France (April) – billeted in Airaines (Somme). Home via Boulogne (May). Sheerness (September and October), Isle of Grain (October), Western Command (October).	Contract terminated (March). Began work for the Admiralty: HMS *Repulse* (July).
Thomas Hennell			WAAC commissioned some drawings.
Eric Ravilious	Castle Hedingham (Royal Observer Corps). Westbury & Uffington.	Chatham (February), Sheerness, Grimsby (April), Norway (May), Portsmouth (July), Newhaven (mid-September), Home.	Dover (July), Scotland (August), Firth of Forth, Dundee (November).
Albert Richards	Wallasey and London.	Royal College of Art, Sapper in Royal Engineers (April), Suffolk, Northumberland.	Wiltshire.
Richard Seddon	Sheffield.	France near Maginot Line (April), Neufchâtel (May/June); home via HMS *Boadicea*. Invalided out of the army.	
John Worsley	Midshipman aboard *Laurentic* (October).	Torpedoed aboard *Laurentic* (November).	HMS *Lancaster*, HMS *Wallace*.

1942	1943	1944	1945
Illustrating aircraft workers, Yate near Bristol (December).	HM Submarine Tribune (June).	Normandy (July), Hospitalised (August).	
	Iceland (August), UK (November), Kent.	Grimsby (March), Portsmouth (May), Normandy (June), Kent (July), France (August).	Chatham (February), Holland. Leaves UK (May), Rangoon (June), Ceylon, Calcutta, Penang, Singapore, Java.
RAF Clifton, York (February), Saffron Walden (April), RAF Sawbridgeworth (May), Somerset, Iceland (August).			
Suffolk.	Ringway, Manchester, Official war artist (October).	Normandy (D-Day), France.	Holland, Germany.
Sailing from USA to Freetown (Spring), HMS *Devonshire*.	HMS *Devonshire*: Indian Ocean, Newcastle upon Tyne (summer), Sicily (July). Captured in the Adriatic (November).	Marlag PoW camp, Germany.	Marlag PoW camp, Germany (till May), Lübeck, UK.

Appendix C

The Paintings in *The Sketchbook War*

A number of war artists' paintings have been a source of inspiration in the writing of this book. They are listed below, together with where they are located and the chapter in which they appear. The Imperial War Museum images can be viewed online.

Title	Artist	Location	Chapter
September 3rd, 1939	Henry Moore	The Henry Moore Foundation	2
Edward Bawden working in his studio	Eric Ravilious	Royal College of Art	3
A Warship in Dock	Eric Ravilious	Imperial War Museum	5
Dangerous Work at Low Tide	Eric Ravilious	MOD Art Collection	5
A Court Martial, Halluin	Edward Bawden	Imperial War Museum, London	5
Leaving Scapa Flow	Eric Ravilious	Bradford Art Gallery	7
Norway, 1940	Eric Ravilious	Laing Art Gallery, Newcastle upon Tyne	7
Au Nouveau Monde Estaminet	Edward Bawden	Imperial War Museum, London	7
Embarkation of Wounded	Edward Bawden	Imperial War Museum	7
Bethune Strategy (Rearguard Defences)	Richard Seddon	Imperial War Museum	7

Signalling HMS *Bulldog* from the Shore	Richard Seddon	Imperial War Museum	7
A Day with the Home Guard	Edward Ardizzone	Imperial War Museum	8
Train Landscape	Eric Ravilious	Aberdeen Art Gallery	8
Coastal Defences No. 2, 1940	Eric Ravilious	Museum of New Zealand, Te Papa Tongarewa	8
RNAS Sick Bay, Dundee	Eric Ravilious	Imperial War Museum	10
Marlag O PoW Camp	John Worsley	Imperial War Museum	14
Road between St Aubin and Benouville	Albert Richards	Imperial War Museum	15
At the village of La Plein	Albert Richards	Imperial War Museum	15
The Search for Rubble	Albert Richards	Imperial War Museum	15
Black Caen	Albert Richards	Imperial War Museum	15
Marmalade Bridge	Albert Richards	Imperial War Museum	15
Ravenna	Edward Bawden	Imperial War Museum	17
Fishing Boats, Reykjavik	Thomas Hennell	Private Collection	17
Flooded Maas	Albert Richards	Walker Gallery, Liverpool	17
Field Marshal the Viscount Montgomery	John Worsley	Imperial War Museum	17
The Wehrmacht, May 1945	Edward Ardizzone	Imperial War Museum	17

A number of sketches in Ardizzone's *Baggage to the Enemy* and Helen Binyon's *Eric Ravilious, Memoirs of an Artist* also provided invaluable inspiration.

Appendix D

Photographs

Brick House, Great Bardfield. (*Author's photograph*).

Edward Ardizzone. (*Christianna Clemence and Tim Ardizzone*).

Richard Seddon.

Bank House, Castle Hedingham. (*Author's photograph*).

Eric Ravilious, Barnett Freedman and John Nash, April 1940. (*Ronald Blythe*).

Digging trenches: a sketch by Edward Ardizzone. (*Ardizzone estate*).

Edward Ardizzone's postcard to his daughter, Christianna, August 1939. (*Ardizzone estate*).

War Office letter of appointment, 1940. (*Barnett Freedman archive at Manchester Metropolitan University Special Collections*).

Freedman's Harrods shopping list, 1940. (*Barnett Freedman archive at Manchester Metropolitan University Special Collections*).

Barnett Freedman's order from Winsor & Newton. (*Barnett Freedman archive at Manchester Metropolitan University Special Collections*).

Eric Ravilious in uniform. (*Ronald Blythe*).

Barnett Freedman's War Correspondent's Licence. (*Barnett Freedman archive at Manchester Metropolitan University Special Collections*).

Edward Bawden in uniform. (*The Estate of Edward Bawden*).

A military ID card, 1941. (*Barnett Freedman archive at Manchester Metropolitan University Special Collections*).

Barnett Freedman at work in France, 1940. (*Barnett Freedman archive at Manchester Metropolitan University Special Collections*).

The Catalogue for the War Artists' Exhibition at the National Gallery. (*Barnett Freedman archive at Manchester Metropolitan University Special Collections*).

The War Artists' Exhibition. (*Getty Images*).

A sketch by Edward Ardizzone of St Paul's surrounded by bomb damage. (*Ardizzone estate*).

Ardizzone draws the bomb squad. (*Ardizzone estate*).

Group Captain Lord Willoughby de Broke at his desk at the Air Ministry. (*Imperial War Museum, CH 8811*).

A sketch of Eric Ravilious by his wife, Tirzah. (*Anne Ullmann*).

A Hudson of 269 Squadron at the RAF base at Kaldadarnes, Iceland. (*Imperial War Museum, CS 112*).

Ardizzone in the Western Desert. (*Christianna Clemence and Tim Ardizzone*).

Geoffrey Keating and Edward Ardizzone outside Villa La Scala, Taormina, August 1943. (*Christianna Clemence and Tim Ardizzone*).

Lieutenant John Worsley, RNVR, at work on an Italian quayside. (*Imperial War Museum, A 20824*).

Anthony Gross in the desert. (*Mary West and Jean-Pierre Gross*).

Captain Anthony Gross. (*Imperial War Museum, H 8511*).

Anthony Gross in Cairo 'against the background of the Pyramids.' (*Mary West and Jean-Pierre Gross*).

Bomb damage at the National Gallery. (*National Gallery Picture Library*).

Berlin: Professor Schweitzer-Mjolnir opens an exhibition of work by German official war artists. (*Imperial War Museum, HU 39484*).

The war artist's dummy: Albert RN. (National Museum of the Royal Navy).

Ardizzone drawing: dining in Cairo. (*Ardizzone estate*).

Ardizzone and Henry Carr. (*Imperial War Museum, NA 14235*).

Captain Albert Richards. (*Walker Gallery, National Museums, Liverpool*).

Barnett Freedman at work in his makeshift studio in Normandy, 1944. (*Imperial War Museum, A 24517*).

Edward Bawden in Rome, with John Aldridge. (*The Estate of Edward Bawden*).

Lieutenant T. Hennell in RNVR uniform. (*Michael MacLeod*).

Thomas Hennell painting in the ruins of Caen, 1944. (*Michael MacLeod*).

Barbara Loxton's drawing of men sheltering from German shelling, February 1945. *(Polly Loxton; image photographed by the London Metropolitan Archives)*.

Edward Bawden photographed in 1946. (*National Portrait Gallery; photograph by Howard Coster*).

The receipt for the return of Ardizzone's pistol, September 1945. (*Christianna Clemence and Tim Ardizzone*).

Thomas Hennell remembered, one of the 18,000 names at the Chatham Naval Memorial. (*Author's photograph*).

Captain Eric Ravilious' name on the Chatham memorial. (*Author's photograph*).

Albert Richards' jeep in Brussels. (*Williamson Art Gallery and Museum, Birkenhead*).

Appendix E

The Colour Illustrations

'September 3rd, 1939' – *Henry Moore*
Reproduced by permission of The Henry Moore Foundation.
'Observer's Post' – *Eric Ravilious*
By the kind permission of the Trustees of Cecil Higgins Art Gallery, Bedford,
England.
'Aircraft Runway in course of Construction at Thélus, near Arras: May
1940' – *Barnett Freedman*
Imperial War Museums (LD 261).
'An Old Battleground' – *Richard Seddon*
Imperial War Museums (LD 988).
'The Bombing of GHQ Boulogne' – *Edward Ardizzone*
Imperial War Museums (LD 215).
'Dunkirk: Embarkation of Wounded' – *Edward Bawden*
Imperial War Museums (LD 177).
'HMS *Boadicea* shelling German Tanks on the Cliffs near Veulette, 10 June
1940' – *Richard Seddon*
Imperial War Museums (LD 5988).
'Dangerous Work at Low Tide' – *Eric Ravilious*
Courtesy of the Ministry of Defence Art Collection, London.
'Submarine Scenes: Diving Controls, *c.* 1941' – *Eric Ravilious*
Image courtesy of Towner, Eastbourne.
'The Landing Pier, Freetown, 1941' – *Anthony Gross*
Imperial War Museums (LD 2093).
'The Battle of Egypt, 1942, No 5 Ambulance Train' – *Anthony Gross*
Imperial War Museums (LD 2553).

'A Convoy in the Pentland Firth' – *Thomas Hennell*
Imperial War Museums (LD 3657).
'On the Road South to Taormina' – *Edward Ardizzone*
Imperial War Museums (LD 3456).
'Grand Harbour, Malta, October 1943' – *John Worsley*
Imperial War Museums (LD 5156).
'The Landing in Normandy' – *Barnett Freedman*
Imperial War Museums (LD 5816).
'Gliders Crash-landed' – *Albert Richards*
Courtesy National Museums Liverpool.
'Calais, 10 November 1944' – *Thomas Hennell*
Imperial War Museums (LD 4754).
'Ravenna: Lieutenant-General Sir Richard McCreery decorates Bulow, the Partisan Leader, with the *Medaglio d'Oro* for conspicuous personal bravery, December 1944' – *Edward Bawden*
Imperial War Museums (LD 4966).
'Naval Officers Filling in a Discovered Escape Tunnel, 1945' – *John Worsley*
Imperial War Museums (LD 5149).
'Flooded Maas' – *Albert Richards*
Courtesy National Museums Liverpool.

Index